sacred food

sacred food

cooking for spiritual nourishment

elisabeth**luard**

MQP
MQ Publications Ltd

previous page: Tamil Sikh bride's henna-dyed hands holding gilded coconut husks. Red, the color of henna as well as of the thread which binds a Sikh to his faith, is the color of happiness.

First published by
MQ Publications Limited
12 The Ivories, 6–8 Northampton Street
London N1 2HY
mail@mqpublications.com

Design by Balley Design Associates
Cover photograph: Rod Shone

ISBN: 1 84072 201 0

Printed in Belgium by Proost

1 3 5 7 9 0 8 6 4 2

introduction

Sacred food is the spiritual essence of all those things that sustain human life on earth—the bite-sized, digestible amanuensis of everything our ancestors couldn't explain. When sacrifice was made to the presiding deity—whatever or whoever that might be—the offering was consumed in essence. What was left, having been touched by the Maker of All Things, was sacred. Consuming sacred food allowed mortals to join the immortals in spirit, if not in flesh.

Our ancestors found the world a terrifying place, and with good reason. How much more terrifying if the world was all there was. How else than by a Creator to explain the raw stuff of human existence—birth, death, famine, plague, the scary, and the unknown? By transforming the sacrifice through the skill of the cook, the offering becomes something more than it was. By creating a new thing—the transformation of water into wine, grain into bread, dead flesh into roast meat—humanity can take on a little of the nature of the divine.

above: The traditional Russian Easter bread, *kuchlich*, with red-dyed eggs—symbols of rebirth in pagan times as well as the Christian metaphor for the mystery of the Resurrection.

Our ancestors saw the propitiation of the gods as a serious business: it was all that stood between the cave mouth and wild wood. In modern times, when so many of the festivals that marked the changing year have turned into municipal events, the primitive purpose of the celebration—the passing of winter storms, the return of the sun—may be airbrushed out, but the shadow remains, a ghost at the table. Although the gods of nature have mostly lost their place at the feast, the founding fathers of organized religions—whether Muslim, Hindu, Christian, Buddhist, Jew, or the humanist belief systems of the East—had the good sense not to ignore them completely. Certainly the priests of the new order preached against the old—but they made sure their festivals did not change out of all recognition, and remained rooted in what had gone before. It is to this adaptability that the festivals owe their strength in the face of those who look for a rational explanation, their survival against all odds.

above: A Bedouin woman makes pitta bread in her tent in the Negav Desert, Israel.

In an age when every school child is aware of the structure of DNA, when our scientists are unraveling the skeins of life itself, why should we need to mark the flowering of a cherry tree in some long-abandoned garden? Or celebrate the gathering of harvest, when our larders—at least, those of the Western world—show no difference between summer and winter? Still less, count the passing of centuries from the inaccurately recorded date of the birth of a baby to a pair of unknown Palestinians in a stable in Judea? Traditions, whether religious or secular, are like spiders' webs—impossible to unravel without destroying the fabric. In this far-from-comprehensive glance—history would claim too great a scope—at why and what we cook when we need to nourish the soul, I have looked to the spirit rather than the substance. The instinct that propels a Muslim to mark the birth of a baby or mourn the death of a loved one is in no way different from the sentiment that draws joy or sorrow from the devout Christian or the worshiper of the animist gods of the ancients.

Certain foods have universal significance but without requiring explanation from professors of ethnology. Seeds, nuts, fruit, eggs, and grains signify renewal; new life from old. Blood, shed or shared, is a metaphor for sacrifice. Sweetness, sugar and honey, makes the heart glad. Wine and strong drink, together with some hallucinogenic substances extracted or obtained by one means or another, are useful to the priesthood, since they allow men to believe they are gods. These foods—presented and prepared in a million different ways, or absent and marked by regret at their absence—are to be found at the heart of all our rituals.

fertility
cultivation
harvest

1

The Cree Indians of Canada, observed the philosopher Claude Levi-Strauss, were in the habit of offering the first fruit of every harvest to the forces of nature, holding the green berries first toward the sun so they might ripen, next toward the thunder so that it might bring rain to make them juicy, and finally toward the earth so that she might bring forth more, and in greater abundance. They made this sacrifice not of their own volition, but because the Supreme Being Who Created All Things told them to do so—thus creating the first act of worship. In addition, before the offering could be found worthy, it first had to be cooked, so receiving the blessing of the purifying fire—a wise precaution when dealing with unripe foodstuffs. In this simple act was all the knowledge a man or woman might need.

"O most merciful Father, who of thy gracious goodness hast heard the devout prayers of thy church, and turned our dearth and scarcity into cheapness and plenty;
We give thee humble thanks for this, thy special bounty, beseeching thee to continue thy loving-kindness unto us, that our land may yield us her fruits of increase, through Jesus Christ our Lord. Amen." **Early prayer of thanksgiving**

If the oldest act of worship is the giving of grace before meat, whether spoken or unspoken, then the act of blessing food is a response to a universal need. The closer people live to their source of sustenance, the better is their understanding of the natural world. The greater their respect for those things over which they have no control, the more they crave a higher authority.

Of all disasters that could ever befall mankind, famine was the greatest. The specter of famine haunts us still. In the days when we needed to know exactly where our next meal would come from, we gave thanks for the food on the table today in the fear that tomorrow the larder might be empty. At festivals and family gatherings, although there may be no formal summoning of the deity, an unspoken blessing is invoked simply by obeying the rules of courtesy that require us to wait and not raise a forkful to our lips before others have been served. This, a momentary

previous page: Japanese rice-planting ceremony in flooded fields near Kyoto, Japan. Rice is regarded as a sacred food in its own right throughout Asia.

pause that goes against our natural inclination to fill our bellies, permits not only the gods, but the spirits of our ancestors to join the feast. The penalty, if we don't wait for our companions to be served but plunge immediately into the plateful set before us, is to be considered greedy; if we are children, we're told to mend our manners.

Other gestures across the globe serve the same purpose among them, in Christian societies, the cross the village baker marks on the crust before he slips a loaf into the oven; among the rice-eaters of the East, the sacredness of the grain is acknowledged by the care with which the chopsticks convey it to the mouth; in the traditional street markets of Mexico—now fast-vanishing—the incantations muttered by the *tortilla*-maker as she grinds the corn; in the cold lands of the Celts, where, in the depths of the long winter, it was once the custom to toast oats at the fire and then scatter them abroad—to encourage the grain to sprout and bring a good harvest. In the hot lands of Africa, where fertility depends on unreliable rainfall, water was poured on a dry riverbed in the hope that the spring might rise and provide water for the parched soil. In the land of the vine, wine was poured as a libation on the ground to coax the grapes to grow plump; while pastoralists hoped that by shedding the blood of a young animal on a mountaintop the rest of the flock would be saved from harm.

In a hostile world, you need all the friends you can get.

hunting

There was a time, no more than a few thousand years ago, when a lord-of-the-universe was whoever had amassed the largest stock of bear meat.

Our hunter-gatherer ancestors probably looked for little more than a decent feed and a dry cave. While those who sow can be reasonably confident of reaping, hunting is less certain of success. Any hunter knows that his business is best left till the end of the grass-growing season, when the prey animals have put on a little flesh and the females are no longer suckling.

Among primitive societies, the gathering of staple grains and roots was primarily the task of the women, while the men—and, among some societies, young women before marriageable age—were responsible for the provision of meat. The elemental spirits of nature, though useful to the gatherers, were of less relevance to hunters, who needed the more human attributes of strength, cunning, and bravery. There are no records to tell us exactly when the gods took on human form, but it can only have been in response to a need. These superior beings became endowed with human vices as well as virtues. The Greek gods were expected to behave more like spoiled brats than wise parents—promiscuous,

below: Paleolithic depiction of a shaman disguised as a goat and pursuing prey animals, possibly in anticipation of a successful hunting trip. Cave-painting executed between 15,000 and 10,000 B.C. at Trois Frères near Montesquieu-Avantes, Ariege, France.

blood-hungry, careless of the welfare of their mortal doppelgangers—whose attention could be attracted by the sacrifice of a prey animal in much the same way as grains sprouted before their season could guarantee harvest. And, if all else failed, the goodwill of the gods might be bought by the blood of a handsome youth or a beautiful maiden.

Even so, the gods' reactions were never predictable, still less loving or forgiving, and it was only to be expected that one of the most ancient of our festivals—the lighting of fires on the longest night of the year—had to do, quite literally, with keeping the man-wolf from the door. If fires were first lit at the cave mouth for protection and warmth, we soon began to love what the fire could do to our food. We learned to appreciate the scent of roasting meat, the flavor of the rich, buttery fat as it browns and crisps, and turned grain soft and chewable. As with animals around a kill, those who dip their hand in the same pot are declaring their allegiance to the group. After the eating comes the storytelling. When the belly is full, the heart can roam. It was in the night, when the flames had died to glowing embers, that the storyteller came into his own.

At night, under the stars, bears are bigger, tigers fiercer, men braver, and women more beautiful. How much more captivating are the voices of the tale-tellers when their stories are told in the firelight to an audience grown drowsy and plump on the rewards of the chase. From Homer to Hollywood, we have honored our storytellers, rewarding them with belief. From this, the strange alchemy created when we listen well to a tale told well, came the power of the shaman, the priests who held the power to anoint the king—a mortal man, who by divine blessing, became the representative on earth of old gods, the elemental forces among which the sun was always the first.

So important was the sun to our ancestors that their leaders crowned themselves with the only substances found on or beneath the earth that can match its brilliance. Foods considered suitable for sacrifice to such a god were inevitably round and golden—pancakes, yellow with eggs; round breads, baked as golden as sunshine; foods made golden with saffron or some other means. And, of course, there was the metal itself. The golden halos that frame the faces of the painted images of the Christian saints could be counted on to remind all who saw them— converted or yet to be brought into the fold—of the life-giving rays of the sun. When the first conquistadors arrived in Peru, they found that the Inca people regarded the Emperor as a deity and worshiped him in the form of a great golden disk—the very incarnation of the sun—who feasted on corn, called *maíz* by the Spanish, the golden food of the sun.

right: Priestess offering the god a ritual
meal of yam and eggs at the Akonedi
shrine in Larteh, Ghana.

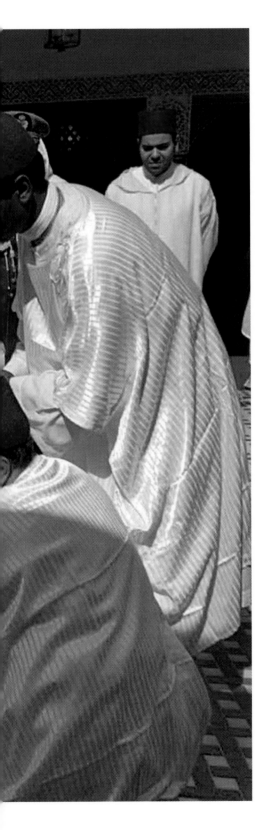

left: King Mohammed VI of Morocco, a direct descendent of the Prophet, sacrifices a sheep at the festival of Eid al-Adha, the Feast of the Sacrifice, a ceremony that marks the end of the annual Muslim pilgrimage to Mecca.

The sharing of sanctified foods, particularly the consumption of meat that had been offered in sacrifice, was the way in which a nomadic people obtained union with nature, and through nature, might hope for some control over the forces that governed their lives. The killing of animals was never taken lightly. To this day, among rural communities, although the slaughter of household creatures such as chickens and rabbits is considered women's work, the slaughter of herd animals, from pigs to cattle, is seen as men's work; and not simply for reasons of physical strength, but also because of the ritual, priestly significance. Among Jews and Muslims, both of whom look to a pastoralist tradition, ritual is particularly important, and meat killed in any other way than that laid down in the Holy Book is considered unclean.

In many cultures, including those of the East, killing must be done with respect: before knife is applied to throat, the victim's forgiveness must be sought. While the religious requirements of *halal* butchery are not usually associated with fertility rituals, the connection between blood spilled on the ground as part of ritual slaughter and blood spilled as sacrifice in expectation of reward is not overlooked, even in modern times. The distinguished author Jeffrey Steingarten, visiting the estate of an Algerian grandee a few years ago, described the sacrifice of a sheep that was designed to ensure the success of the olive harvest. The meat was always eaten, the grandee assured his visitor; it was only the blood that was wasted.

Pastoralists eat meat; you will find no vegetarians in a Kurdish *yurt*, still less among the hordes who followed Gengis Khan. Farmers know that vegetables can be made flesh by the simple process of feeding them to warm-blooded creatures, a miraculous transformation that gave rise to many of those elliptical folktales of the tribes of Africa: that blood sprinkled in the wind carries the seeds of life. This simple belief—that a drop of blood shaken on the earth will bring forth good things—lies at the heart of many of our sacred rituals.

appeasing the spirits

In the subtropical lands of southeast Asia, the islands of the Pacific, and the lands of Equatorial Africa, people concerned themselves not so much with the agricultural year as with the propitiation of the elements. Keeping on the right side of willful gods was a matter of urgency. Heaven only knew when the gods of wind and weather would dump a cloudful of hailstones on a plantation of mangos, send a tidal wave to sweep away a deltaful of young rice plants, a hurricane to uproot the year's banana crop—or, worse, rip the people from their beds and deposit them in the swamp. In the tropics, the business of planting and harvesting does not depend on the heat of summer and the cold of winter, but on dry and wet, monsoon and drought.

In the Americas, unencumbered by Christianity until the arrival of the conquistadors, the rituals of planting and first harvest could be observed in the raw: "Formerly, before the Spaniards came," wrote Elsie Parsons, documentor of the folkways of the people of Mitla, Oaxaca, southeast Mexico, in the 1930s, "before planting a field, a man buried a plateful of food, tortillas, and tamales, in a round hole in the middle. Afterwards, a turkey was decapitated and its blood sprinkled on the offerings." When the ritual was done, the ladies prepared a savory stew—a *mole*, says Ms. Parsons, with chocolate and green tomatoes. Sacrifice is easy to bear when the spoils are shared. Later in the year, as soon the corn swelled in the husk, came the Fiesta de los Elotes—the feast of green corn: "In October when the corn is green, before it dries, people may harvest one hundred ears or more and invite relatives and compadres to their house and give each guest two cooked ears of corn with salt and chilli. And when the man of the family brings the green ears into the house, he must say 'Dear God, abundance has come to my house.'" Landless people would buy corn so they too might celebrate—even in Mexico at a time when many still worked the land, townsfolk did not want to be left out.

below: A Peruvian woman, a descendant of the sun-worshipping Incas, pours a libation of *chicha* on the corn, as a blessing on the harvest.
right: Mural in Chiapas, the last Mexican stronghold of the ancient civilizations, showing precolumbian worship of the maize god.

Nature in India is by no means motherly—most of the time she seems hell-bent on man's destruction, expressing herself in a terrifying cycle of wind, tempest, earthquake, storm, drought, and flood. Perhaps in response to this, the people developed a pantheon of deities invested with superhuman capacities through whom they could appeal directly to the forces of nature in the form of offerings, prayers, and festivals. In India, the solar calendar divides the year into six seasons of two months each—a twelve-month period during which, just for good measure, thirteen harvest-related festivals are celebrated, and in and among these food-related festivals are scattered the feast days of the minor and major gods of the prolific Hindu pantheon, many of whom have different incarnations and alternative names.

The festival of Rathajatra, a commemoration of the chariot journey undertaken by the Lord Jagannath, a late incarnation of the Lord Krishna, who made the trip with his sister and brother to recover from a bout of monsoon fever, is celebrated in the monsoon months. At the temple of Jagannath in the the town of Puri in Orissa, a gigantic wooden chariot—the juggernaut—loaded with three wooden figures is dragged through the streets. The food appropriate to a rainy day festival is *khichuri*, a dish of rice and dal cooked together, eaten with eggplant fritters. The festival of Kanu—held in January, at the end of the monsoon season when most of India's rice crop is gathered—is celebrated with a pilaf cooked with nuts and tamarind, each element—soft, strong, sharp, bland—representing one aspect of the deity.

Hemanta, the Hindu season that forms the last two months of fall, brings to maturity the all-important harvest of pulse vegetables—chickpeas, lentils, yellow and black-eyed peas, and mung beans. At Dashrana, the festival sacred to Saraswati, goddess of knowledge and wisdom, the temple offering is chickpeas—although any of the other pulses are perfectly acceptable as an offering. In celebration, the temple cooks prepare *shondal*, a deliciously spicy bean salad dressed with sesame.

Of the Hindu harvest-related festivals, Navami, the last day of the goddess Durga's residence on earth, is sacred to meat-eating. In more robust times, the goddess demanded offerings of live animals—young male goats, or buffalo—today, the meat is bought in the market and taken to the temple. In the old days, for the sacrifice to be worthy, the sacrificial beast had to be beheaded with a single blow: a bungled execution was taken as a sign of the goddess' displeasure and a warning of trouble to come. Temple offerings of meat were—and are today—prepared immediately by the temple cooks and eaten on the same day. Afterward, when sacrifice has been made and the goddess' effigy has been floated away on the river, sweet things are eaten to speed her on her way.

The feast day of Durga's daughter Lakshmi, goddess of wealth and prosperity, follows. Lakshmi's special food is a creamy rice pudding, *payesh*, made with milk cooked down to a thick cream, flavored with cardamom, enriched with butter and sugar, and finished with almonds and raisins.

Nature's bounty, the food without which man cannot survive, plays an essential role both as sacrifice to the gods and as an encouragement to devotees. A reputation for serving good food affects the capacity of the temples to attract worshippers, whose presence will, in turn, flatter the deities. While the temple food, *prasad*, served to pilgrims is by no means luxurious, there is an obligation on the temple cooks to prepare nourishing and balanced meals. Food is prepared according to the Hindu principles of Ayurveda—a 5,000-year-old philosophy of life designed to achieve enlightenment by balancing the life forces. This highly sophisticated system takes into account the seasons and the three *doshas*, or forces, that give rise to the constitutional types—*vata* (active), *pitta* (intense), *kapha* (heavy)—that a person, male or female, can be one, other, or a mixture of. In recognition of this, Ayurvedic meals must provide three categories of food: stimulating, tranquilizing, and fortifying; six tastes: sweet, salty, sour, bitter, pungent, astringent; and six qualities: hot, cold, dry, oily, heavy, and light.

Shondal **indian chickpea salad**

A spicy dish from southern India, made with the temple offerings brought to Saraswati, goddess of wisdom, during her festival of Dashrana in the last months of fall. The foods offered to the goddess are prepared by the temple cooks and served to devotees in return for a small payment.

Serves 4–6

4 cups / 900 g cooked chickpeas (boiled without salt)

Juice 2 lemons

2 tablespoons coarse-grained salt

2 tablespoons sesame oil

2 teaspoons black mustard seeds

6–8 small dried red chilies, crumbled, or fresh chilies

Generous pinch ground asafetida

2 tablespoons flaked coconut, lightly toasted

2 tablespoons chopped cilantro/coriander

❶ Combine the chickpeas with the lemon juice and salt.

❷ Heat the oil gently, then add the mustard seeds—they jump like fleas when they feel the heat, so have a pan lid handy.

❸ Add the chilies and allow to sizzle for a few seconds. Add the asafetida and immediately pour the contents of the pan over the beans. Toss to blend, and finish with coconut and cilantro/coriander.

Pitlai **ayurvedic vegetables with dal**

This aromatic curry combines all the qualities necessary for an Ayurvedic meal: stimulating, tranquilizing, and fortifying. The Ayurvedic diet should balance the six tastes: sweet, salty, sour, bitter, pungent, astringent; and six qualities: hot, cold, dry, oily, heavy, and light.

Serves 4–6

3 tablespoons ghee (clarified butter)

1 tablespoon Madras curry powder

3–4 medium carrots, scraped and diced

3–4 smallish zucchini, wiped and thinly sliced

1 handful green beans, cut into short lengths

4 tablespoons shelled peas

1 teaspoon salt

3 tablespoons sesame or other seed oil

1 teaspoon turmeric

1 teaspoon ground cumin

1 small cauliflower, broken into florets

1 eggplant, diced

6 medium-size tomatoes, skinned and diced

2 cups / 450 g red lentils, cooked to a puree

❶ Melt the *ghee,* or butter, in a roomy saucepan and add the curry powder. Stir briefly, and then add the diced carrots and zucchini. Turn the heat to low and toss with the butter for a few minutes. Add the green beans and peas, salt, and just enough water to submerge the vegetables. Cover and leave to simmer while you prepare the remaining ingredients.

❷ Heat two tablespoons of the oil in a small skillet or frying pan. Sprinkle in the turmeric and cumin and let them feel the heat for a second. Add the cauliflower and stir-fry for a couple of minutes—just enough for the cauliflower to drink the oil. Push the cauliflower aside and add the remaining oil. When it's sizzling, drop in the diced eggplant. Toss till lightly browned, and then add the tomatoes. Bubble up and combine with the cauliflower. The mixture should be soupy—if not, add a little water. Simmer for about 10 minutes before mixing with the other vegetables, which should be perfectly tender by now. Mix in the cooked lentils and simmer for a couple more minutes to blend the flavors.

Serve with plain, boiled rice and *chapattis* for scooping.

right: Balinese women transporting beautifully arranged offerings on their heads, en route to a temple ceremony.

The principles on which offerings are made to the heavenly father, in whatever guise he is worshiped, is that since all good things belong to him, if food is offered in its natural state, he is simply being asked to receive his own. For this reason, it is not enough to offer things as they are, they must be enhanced in some way; transformed, and made other than what they are—thereby making them worthier than nature left them.

As a general rule, this applies to all ritual offerings in the East. The principle that sacred foods must somehow be made more worthy is clearly seen in the temple offerings of the women of the Indonesian archipelago, whose exquisite arrangements of fruit and other good things, when carried in baskets balanced on heads down dusty roads, end up covered in a thick mantle of inedible dirt and flies.

Among the people of the southeast Asian islands, there is a belief that while everyday cooking is a chore that can be left in the hands of women, the preparation of festival food is a rite that can only be properly performed by men. As befits a function that has all the trappings of the priestly rather than the practical, feast-day foods cooked and served in a place of spiritual significance are prepared according to secret rituals that are never divulged to outsiders.

The myth is part of the mystery. Sounds familiar? This transformation—the elevation of chef to the status of shaman—has nothing to do with the day-to-day business of the kitchen, and quite rightly so. An altar without a priest serves no useful purpose. A festival feast is no ordinary banquet, but a sacrificial meal to be consumed in the company of very old gods indeed.

Although location and gender are of paramount importance, so too is the way in which heat is applied. While everyday cooking is done on top-heat, using whatever pots and pans come to hand, it is a characteristic of men-only cooking that the method is kept as primitive as possible. Hence, the instinctive feeling that barbecue cooks should always be men. Women never cook the Spanish *paella*, the Corsican lamb roast, the Hungarian *bogracs-gulyas*—all dishes descended from the alfresco feasts of nomadic peoples to whom cooking was not an everyday occurrence but a special event, an occasion for rejoicing.

planting

The rituals that mark the start of spring fall on or around the first date on which it is possible to plant seeds. For those who date their festivals by the solar calendar, it is also the first day of the new year.

The Iranian new year, No Rooz, falls on March 25, at the moment when the earth passes the vernal equinox.

The tradition of tolerance among those who follow the teachings of the Prophet—evident throughout the Moorish ascendancy in Andalusia, probably the only time and place when Christian, Muslim, and Jew lived and worshiped side by side in harmony—ensured that the rituals of No Rooz survive in modern Iran in a form that today would be perfectly recognizable to the ancient Aryan worshipers of the sun as the bringer of light, the life-giver, without whose goodwill nothing would grow. For those who observe No Rooz, the new year begins as soon as the earth feels the warmth of the sun. As it was in ancient Persia, so it is in modern Iran: preparations for the festivities start with a thorough spring-cleaning of mind and body—personal, professional, and practical. New clothes are purchased, dwellings repainted, floors scrubbed, carpets beaten, cupboards tidied, furniture polished; in the kitchen, pots are scrubbed, pans polished, knives sharpened, storecupboards emptied and renewed.

In addition to these household precautions, deals are done, bills settled, quarrels resolved, enemies reconciled, while all the while, the path is made smoother by the sharing of sweetmeats. In anticipation of encounters that might otherwise be unfriendly, prodigious quantities of sweetmeats are prepared in the weeks preceding No Rooz. In every household, up and down the land, kitchens fill with the delicious scent of hot almonds, caramelized sugar, and buttery pastry, although today—with fewer people to help in the home and less time for domestic duties, the more complicated confections—the delicate *loukums* and exquisite *halvas*, nut-layered pastries, and honey-drenched fritters—are the business of professional bakers.

Meanwhile, in city markets, flower sellers sell sweet-scented bundles of spring blossom—cyclamen, hyacinths, narcissi, and forsythia. The fruit merchants do a brisk trade in late-winter fruit: rosy pomegranates, oranges, overwintered grapes, sticky black dates, persimmons, brown-skinned frost-bletted medlars no bigger than a wild bird's egg. Fish vendors do a busy trade in luxury fish, both fresh and salt—not something Iranians eat every day. But the stalls that attract the longest queues are those piled with edible green-ery—nettles for soup, young spinach, tender shoots of spindly green asparagus, and infant fava beans to be cooked whole in their pods. In all cultures, ancient or modern, the first shoots of spring are endowed with a mystical significance that has little to do with their capacity to nourish.

From the shadowy interiors of the seductive little shops that sell dried fruit and nuts—quick snacks to be enjoyed on the way home, treats for both adults and children—wafts the irresistible aroma of roasting pistachios, cashews, almonds, chickpeas, hazelnuts; the seeds of sunflowers, pumpkins, and melons. Persian pistachios are huge, with smooth, ivory shells from which bursts luscious pale-green flesh husked with carmine. The variety of dried fruit is astounding: apricots, cherries, peaches, a dozen different grapes, pears, figs, and, most delicious of all, white mulberries, chewy and intensely sweet, like little drops of golden toffee.

On the festive table, *Haft Seen*, are placed the seven "Ss" —seven dishes containing the seven sacred substances that represent the seven spirits that guard mankind: birth, life, health, happiness, prosperity, beauty, light. The seven substances—the name of each of which begins with an "S"— are *sumac*, a sour-flavored powder milled from the dried fruit of the *sumac* bush, much prized as a seasoning; *serkeh*, a soured juice or vinegar; *samanou*, a sweetmeat made from sprouted wheat; *sabzi*, herbs, a peculiarly Persian combination of edible leaves, among which is included costmary, an aromatic member of the daisy family valued in the medieval pharmacy for its ability to cure headaches; *seeb*,

above: Table setting for the Zoroastrian festival of new year, still celebrated in much the same way as it was in ancient Persia; each element has its own ritual significance.

the apple, the fruit of the Garden of Eden; *seer*, garlic, the herb that protects against evil; *senjed*, the root of the lotus plant whose blossom resembles the sun; or *sonbol*, the edible root of a wild hyacinth, the first flower of spring. In addition, there will be a bowl of cooked eggs; a dish of sprouted grains; a live goldfish or an orange in a bowl; a book of poems; lighted candles, one for each child; a mirror to reflect the light. Last, but by no means least—endowing the ritual with the approval of the Prophet—a copy of the *Koran*.

At nightfall, when the transition from day to night marks the moment the feast can begin—the senior reveler rises to greet the new year with a reading from the Muslim holy book. Afterward, sweetmeats are handed to all present, with a gift of

gold or silver for the children. The *Haft Seen* with its sacred offerings is then removed to make way for the table to be laid for the first meal of the new year. In modern Iran, the festive dish is a *sabzi polow*, Saffron Pilaf (*see page 29*): a dish of rice, rich with butter and layered with spring herbs—tasting marvellously fresh after the dusty spices of winter. The usual accompaniment, for those who can afford the luxury of fresh seafood, is fried fish, and *kookoo-ye sabzi*, a thick egg-cake of a size perfect for sharing. Some households serve seven dishes—*Haft Meem*, the seven "Ms", in which the main ingredient is a food whose Persian name begins with "M"—rice, chicken, yogurt, fruit, preserved fruit, raisins, and rosewater.

In addition to these good things, a festive soup-pot is kept simmering on the stove throughout the twelve days to mark the transition from the old year to the new. Using *reshteh*, noodles, as the main ingredient, it is constantly renewed and never allowed to cool for fear the larder will not be refilled. This venerable and nourishing soup, *Shuli* in Zoroastrian Persia, *ash-e reshteh* in modern Iran, is similar in composition to the Italian *pasta-e-fagioli*, made to a recipe so ancient it might well have been that same pottage for which Esau sold his birthright, combining in a single pot the sacred trinity of the ancestral larder: beans, grains, and greens. The recipe follows the natural order: first to be added to the simmering broth are the traditional pulses of the old-world storecupboard—chickpeas, mung beans, and lentils—conveniently emptied from their storage jars during the new year spring cleaning. Next is added the grain—in the old days, it was flour mixed to a paste with water. Into the broth is stirred freshly gathered new greenery—spinach, the leaves of young beets, baby leeks, and scallions—an edible proof that spring is well on its way To complete the picture, the broth is delicately tinted with

below: A copy of the Koran completes the abundant festival table at No Rooz.

saffron or turmeric, the color of sunlight.

As is to be expected of so estimable a recipe, changes have been made over the centuries. Cultivated greens have replaced the wild-gathered clovers; new-world beans have joined the old-world pulses. In its earliest form, the soup was thickened with flour-and-water paste rather than the modern thread-pastas, *reshteh*, although these continue to serve the same function and are made with identical ingredients. The process by which a flour-and-water paste became a pasta is not hard to unravel. The dough-pellets, *omåj*, tiny finger-formed pastas that replaced the original thickening, were simply the result of flicking droplets of water over milled grain and rolling the result into storable form. From the finger-rolling technique to the roll-and-cut method is another short step, but an important one since it gives final form to the narrow thread-noodles used in Persian cookery to this day. Who actually invented the process is a matter, as they say, for continuing historical debate. Whether or not an ancient Persian housewife thought the trick up for herself, or whether

Sabzi Polow **saffron pilaf**

A buttery pilaf rice layered with fresh spring herbs served at the outdoor picnic that marks the festival of No Rooz, new year, celebrated in March in modern Iran as in ancient Persia. Traditionally it was served by those who could afford the luxury of fresh seafood with fillets of white fish, dusted with turmeric, and fried golden in clarified butter.

Serves 12

5 cups / 900 g basmati rice (long grain)

Salt to taste

6–8 cups / 500 g parsley, cilantro/coriander, dill, and chives

1 tablespoon chopped fenugreek (dried or fresh)

Handful fresh garlic leaves, shredded, or 2 garlic cloves, finely chopped

1 cup / 250 ml sunflowerseed oil

1 teaspoon powdered saffron, soaked in 4 tablespoons boiling water

½ cup / 125 g clarified butter (ghee)

❶ Wash the rice thoroughly in several changes of water. Put in a bowl, cover with water to the depth of one finger, add 3 tablespoons salt and leave to soak for 3-4 hours. Meanwhile, destalk and rinse the herbs, pat dry, chop finely, and spread on a clean towel to evaporate any remaining moisture.

❷ Bring a large pan of water to a boil and add 3 tablespoons salt. Drain the soaked rice and stir it into the boiling water. Return the water to a boil, bubble for 2 minutes, and test to see if the grains are soft on the outside but firm in the middle. Drain thoroughly in a colander, rinsing with warm water.

❸ Rinse out the pan and return it to the heat with the oil, together with a couple of spoonfuls of water. Heat till the water has evaporated. Cover the base with one third of the drained rice, top with half the chopped herbs, spread on another layer of rice, top with more herbs, and follow with another layer of rice, mounding up the last layer into a dome shape. Poke 3 holes right through the rice with the handle of a wooden spoon. Wrap the saucepan lid in a clean dish cloth and cover the pan tightly. Leave the heat high for a couple of minutes to reheat the rice right through, then reduce the heat to minimum. Leave on the gentle heat for 30 minutes. After you remove the pan from the stove, set it on a cool, wet slab to loosen the crusty base.

❹ To serve, remove a generous ladleful of the rice and toss with the saffron water. Heat gently to evaporate excess liquid. Melt the butter in a small pan. Lightly toss the remaining rice with its herbs and pile on a dish (leaving behind the thick crusty golden layer that has formed on the base of the pan). Top with the saffron rice and trickle with the melted butter. Unstick the crust in a single piece, if possible, and serve separately. Hand around a bowl of thick yogurt, deliciously cool and refreshing, and a thick wedge of *kookoo-ye sabzi* [herb omelet] (*see page 31*).

she learned it from a traveler who came from China, or whether the technique was first discovered in another place altogether, or whether all cooks involved in the conversion of milled grain to storable, palatable foodstuff came to the same conclusion simultaneously is a question suitable for those who wish to know how many angels might safely dance on the head of a pin.

Whatever its place of origin, the servant outgrew the master, and the pasta gave its name to the soup itself. In any event, the appearance of the broth after the addition of the noodles led to its versatility. It has been adopted as the dish served at the farewell feast for pilgrims before they embark on their journey to Mecca; to celebrate the return of a long-lost relative or friend; and at all festivities when Allah must be shown gratitude for some specific intervention. So important a ritual is this that friends and neighbors will often bring a bowl of noodle soup to the door of a respected household at times of family celebration. Etiquette demands that, when the bowl is returned, it must be filled, by way of thanks, with some of the recipient's own good cooking.

No Rooz lasts for twelve days, the same period allotted to the holy days of the Christian Christmas, and shares with it some startlingly similar rituals, including, in Provence, a *soupe de lasagnes* whose composition exactly mirrors the Persian ancestral pottage. Throughout this time, while householders put their affairs in order, the young are expected to visit their elders, and to be rewarded with sweetmeats for their respect.

On the thirteenth day, houses are emptied of all greenery—the budding branches, the yellowing dishes of sprouting greens that might by now afford the devil a hiding place—and everyone heads for the hills. Provisions are packed, together with tables, chairs, carpets, cushions, cutlery, plates, glasses, portable stoves, and cooking utensils—the creature comforts

necessary for a night under the stars. The food, of course, is stupendous, the menu a rustic rerun of the first-day feast: the buttery golden *pilaf* still swaddled in its cooking pot; eggs for the omelet transported carefully in a basket; jars of yogurt to be set in the stream to keep cool; the bread still warm from the oven wrapped in a thick, white cloth to keep it fresh. In addition, there is fresh fruit to be squeezed for juice, jars to be filled with fresh water from the stream, the makings of little cups of bitter coffee, syrups for sherbets, and tea for the *samovar*.

Later—when the feast is over, after the last grains of rice have been rolled between buttery fingers into little savory balls to be popped into mouths no longer capable of protest, as the sun dips below the desert's sandy horizon or drops below the blue edge of the hills—richly woven carpets are rolled out and the revelers take their ease under the stars. As midnight approaches, fires flicker and candles are lit, each one to mourn a death or speak of a birth in the year just passed. This is a time for hope no less than a time for regret. The old remember the loves they have lost; the young wonder what love the future may bring. Newlyweds look for portents —the call of a night-bird seven times repeated, seven white flowers shining under the moon, a piece of bread torn into seven pieces—that speak of a new candle to be lit, a new infant to be born, and doubly blessed if conceived under the dome of heaven. And, all the while, there are sherbets to be sipped, hot tea to be savored; almond-pastries, *baklavas*, *halvas*, and exquisite ices, made with the powdered roots of wild flowers, that, even in the lands where they grow in profusion, are both beautiful and rare. And all the while it will not be forgotten that—long ago, before the festival acquired its modern trappings—the purpose of a night under the stars was to speed the ancestors on their return to the heavens.

left: Early seventeenth-century Persian miniature by Abassi Saavia of a nobleman and his retinue enjoying the alfresco feast customary at the time of the spring plantings.

Kookoo-ye Sabzi iranian new year omelet

A thick round egg-cake served at the picnic celebrates the ancient Persian festival of No Rooz, that combines the new year with the spring plantings and the remnants of ancestral visitations. The omelet is never less than the size of a dinner plate, perfect for sharing, with a crisp, buttery, golden crust and a juicy, green interior. For this quantity of eggs, the volume of green herbs when destalked, and chopped, should fill 4 cups / 1.2 liter pitcher.

Serves 8

1 handful parsley, finely chopped

1 handful cilantro/coriander, finely chopped

1 large bunch scallions, chopped with their green tops

2–3 sprigs fenugreek, finely chopped (optional)

1 tablespoon shelled walnuts, roughly chopped (optional)

1 small handful spinach leaves, shredded

1 tablespoon dried barberries or cranberries

1 tablespoon all-purpose flour

10 medium eggs

1 teaspoon powdered saffron, soaked in a splash of boiling water

Salt and freshly ground pepper

3–4 tablespoons olive oil

❶ In a large bowl, toss the chopped herbs (they must be really dry), scallions, fenugreek, nuts, spinach, berries, and the flour. In another bowl, whisk up the eggs with the saffron water and season with salt and pepper.

❷ Heat the oil in a large skillet—one with a good nonstick surface. When the oil is hot, pour in the egg mixture slowly, stirring the herbs in as you pour, so the base is still golden but the interior is green. Shake to loosen the base, turn the heat right down, cover loosely, and leave to cook very gently for 20–25 minutes. If the heat is too high, it will make the eggs leathery. As the omelet cooks, shake to loosen the base, and neaten the sides with a spatula to build up a deep, straight edge.

❸ When the top looks set, invert a large plate over the pan and flip the whole thing over so the omelet ends up on the plate, cooked side uppermost. Be brave. It's no harder than flipping a pancake. Slip the omelet back in the pan for another 5–10 minutes and brown the other side (you may need a little more oil). When it feels firm, slide it out onto its plate. It will set a little more as it cools. Pat off excess oil with paper towels.

Serve at the temperature of a warm sunny day, with the Saffron Pilaf (see page 29) and a bowl of thick, creamy yogurt.

Bastani Sa'labi saffron salep ice cream

Throughout the Middle East, the usual thickening for a creamy ice is *salep*, the powdered root of a ground orchid that is not only beautiful, but has the added distinction of being remarkably high in protein—all the better for celebrating No Rooz.

Serves 6

1 teaspoon salep [powdered orchid root]

2 tablespoons rosewater

2 cups /1 pint whole milk

6 tablespoons sugar

1 teaspoon powdered saffron soaked in a splash of boiling water

❶ Mix the salep with a little of the milk and the rosewater.

❷ Bring the rest of the milk to a boil, remove from the heat, and whisk in the *salep* mixture. Reheat gently, whisking till it thickens, which happens immediately. Stir in the sugar and the saffron water, and leave to cool.

❸ Tip into a metal container and freeze. If using the freezer, take the ice cream out when it is nearly solid, and beat it thoroughly (or liquidize) to break down the ice crystals and incorporate as much air as possible. Take it out of the freezer and put it in the refrigerator half an hour before you are ready to serve.

Particularly pretty when sprinkled with chopped pistachios and pomegranate seeds.

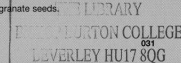

left: Chinese housewife preparing dumplings; at new year, these must be prepared in quantities sufficient to carry the household through the two-week holiday, when all domestic activity ceases—cooks and servants alike leave their aprons on the hook.

chinese new year

In China, as in ancient Persia (and modern Iran), the festival of Sun Neen does double duty as the first day of spring and the start of the new year, falling around February 5, which, incidentally, coincides with the spring festival celebrated by the ancient Celts in western Europe.

In pre-revolutionary China, festivities followed a traditional pattern, although the detail varied from household to household and region to region. In modern post-revolutionary times, it has more to do with what may or may not be permitted. In old China (to make the difference between pre- and post-revolution), beliefs were a tolerant blend of ancestral superstition allied to Confucian good sense, and overlaid by Buddhist concerns over the sanctity of life—all of which were applied according to Taoist principals of non-interference, that could also be applied to what happened in the kitchen.

It will come as no surprise that foods considered suitable for this ancient festival of renewal follow the ancient rule that all should be sunny in both color and shape, and that seeds should figure somewhere in the recipe. Dumplings and little steamed buns are the obvious candidates—among which, *Jien Düy*, little round doughballs stuffed with sweet beanpaste, rolled in sesame seeds, and fried golden are the most popular.

One week before the festival, in those households that still observe the old ways, the custom is for the family to gather around the fireplace, over which is pasted a picture of the household deity, the Kitchen God, to eat *Jien Düy* and speed him on his annual visit to heaven. Honey is rubbed on the lips of the image so that the god may speak sweetly of the household's doings to the Supreme Being, while firecrackers are let off to chase any negative thoughts from his mind. The picture is then taken outside and set alight so that the god may ascend directly to the heavens by way of the smoke. A week later, on the thirtieth day of the Twelfth Moon, the family gathers together again to paste up a new picture and welcome their protector back with more firecrackers, honey, and sweet dumplings.

Hsiang Ju, daughter of author Lin Yutang, remembers new year as the best time of her childhood. In old China, New Year was also a good time for the servants—

often the sole object of children's affections in large and busy households—who were allowed to return home to visit their relatives: "The joy of New Year came from many directions. Creditors looked forward to getting their debts paid, debtors to settling accounts somehow. Madames of certain houses were paid at New Year. Children were given new clothes made specially for New Year's Day, and some entered in close alliance with the servants in their expectation of red packets of money, counting the number of visitors."

A full month before the holiday, preparations began. Not only did the house have to be scrubbed, linen laundered, and clothes pressed, but all the food had to be cooked and stored to be eaten at a time when even the women of the household did no work.

The women, mistress and servant alike, gathered together in each other's kitchens to make *chiatotse*, the savory new-year dumplings, rolling the little glutinous balls of rice flour in their fingers and gossiping, though without

unkindness, malicious talk being unlucky at new year. Enormous quantities of these little pork-and-cabbage dumplings, shaped like the crescent moon, were prepared, packed in earthenware jars, and stored outside so the contents froze hard, an easy way to keep the dumplings fresh. Meanwhile, throughout the holiday, butchers and public eating houses maintained a constant supply of chickens, ducks, and pork cooked in great pans of soy sauce and hung up in the windows to drip.

Recipes, naturally enough, had to obey religious dietary prohibitions, although in China these were always less strictly observed than elsewhere. Chinese Buddhists, for instance, observed the rules of vegetarianism only on the first and the fifteenth day of every month. Nevertheless, new year was considered special, and meat was prohibited throughout the run-up to the festival. Even in non-Buddhist households, it was considered unlucky to slaughter any living thing at a time when the new year was waiting to be born.

"On the morning of New Year's Day, one did not sweep, light fires or pour water, these being unlucky. Fragrant candles were lit, everyone put on his best new clothes and received callers. Housewives settled down at the *mahjong* table, telling people to help themselves to cold food." Visitors brought gifts: of tangerines (symbols of good luck), luxurious fresh fish, deliciously glutinous pig's trotters, chickens to be eaten cold with exquisite little sauces. There was always *nienkao*, a steamed cake made from brown sugar and glutinous rice flour that was stamped with a lucky word in red and was palatable only when sliced and fried and even so, Hsiang Ju recalls, it took a long time to go away. "Those who did not wish to stay at home and gamble milled around at the temple, visiting the fortune-tellers, watching the jugglers and acrobats, listening to the storytellers. And so it continued until around the 16th of the month, after which everything returned to normal."

left: Chinese temple-offering of suckling pig, red apples, red glass goblets, and red chopsticks; red ensures happiness and prosperity.

Chiaotse chinese new year dumplings

Little crescent-shaped dumplings made in great quantities to carry guests throughout the holiday. Prepare them in advance and store in the freezer—they defrost rapidly in the steamer.

Makes 60 dumplings

The filling:

1–2 Chinese cabbages (about 2 lbs / 900 g), finely slivered and chopped

1½ lbs / 675 g finely ground pork

1–3 scallions, finely chopped

2 teaspoons finely chopped fresh ginger

3 level teaspoons salt

4 tablespoons soy sauce

1 teaspoon sugar

The dough:

Generous 3 cups / 500 g all-purpose flour

1½ cups / 350ml water

❶ Blanch the cabbage in boiling water and return the water to a boil. Allow 3 minutes boiling before draining thoroughly. Rinse under cold water.

❷ Mix the cabbage with the rest of the ingredients, kneading thoroughly with your hands.

❸ Sift the flour into a roomy bowl, and pour the water into a well in the middle. Work thoroughly with your hand or in a food processor to make a smooth, elastic but still quite firm dough—allow 10 minutes' kneading time.

❹ Form into a ball, cut into quarters, and roll each quarter into a thick rope. Keep each rope covered with plastic wrap or a damp dish cloth to stop it from drying out while you work. Cut the first rope into 15 equal pieces and work each piece into a ball—flour your hands first—and drop onto a floured board.

❺ Roll each out into a thin disk the diameter of your hand with a stroke or two of the rolling pin. Holding a disk in the palm of your hand, drop in a teaspoonful of filling. Pleat one side of the disk to make little gatherings, and bring it up over the top of the filling to meet the other side. The result should be a plump little crescent with a seam over the top and one side fatter than the other.

❻ Transfer to a lightly floured baking tray, and continue till the dough and the filling are all used up. Freeze in batches and bag up when perfectly firm.

❼ Treat as ravioli: drop in plenty of boiling water and cook for 20 minutes, till the filling is cooked right through. Serve with a dipping sauce of vinegar and soy sauce.

Alternatively, make pot-stuck dumplings. This technique combines frying and steaming, and gives the little dumplings a deliciously crisp base and a tender crown. Pour 2 tablespoons of oil into a roomy skillet (a 10 inch / 25 cm skillet will accommodate about 15 dumplings), heat the oil till nearly smoking, and arrange the dumplings in the pan, seamside up in concentric circles. Turn down the heat and fry gently for 3 minutes, till the base is lightly browned. Add enough boiling water to come halfway up the dumplings, turn the heat down again, cover, and simmer for 10 minutes, till the dumplings are perfectly tender. Remove the lid and bubble up for another 5 minutes, till the dumplings are frying again. Reverse the contents of the pan onto a plate to make a round cake with a crisp, golden top that falls easily into its component parts. Serve with a dipping sauce of vinegar and matchstick-cut ginger.

rosh hashanah, the jewish new year

Jewish households celebrate Rosh Hashanah, new year, in late September or early October, at the time when nomadic shepherds return home to overwinter their flocks. The festival begins at sunset on the eve of a day chosen according to the lunar calendar, and lasts for forty-eight hours. At some time during the allotted two days, it is customary to eat a piece of apple dipped in honey or sugar to ensure sweet times ahead. While the men commit to studying eternal truths in the holy book, the women write their history in the dishes they prepare—a method of communication as eloquent as it is subtle, but which, being nowhere else but in the mind of each woman, has the virtue of indestructibility. Because of this, the Jewish new-year menu is both variable and regional, reflecting the wanderings of the diaspora. According to the affluence, disposition, or the allegiances of the household, the feast will include one or many dishes that feature foods that have a particular symbolism, or whose composition or shaping is of special significance to the participants. For the Ashkenazim, the Jews who settled in northern Europe, the festive bread, *hallah*, is the chief vehicle for the transmission of ancestral memory. A braided ringbread sprinkled with raisins can be a simple symbol of the year's turning, or serve as a reminder of the inevitability of life and death, or it might be a crown of fertility (among the Slav communities of eastern Europe, young matrons with babes-in-arms are permitted to wear wheat in their Easter garlands). When slashed like the rungs of a ladder, it reminds the people of Jacob's direct ascent into Heaven, which speaks of the possibility of eternal life; when baked in the form of a bird with spread wings, it is at once the protector of the people and represents the Lord's promise to defend Jerusalem as a bird defends its nest.

There are other dishes whose symbolism is less obvious but which are, nonetheless, emotionally significant. A chicken soup with *mandlen*—small, round dumplings, handrolled—serves to remind those who share it of the need for unity and strength. A fish, cooked whole and with its head still in place, reminds the father to exhort his sons to be first in everything, while a dish of carrots sliced thinly reminds the mother to tell her daughters of their duty to refill the household purse with golden coins. Meanwhile, the Sephardim, those who took refuge among the Muslims in the Moorish lands of Spain and Portugal, eat a roasted sheep's head for the same

right: A young girl learns how to braid the *hallah* bread eaten on the Jewish Sabbath; the duty of all adults at this time is to instruct the young in the ways of their forebears.

reason as the Ashkenazi households serve the fish head: as a reminder to be at the head rather than the tail, although the underlying reason is economic rather than intellectual.

The sheep's head can also be taken as a symbol of Abraham's willingness to sacrifice his son Isaac on the altar of his God, a tragedy averted by the intervention of the Almighty and the appearance of an alternative sacrifice, a young ram. Sheeps' heads being a little hard to come by in modern times, it is more usual, even in Orthodox households, to serve just the brains and tongue. Those who have no stomach for such meats might care to follow the example of the Sephardim of Morocco, and give thanks for the year's good things with the Muslim Sabbath dish, a seven-vegetable *couscous*—seven being the number of good fortune in every culture that takes its lead from ancient Persia. The threads were knotted even more confusingly when the diaspora reached the new world and communities long separated mixed and matched regional habits. As at the various renewal festivals of other cultures, all manner of seeds and grains continue to be eaten to encourage fertility in both land and people, along with green things—vegetables, green olives, green tea—as a reminder to the earth not to stay dormant for too long. The many round foods that feature in the new-year customs of other cultures appear in the guise of meatballs, dumplings, donuts, bagels, *knishes*, and *piroshki*—all of which, because they are circular and self-contained, can be read as symbols of unity and continuity.

At the end of the meal, sweet things must be enjoyed—dates, pomegranates, and figs—all the Biblical foods that ripen at this time. Even now, with the Promised Land no longer a dream, the rituals and food ways of Rosh Hashanah still speak to the heart as well as the stomach.

Among sophisticated cultures, sacred foods whose spiritual significance comes from sophisticated culinary expertise—the combinings, layerings, shapings, and bakings of the festive dishes prepared by Jewish, Chinese, Indian, Persian, or French cooks, or indeed by anyone schooled in one of the world's great gastronomic traditions—are the culinary equivalent of the written word designed to tell the people what they should be told. As with the holy books of all the great religions, they are ultimately created to limit rather than expand the human consciousness. In contrast, the significance of the bowl of berries prepared as a sacred offering to the spirits of nature by the Cree Indians seems scarcely worth discussing—lacking the layers of intellectual reasoning applied by other cultures. And yet, in that simple gesture, the expression of expectation, that by offering up a handful of sour fruit to a higher power, it will be made sweet—is all the longing of the human spirit, the hope that we, and our kind, are not alone in a hostile universe, that something stronger and better will make it good.

food as a communal memory

Ancestral memory is much like the stuff we keep in a trunk in the attic—we know it's there, but we don't open the lid till we need it, and, when we do, all we find is the remnants left by the rats. So it is with the knowledge that survived in many cultures other than those of the developed world—but which, when first stumbled upon in modern times, the developed world saw no reason to value. There is no doubt that the knowledge possessed by the aboriginal peoples of Australia and the indigenous tribes of the Americas cannot easily be replaced. Perhaps much of it is lost forever, however hard our scientists try to reconstruct it.

The wild gatherings that sustained the original inhabitants of the Antipodes were far more than a food source; they were life itself. To a people whose ancestral belief is that their very existence depends on the union of all living things, survival depends on the capacity of all who share the earth to live in harmony. Ritual energies are

right: Aboriginal woman preparing the *bunya-bunya* pinenut harvest—a moment of glut that allows the menfolk the luxury of hunting and young people an opportunity for marriage.

directed toward the encouragement of this harmony—the ultimate aim of religious ceremonies that have to do with the cycle of life.

Information on the harvesting of aboriginal foodstuffs is never lightly divulged, since, to do so is to betray what are, effectively, state secrets—and not only because it is inadvisable to allow outsiders to trample all over the song-lines (totemic and sacred sites that define the territorial rights of a tribe). To speak idly of the where-abouts of crops, the seasons in which they may be found or harvested (not necessarily the same thing) is to open these precious resources to exploitation by those who do not understand their rhythms. This is not the same emotion as that which governs the sharing of food. Transients, travelers—including the white settlers from across the sea—might be welcome to partake of what is already in the pot, but it would be folly to tell them where to find it for themselves.

There is evidence that some foodstuffs that were particularly abundant locally— pigweed and hogweed, for instance, whose seeds are unusually protein-rich, were cultivated through the simple method of digging irrigation channels and, where nec-essary, discouraging competing growth. Large quantities of the seeds could then be stored, coated in grass and mud for protection, to provide food during ceremonial activities, among which was hunting. The pursuit of live prey is always a risky busi-ness. Success can never be guaranteed, making an alternative foodstore advisable, if not essential. Hunting is a secondary activity to gathering, since the results are less predictable. Respect is paid to those warm-blooded creatures that share the earth's resources, from whom life is taken for the sole purpose of feeding another. The men hunted the larger animals—kangaroo, emu, wallaby—and the meat was shared according to traditional laws. Young boys were not permitted to eat strong meat like emu or the internal organs of other animals. These were reserved for the elders, while women and children were permitted to eat certain foods at certain stages in their lives and not at others. Within these rules, no member of a group went hungry.

The sites of opportune harvests such as witchetty grubs—from the aboriginal word, *witjuti*, the larvae of any species of insect that bores its way into rotten wood —are carefully noted and communicated at the proper time. Packed with protein, insects are particularly valuable foodstuffs.

The celebration of voluntary rites of passage—such as initiation rather than the

involuntary rites of birth or death—were timed to coincide with whichever harvest was of particular importance to the people's survival. Information on the harvest was transmitted orally and visually by the senior to the junior members of society—an essential task since many of the foods need lengthy processing to render them palatable or, in many cases, to remove toxins. Where preparation of a foodstuff is simply a matter of deciding whether to cook it or eat it raw, ritual is of minor importance, but it is a different matter when knowledge makes the difference between life and death. Often the preparation processes were dangerous in themselves, since volatile and poisonous substances had to be neutralized. That the methods by which this was achieved were both complicated and lengthy was a reason to render them sacred, thus committing the ritual to communal memory. If the food were no longer harvested, the knowledge would be lost; if, however, the method were recorded in a way that can be read by others, it would be vulnerable to exploitation. Oral information is easily abandoned, written information is easily stolen—there are no easy answers.

Certain records, however, do exist. Among the Tiwi people of Melville and Bathurst Islands, the harvesting of a certain species of wild yam, the underground tuber of a vine, is an intrinsic part of initiation ceremonies—not only for its mystic significance, but also as an opportunity for girls to be taught when to gather and how to prepare a food on which their people depend. The harvest follows the natural cycle of spring growth and winter fallow: tubers are dug when the seed has been set but before the vine has withered. This particular yam, unlike other yams that are immediately palatable, has to undergo considerable preparation, not only to make it edible, but also to ensure the flesh is leeched of all toxins. The tubers are first steam roasted in an earth oven, the outer husk removed, the flesh pounded till soft, and washed in running water till no trace of bitterness remains. The mash is then drained by packing it into a hole dug in the sand, after which it is ready to be eaten immediately, or dried for storage.

Among the truly dangerous foodstuffs, the *burrawang*, a palm—like cycad whose fruit, after lengthy preparation, tastes a little like mild cheese, is so toxic in its original state that aboriginal mothers taught their children not to touch it at all. A fast was observed by those who prepared the fruit—a process of soaking and draining that lasts several days, after which the food was buried in sand to leech it of remaining toxins for at least a month—some reports stipulate nine. In northern Australia, this was a ceremonial foodstuff only, but in other places, the prepared kernels, aged until chalky, a process assisted by natural events such as bushfires, were dried and milled into flour of excellent keeping qualities. It was used to make *dampers*, unleavened breads that were baked under hot ash— a process adopted by Australia's first white settlers.

Less predictable harvests, such as the *Bogong* moth that flies in huge numbers in early summer estivating in the mountains of New South Wales, provided vast quantities of food for a very short time. The aboriginal peoples treated these periods of plenty—the early equivalent of boom following bust—as an opportunity for social interaction. The most important of these opportune harvests, and the one that could feed the largest number of people for the least possible effort, was that which followed the three-year fruiting cycle of the *bunya-bunya* pine. The *bunya-bunya* nut, although not the most important food plant in the antipodean larder, is certainly the aboriginal foodstuff possessed of the highest degree of spiritual resonance.

The tree that supplies this miraculous foodstuff belongs to one of the most primitive of all botanical families, of which there are many in this ancient land. The group includes the monkey-puzzle—a tree native to the continent of South America, once part of the Australian landmass—whose nuts provide the Araucani people of Chile with a major food source. *Bunya-bunya* pines are mainly to be found in the mountain ranges of southeast Queensland, where the trees, tall and stately, fruit profusely one year in every three. The cones look like huge green pineapples, inside which are large quantities of creamy-fleshed seeds that need no preparation, can be eaten at any stage of ripeness, raw or roasted, and are an excellent source of protein. They taste, I'm told, rather like pine-flavored chestnuts.

All was well with the *bunya-bunya* nut harvesters until the arrival of the white settlers, whose accounts of thousands of native people flocking from many hundreds of miles for no obvious reason caused great alarm in the homesteads. The fear that the native people were up to no good was fed by the fact that the harvesters did not sleep in the nut groves at night but, unwilling to risk a crack on the head by a twenty-pound pine cone, withdrew to surrounding valleys. From here, they dispatched hunting parties to kill the meat animals required for initiation ceremonies and the other ritual activities that could not be risked at any other time. As was also customary, the presence of the elders was used to settle arguments and reconcile differences. These seemingly sinister activities gave rise to considerable alarm among the new settlers, who circulated stories of cannibalism and other nameless horrors performed to appease gods of unimaginable savagery. Calls for the wholesale banning of such gatherings were implemented after three particularly prolific harvests in the 1880s. This action, backed up by physical force, spelled disaster for the native people. For an oral tradition to survive, the lessons learned by one generation must pass directly to the next. Among the aboriginal peoples, the process by which essential knowledge is conveyed is by following the natural cycles of fallow and harvest that also dictate the movements of people and animals. Information of historical and practical value, because it is intricately bound up with the way people live, swiftly disappears if lifestyles change. At the point of change, information can only be preserved artificially.

The care and use of the land is woven into the legends of the Dreaming, the song cycles that tell of the creation of land and ocean, valley and mountain, trees and plants, man and beast. Such talk is not idle, but a blueprint for survival. Song, dance, and paintings on rock, bark, and bodies as well as, in modern times, more conventional materials fulfill this conservatory role. Into the seemingly abstract patterns— beautiful in their own right, and endowed with a symbolism easily recognized by the initiated—can be read topographical instructions, even specific directions, for reaching a valuable food source, along with its identity, quality, and quantity.

The sacred nature of the harvest is unspoken, since it is already venerated as indivisible from the sacred whole.

harvest of the waters

Opportune harvests—of which the fisherman's catch is surely the most unreliable—have always been considered to have a spiritual connection, since they must be assumed to be the result of some form of divine intervention.

All who risked their lives at sea developed rituals to ensure the forces that governed the deep were friendly. Sometimes these involved the whole community, from the dipping of holy images in the waters, to the scattering of specially baked breads or other sacrificial offerings on the waves, to the full-scale immersion of all people involved. Sometimes in harbors, or rivers, or where the waters are protected, rituals include the enactment of mock-fights in which the home team—good— triumphs over the outsiders—evil. Other rituals can be more private; small gestures designed to avert trouble, such as the wearing of a certain garment, or the possession of a talisman. Disaster can be attributed to many things: failure to observe the proper rituals, the slaughter of certain seabirds, the presence of a female onboard ship, even uttering certain words that permitted the forces of evil to gain a foothold.

Just as those who scattered seed on the cold earth were making an act of faith, so those who cast their nets in the waters did so in the hope, but without certainty, of success. Fishing communities were rarely monocultural, cropping the land—farming and shore-gathering—at times when the waters were dangerous or unproductive. Traditionally, fishermen provided the same service as hunters. They cropped a protein source, that, although unreliable, afforded the community a period of freedom from labor. With leisure comes the chance to consider the great philosophical questions—the nature of God, the purpose of Man—on which are laid the foundations of all religion.

Of the four elements on which humanity depends, water is the most mysterious. To our ancestors, driven by hunger to harvest the oceans as well as the rivers and lakes, the deep was a dangerous place. While inshore fishermen are dependent on the tides, leaving and returning to harbor according to the pull of the moon, deep-sea fishermen follow the shoals. trawling the two great oceans, the Atlantic and the Pacific, which span both northern and southern hemispheres. Until modern times, Antarctica was out of bounds to all but the most narrowly adapted of warm-blooded creatures, while the islands and frozen seas of the Arctic proved capable of colonization by the hardier breed of nomad—hunters, herdsmen, and fishermen. Among these are the reindeer-herding Sami, a people from the far northern reaches of Scandinavia who speak an ancient language and have managed to preserve much of their culture into modern times. Otherwise known as Lapps—not a word much liked by those to whom it's applied—their sacred food was *Amanita muscaria*, an hallucinogenic mushroom that grows freely in the pine forests, although, as with all fungi harvests, some years are more prolific than others. It was an infusion prepared with this fungus that drove the Vikings to the state of mind they called berserk—a frenzy that endowed the longshipmen with what seemed like superhuman savagery and strength.

While it can only have been hunger that first drove a man to risk his life on the ocean, curiosity kept him there, and a belief in a higher power drew him on. Among the most resilient of the ocean-going gatherers were the fishermen of the Lofoten islands, an ice—bound archipelago high above the Arctic Circle, toward whose shores the female codfish, fresh from overwintering in the ocean, drift on the Gulf Stream to spawn. This inshore catch—firm-fleshed, muscular, with buttery livers as rich and sweet as bone marrow—is one reason for the original settlement of the islands. When dried and salted, the cod provided the fishermen with fuel-food that allowed them to undertake impossibly arduous sea voyages. It was the long trawl for the cod that led Leif Ericson, the Norwegian explorer, to stumble into the Americas a full five centuries before Columbus made landfall. The haul also provided the islanders with a valuable trade item that, when exchanged for gold and good red wine, compensated for the hardship endured for the rest of the year.

Skrei-molje norwegian spring cod

The inshore fishermen of the Lofotens—the snow-covered islands off the northern coast of Norway—traditionally celebrated the arrival of the shoals of spring cod, *skrei*, by cooking the first of the catch straight from the nets. The liver cooked in a little of the fish liquor provides a delicious rich sauce, with the consistency and flavor of beef marrow. Failing this, the fishermen's wives recommend melted butter with egg.

Serves 4 hungry fishermen

4 thick middle-cut cod steaks, chopped through the bone

1 fresh cod's roe (both wings— the whole thing)

6 large potatoes, peeled and thickly sliced

Water

Salt

Vinegar

The sauce:

1½ sticks / 175 g unsalted butter

2 hard-boiled eggs, peeled and chopped

❶ Wipe the cod steaks and salt them lightly. Wipe the roe and wrap it in a double envelope of waxed paper.

❷ Bring a pan of salted water to a boil and lay the roe in it. Bring back to a boil and then turn down the heat immediately. Simmer until the roe is firm—a medium-sized roe takes about 25 minutes. Leave the roe in the water to cool. Meanwhile, cook the potatoes until soft in plenty of boiling salted water. Drain, dish, and keep warm. Slice the cod's roe—it should be cool and firm by now—and put to warm with the potatoes. For the sauce, melt the butter in a small pan; stir in the chopped hard-boiled eggs.

❸ Bring a shallow pan full of well-salted water with a tablespoon of vinegar to simmering point. Add the cod steaks. Bring back to a simmer, and cook the fish for 4–6 minutes, depending on the thickness. Drain, and pile on top of the roe and potatoes.

❹ Hand the butter sauce separately in a jug. Accompany with thin crispbreads—Norwegian flatbread.

Norwegians drink claret with their cod, although beer with a chaser of *aquavit* is acceptable. Traditionally, you may not drink at all unless your host engages your eye and raises his glass—to which courtesy, the proper response is *Skål!*

The Norse equivalent of a planting ritual, the celebration of the first catch of the codfish is a feast. The central dish is *skrei-molje*, freshly caught cod cooked in seawater (*see above*), fortified with potatoes and rich with cream, in a fisherman's cauldron, a round-bellied pot that sat on a fire lit in the bows of the old longboats—primitive, practical, and universal. The dish, as with all one-pot stews, can be served in as many courses as you please, and the traditional accompaniment is not, as might be supposed in those parts, beer with a chaser of *aquavit*, but Mediterranean claret, the ballast that loaded the trading vessels of the Hanseatic League, controllers throughout the Middle Ages of the profitable salt-cod trade.

The celebrations continue through the night while the participants tell and retell in song and verse the story of the search for the shoals. I first attended the feast in 1985, the year that the town fathers of the island's capital, attempting to preserve a tradition in danger of vanishing, decided to convert a private household festival into a municipal event. Although the celebrants were mainly local and there was already concern over depletion of the cod stocks, the money had been found to fly in a famous contralto from Oslo, a specialist in the sagas of the Norsemen, to add a touch of class to an event that might otherwise have been unworthy of the media's attention. During the course of the long night—and few nights are longer than those of the Lofotens in winter—innumerable cod fishing sagas were both sung and spoken.

While the Norsemen put to sea at the end of February, long before the snows melt and the sun returns to warm the earth—in fact, as soon as the ice cracks and the ships are freed from the floes—in warmer climes, it was the abating of winter storms that allowed the fisherman to leave harbor. In Russia's southerly ports on the Black Sea, the festival food was *blinis* and caviar for those who could afford it; and the first catch of river fish for the rest. In the maritime city of Amsterdam in the Netherlands—whose proudest boast is that its foundations are composed of fish bones—the feast is *groene* herring, the first catch of the seasonal herring shoals, which have flashing emerald flanks and a layer of rich fat beneath the silvery skin. The fish is filleted on the quayside and eaten raw by the enthusiastic citizenry, who consume it with a relish of onion, a nip of *aquavit*, and a heartfelt thanks to God.

The opening of the harbors of the more temperate zones of Europe was a signal for water-born workers—the boatmen of the inland waterways of Germany, the gondoliers of Venice, the churchgoing communities of the lakes of Sweden, those who navigated the water highways of the Volga, the Rhone, the Rhine—to organize boat fights, the watery equivalent of the fieldworkers' planting rituals that, through banging drums or making loud noises and letting off fireworks, are designed to scare away bad spirits. Call it the northern version of the Maori *hakka* ; it is a way of unnerving the opposition.

One notable survivor of the ancient water fights is the gladiatorial punt race at Sète on the edge of the Camargue at the mouth of the Rhone, southern France, where rival captains pass and repass till one topples the other from his perch. The victors celebrate and the vanquished drown their sorrows in *vin de sable*, a sharp, pink wine made from the tenacious little vines that survive in near-desert conditions. All fortify them-selves for the journey home with steaming bowls of *tellines*—exquisite little shellfish gathered from the shoreline, distinguished from other bivalves by the delicacy of their saffron-tinted flesh and almond-shaped shells.

left: Sturgeon fishermen being towed out to sea on the Danube Delta in Romania—the first crop of the year is caviar, the fish eggs that fetch absurdly high prices from connoisseurs.
above: Home-conserved caviar, lightly salted, prepared by Romanian fishermen for transport to market.

In China, the water festival held to ensure the safety of fishermen is Loong Shün Jeet, Dragon Boat Festival, that honors a virtuous minister of the State of Ch'u, one Wut Uen, who drowned himself in protest about corrupt government practices. This took place during the Chou Dynasty, in 295 B.C. The food of the festival is *Joong*, a sticky-rice dumpling wrapped in leaves that is dropped into the waters as sustenance for the martyr. Wut Uen sent a message back from the spirit world to say that the river dragons had eaten all the packages, so could they please, in future, be tied with brightly colored string and accompanied with the beating of drums and the clashing of cymbals, since dragons were scared of loud noise and color. From then on, the gifts of sticky rice bundles were fixed with ribbons, spectators made as much noise as possible, and the boats, carved and painted like dragons, raced each other to the scene of the sacrifice.

next page: Jewish families celebrate Purim in Israel with an open-air picnic—the equivalent of May Day which is celebrated in similar fashion in other cultures.

the farming year

When the herdsman harnessed his horse to the plough, his festivals began to reflect a new preoccupation, the cyclical farming year. Once he had chosen his pastures, tilled his earth, and thrown up a dwelling to shelter his family, there was no going back. The need to persuade nature to turn an amiable face to his endeavors became a matter of life or death. The planting, husbandry, and gathering of such crops as could be relied on not only to provide the daily dinner, but which could, in times of plenty, feed his domestic animals as well, became his life's work. His sacrifices reflected this need. Foods that encourage the earth to put forth abundance include all the obvious fertility symbols—seeds, nuts, eggs— reinforced with water-sprinkling, making loud noises to scare away evil spirits, and taking food out into the fields to encourage fertility in all things under the sun. In contemporary terms, a barbecue, a picnic, or a pilgrimage to the hills, with a loaf of bread, a jug of wine, and thou are all a primitive response to an urge to worship at nature's shrine. In Copenhagen, Denmark, the Danes celebrate May Day, the first day of spring, with a picnic in the Tivoli gardens, carrying with them chairs and tables and whatever else is needed for the preparation of hot drinks, with baskets of sweet things for pleasure—airy, crescent-shaped pastries sprinkled with nuts or centered with soft egg custards, and butter-rich cookies baked in the shape of lucky stars or horseshoes.

Northern Europeans see the cow as their principal milk animal, expect the early lactation in April or May, and convert the first of the year's milkings into fresh, sweet butter (saving the buttermilk for cake-baking). Those who live in the hot lands of the Mediterranean keep sheep and goats as their primary milk animals, expect them to lactate when the first young animals of the year are born, just before Christmas, and conserve the early milkings in the form of yogurts and fresh curd cheeses. In the mountains of Greece at Christmas, circa 1970, Joan Bouza Kosta shared the villagers' anticipation of the fresh milk products that followed the November lambing; in particular the delicious phyllo-pastry pies prepared with the fresh, white curds made with the creamy, new milk: "Eyes shine as people describe the rich yogurt and sweet milk pies, *galopita*, traditionally made for the New Year's celebration, huge round pies, each requiring three liters of milk and thickened with eggs, ground almonds, and semolina. No one goes without. On New Year's morning, shepherds are busy delivering pails of milk to their friends, neighbors, and patrons who do not have flocks of their own."

The pies are baked in a *tapsia*, a flat round copper pan about the size of a donkey's pannier, a design that would be familiar to the cooks of Classical Greece. They are baked, in the round stone ovens that stand in every backyard, and are made again for Aprokreas, or carnival, the two weeks of festivities that, in Greece, precede the beginning of Lent.

Butterkakker **danish may day cookies**

Lucky horseshoe cookies to be packed for the traditional spring picnic in Copenhagen's Tivoli gardens, made with fine flour, imported almonds to make it special, real vanilla, pure white sugar, and the beautiful pale butter yielded by the year's first milkings.

Makes about 30 little cookies.

1¼ sticks / 150 g softened unsalted butter

Scant ½ cup / 100 g sugar

⅔ cup / 100 g ground almonds

Scraping of vanilla bean or 2 drops vanilla extract

⅔ cup / 100 g all-purpose flour

1 teaspoon baking powder

A pinch salt

❶ Preheat the oven to 375 F /190 C / Gas 5.

❷ In a warm bowl using a wooden spoon, beat the butter with the sugar till light and white. Beat it some more as you work in the almonds, vanilla, and the flour sifted with the baking powder and salt. Keep on beating till you have a softish dough; you may need a little milk. The whole business can be done in the food processor if you prefer.

❸ Butter the baking sheet.

❹ Cut off nuggets of the dough and roll them into little ropes about as long and thick as your middle finger. Arrange these on the baking sheet in the shape of lucky horseshoes.

Bake for 20 minutes. Transfer to a wire rack to cool and crisp. Delicious when accompanied with camomile or lime blossom tisane sweetened with meadow-flower honey—the essence of spring.

Galopita **greek milk pie**

Milk pies, baked for Christmas and New Year in big, round copper pans called *tapsia* are a specialty of the shepherding communities of the Peloponnese region of southern Greece. The filling is made with the first creamy milkings of the new season and never includes eggs, though city dwellers are known to do so. You can use phyllo instead—you'll need about 20 sheets.

Serves 3 Greek villagers and 5 outsiders

The pastry:

1⅓ cups / 200 g all-purpose flour

About ¾ cup / 175 ml water

The filling:

3 cups / 750 ml very rich milk (half-and-half or light cream)

1⅓ cups / 200 g all-purpose flour

Scant ½ cup / 100 g sugar

To finish:

Olive oil

Ground cinnamon

Sugar

❶ Make the pastry first. Heap the flour on the table, make a well in the center, sprinkle in the water, and work till smooth and elastic, about 5 minutes. Or use the processor to make a softish dough ball.

❷ Divide the dough in half. Work each piece into a ball, cover one with plastic wrap, and roll the other out into a circle about as big as your hand, using a long, thin rolling pin (a well-scrubbed broom handle is perfect). Flour the dough well, and roll it up onto the broomstick. Applying pressure from the center outward with the palms of your hands, roll it out, slowly stretching the dough; rotate the broomstick through a half circle, and repeat. Continue, rotating regularly, till you have a thin 12 inch / 30 cm disk through which the grain of the table might be visible. Repeat with the other dough ball.

❸ Oil a 10 inch / 25 cm pie pan and lay in a circle of pastry, leaving the edges flopping over the sides. Brush generously with olive oil and sprinkle with cinnamon. Cover with the remaining disk of dough (if using commercial phyllo, you'll need 5-6 layers). Cover with plastic wrap and set aside to rest.

❹ Make the filling. Use a little of the milk to blend the flour to a thin paste, then whisk it into the remaining milk along with the sugar. Bring to a boil in a heavy pan, whisking as it thickens, and bubble gently till it no longer tastes of raw flour. Preheat the oven to 375 F / 190 C / Gas 5.

❺ Spread the filling over the pastry, folding over the edges to enclose—it won't completely cover the filling. Trickle the exposed window of filling with more oil, and dust with cinnamon. Bake for 40–45 minutes, until the pastry is crisp. Cool to room temperature, then cut into bite-sized diamonds.

rituals of harvest home

Planting is followed by harvest—or so we must hope. In the temperate lands of the northern hemisphere, harvest home, the festival that marks the safe gathering-in of the foodstuffs that serve to carry a sedentary household safely through the winter, could not take place at any other time of year than the beginning of fall, the end of the growing season.

Among those who still retain a folk memory of their nomadic roots, the rituals of harvest home serve to remind the people who they are and where they come from. It's easy to lose a sense of direction when you spend your life going around in circles, however broad. One such is Sukkot, the Jewish Feast of the Tabernacles, that doubles as a celebration of harvest home. As remembered by Claudia Roden from her Egyptian childhood, the festival—that falls in early October, at the time of the harvest moon—involved the men of the family leaving the shelter of their homes and camping out for a week under the stars. This voluntary exile serves both as a mark of gratitude for the refilling of store-cupboards and a reminder of the time in the wilderness that followed captivity in the land of the Pharoahs. The temporary dwelling of reed and green branches that Claudia's father and brothers built on the flat roof was, to a child, the most excit-

above: Choosing the myrtle for Sukkot, the Feast of the Tabernacles —celebrated to remember the time when tents were pitched in the wilderness during the Children of Israel's wanderings in the desert. This celebration also doubles as the Jewish harvest festival.

ing thing in the world. Those without access to roofs pitched camp in courtyards, gardens, wherever was convenient. Here, the men took up residence throughout the seven days, decorating the interiors of their makeshift dwellings with the best carpets and richest hangings. The evenings were spent around the campfire, drinking wine, singing, storytelling, and praying. Claudia remembers the fragrance of citron fruit and the scent of myrtle twigs, the willow fronds that held the promise of spring. Among the Ashkenazi Jews who fled Germany to escape persecution—a land in which they had taken refuge in medieval times—the festive dish is *tzimmes*, a fragrant stew made with beef, spiced with cinnamon, and sweetened with prunes. Young beef—the fatted calf, the sacrifice made to welcome home the Prodigal Son—is particularly apt at a festival of harvest. Within the recipe—the choice of meat, the spice, and a little sweetness—is the history of a people who, although dispossessed, never forgot the land of plenty from whence they came.

Sukkot chicken soup with dumplings

A chicken soup with *kreplach*—ravioli-like dumplings—eaten on the seventh, and last day of the feast of Sukkot. The veil of dough that hides the filling symbolizes God's forgiveness of man's mistakes. At other times during the holiday, vegetables and fruit take pride of place. Among the Ashkenazim from the North African coast, Egypt in particular, a broad bean soup was eaten on the sixth day.

Serves 6

8 cups / 2 liters clear chicken broth

The dough:

(makes about 20 dumplings)

1 cup / 150 g all-purpose flour

½ teaspoon salt

1 large egg

The filling:

1 cup / 150 g finely chopped cooked chicken

or raw chicken, minced

1 tablespoon chicken fat or oil

1 small onion, finely chopped

1 tablespoon finely chopped parsley

1 egg, forked

Salt and pepper

❶ To prepare a clear broth, simmer a chicken with aromatics—onion, leek, carrots, parsley, celery—in enough water to cover generously for at least 2 hours. Strain, leave to cool, and lift off the hat of golden fat (reserve for other purposes).

❷ Work the dough ingredients together till perfectly smooth and elastic—you may need a little more flour or a dash of water—pop into a plastic bag and leave to rest while you prepare the filling.

❸ Heat the fat or oil in a small pan and fry the onion gently until it turns transparent. Add the chicken, and fry gently if raw. Work all the filling ingredients together, and season with salt and pepper.

❹ Roll out the dough as thin as you can, and cut into squares about the size of the palm of your hand. To do this accurately, roll the pastry into a long, thin bolster and cut into segments, the width of your palm. Unroll the segments to give long thin strips, and pile one on top of the other. Cut into squares right through the full strips. Drop a teaspoonful of the filling into the middle of each square, paint the edges with a little water, and fold over the corners to make a triangle, sealing the edges. Bring the long points together and pinch firmly to make a ring—like tortellini. Leave to rest for 20 minutes.

❺ Bring a large pan of salted water to a boil and slip in the *kreplach*, a few at a time—the water should be boiling so the dumplings don't have a chance to stick to the bottom. As soon as they bounce to the surface, remove with a draining spoon and slip into the hot chicken broth.

Tzimmes jewish beef stew with prunes

Among the Ashkenazi Jews of Germany, the dish served at Sukkot, the Feast of the Tabernacles—a festival that does double duty as harvest home—is a fragrant beef stew sweetened with prunes.

Serves 6

2 lbs / 900 g lean beef, cubed

2–3 tablespoons chicken fat or oil

1 lb / 450 g pickling/pearl onions, skinned

¼ lb / 100 g pitted prunes

⅔ cup / 100 g raisins

3–4 cloves (stick them into one of the onions for ease of retrieval)

1 short length cinnamon stick

2¼ cups / 600 ml hot lamb-bone stock

or plain water

Salt and pepper to finish

A dash of red wine vinegar

❶ Rinse the meat and pat dry.

❷ Heat the oil in a roomy pan and fry the onions gently, shaking over the heat, until they take a little color. Push to one side so that you can fry the meat a little.

❸ Add the prunes, raisins, and the spices, and enough water to cover to a depth of two fingers. Bubble up, turn down the heat, lid loosely, and let it simmer gently for an hour or so, until the meat is tender enough to eat with a spoon.

❹ Taste, adjust the seasoning, and sharpen with a dash of wine vinegar.

To accommodate extra guests, add potatoes, carrots, sweet potato, pumpkin, quince or virtually any other variety of vegetable or fruit that takes your fancy to make the dish go further, although it's advisable to up the quota of spices. Possible additional seasonings include allspice, ginger, and paprika.

the fruits of the harvest

While some foods serve a sacred purpose because they are rich or rare, others are valued for practical, social, or religious reasons, still others for the way they guide us along the paths of ancestral memory—at harvest home, it is the fruits of the harvest itself that take pride of place at the feast.

In the wheat lands of the temperate zones of the northern hemisphere, the sacred food of harvest home is that portion of the harvest offered to the gods as reward, or simply as a way of achieving closer union with the divine. It is not offered in its natural state, but after it has received the benefit of the fire in the form of milled grain, leavened or not, baked as bread.

At harvest home in old England, decorative breads—loaves baked as wheatsheaves, or some other decorative shape that had relevance to the celebrants—were the traditional offering at the safe-gathering-in of the grain. In pre-Christian times, the harvest was celebrated with sacrificial bonfires and the worship of corn dollies, life-sized effigies of fertility gods and goddesses—a libidinous bunch whose carnal appetites were reflected in the behavior of their devotees. In these more decorous days, a festival of eating, drinking, and dancing—particularly the old ring dances, designed to encourage a maid to choose her man—is still considered the proper way to celebrate the gathering-in of harvest, whether the banquet is held in municipal halls or among the hayricks.

In the England of my own childhood, soon after the war, when the countryside still needed all the labor it could get, country schools were closed to allow the pupils to help with the harvest. Even though my brother and I were town-bred evacuees and had no family among the harvesters, we were allowed to walk alongside with the other children behind the reapers, stacking the stooks—wheatsheaves tied with string and bunched in threes. The children walked just behind the reapers—men and women, ten or twelve abreast—listening to the swish of their silver-bladed scythes.

East Anglia was not dairy country: we could not expect to eat beef, the feast of harvest home in other places. But game there was in plenty, fat from the gleanings —plump little pigeons with crops full of stolen grain, rabbits, maybe a brace of bright-feathered partridges. Beyond the reapers, a line of nets was spread to catch the rabbits with a boy standing by with his gun. In those days, country children learned to handle an air gun—pellet-loaded, enough to kill a pigeon but little else—as soon as they were old enough to go to school. Game, and maybe a chicken past her laying days, was often the only meat a country child might taste all year. Every lad knew how to shin up a tree trunk to rob a rook's nest; every country girl knew that a

above: Harvest bread baked in the form of wheatsheaves displayed by the priest in the parish church of Saint Olave in central London.

bundle of fat little fledglings made a fine pie.

Not all game was acceptable. Hares—bigger and bolder than rabbits, with powerful haunches and black-tipped ears— were never killed; there was, and still is, a superstition among country people that killing hares brings misfortune; they are too like men, they said. Only the gamekeeper ever took pheasant, which was left to breed for the landlord's guns. But what we did take, skinned or plucked and stripped from the

bone, was flavored with onions and went to make the harvest pasty, the communal pie that was sent to the baker to be cooked in the bread oven, just in time for the harvest feast.

Then there was the bread, of course, carved into thick, pale slices and used like trenchers instead of plates, as it had been long ago before the Normans came, and used now, as always, to mop up the meat juices, the golden gravy. And above our heads, high up on the rafters, the corn dolly— baked into the shape of a wheatsheaf as tall as a man— presided silently over the feast.

sacred rice

Just as bread is the sacred food of the West, so rice is the sacred food of the East. Rice is not only the most acceptable of all temple offerings, it is also a symbol of wealth and good fortune, and the only food that cannot be spilled or wasted without offending the gods.

rice-planting festival in japan

In Japan, rice festivals take place either at planting time or when the harvest is ready to be gathered. Formal activities center around the acting out of the cycle of cultivation by costumed planting-women to musical accompaniment, from the placing of the young shoots in the paddy fields to the harvesting of the ripe grain. The traditional festival food eaten by both participants and observers—also eaten at new year, and celebrated in February—is *kagami mochi*, little cakes made from sticky rice, washed down with unrefined *saké*—rice-wine, milky white in color since the lees have not been filtered off. Strong drink, not for wimps—but then, who needs wimps at harvest home?

Rice is a sacred food and a symbol of good fortune. The rice god Inari has his own little shrine in households that follow the beliefs of Shintoism. Shinto, or the Way of the Gods, the indigenous religion of the people of Japan, is a very ancient belief system whose roots run deep, drawing sustenance from ancestor-worship, polytheism, nature-worship, totemism, and spiritualism. "At Shinto shrines," explains Shirley Booth in her admirable *Food of Japan*, "gifts of saké, which is made from rice, are offered to the gods and served to the people in golden kettles by Shinto priests." At home, the alcove reserved for the rice god is decorated with snow-white cakes of pounded rice, *kagami mochi*, along with scraps of seaweed and fern fronds. At new year, the *mochi* are topped with *dai-dai* (satsuma oranges)—a name that translates as "long life," making the display doubly significant. Since the arrangement includes ingredients from land and sea, with satsumas hanging, as it were, from the sky, it can be seen as embodying all that which nature has to offer, adding yet another layer of symbolism. *Mochi* themselves, being made with steamed rice reduced to a smooth glutinous paste by lengthy pounding, are the very essence of sacredness, since the spirit of the grain has been reduced to its purest elements. Although the technique is now vanishing as a domestic new year ritual, Ms. Booth visited a Shinto temple at Nenogongen in the mountains above Tokyo where they still make *mochi* every winter in the traditional way, to watch the process for herself: "Snow was falling outside, and the huge old wooden kitchen was a mass of steam, as the rice was steamed in square wooden steamers which were lined with cotton and the water was heated over wood fires, stoked by hand with logs. When the rice has finished its steaming, it's turned out of its cheesecloth lining and dumped into a wooden tub called an *usu*, ready to be pounded with the *kine*, a huge wooden mallet.

left: Rice farmers eating newly harvested rice next to their rice fields in Shirakiyama, north of Hiroshima City, Japan.

right: Pounding the rice for the new year rice cakes to be offered at a Shinto shrine in Tokyo, Japan.

"Traditionally," she continues, "the pounding was done by a man and his wife—the woman reaching down into the rice-mass and turning it, before the mallet, wielded by the man, came crashing back down—a dangerous exercise, requiring perfect understanding and unswerving marital trust. And then, after much pounding, grunting, and sweating, the rice turns into *mochi*—in fact, it's hard to believe it was ever rice." After the festival, the rice cakes that have been offered to the rice god are eaten—their hardness and chewiness making them doubly sacred.

the rice harvests in bengal

The rice growers of the Bay of Bengal, the most prolific rice-producing area of India, plant and harvest three crops a year. When the monsoon rains swell Bengal's eight mighty rivers that empty into the great circular bay, they create a vast flood plain that yields ample catches of fish, particularly shrimp, water-tortoise, and crab. When the waters recede, they leave temporary islands of rich alluvial silt to be fought over by the rice farmers. Naturally enough, harvest home is celebrated with a feast of new rice. As the cauldron comes to the boil on its fire of rice stalks, the cooks chant *"pongol pongol"*, the name given to the dish itself that mimics the noise the grains make as they rattle against the sides of the pot.

Among Hindus, the rice feast must first be sanctified by paying dues to those who might otherwise go hungry, a very practical way of earning the approval of the gods. To the birds, denied their share of what should have been a natural grainstore, is offered a five-course meal, while eleven courses must be laid out for the cattle. If the giver of the feast is a high-caste *Brahmin*, a full eighteen courses must be offered to the cattle, which are first garlanded with roses and bathed in water perfumed with sandalwood.

In the Hindu Tamil regions of Sri Lanka, anthropologist Dennis McGilvray noted in the 1970s, the ritual rice dish offered to the gods at harvest home is *pukkai*. This, he reports, is a sweet milk pudding prepared at the temple according to the *pongol* method, a Tamil word meaning "to bubble and boil," and is made with new rice set aside from the first threshings, and fresh milk, preferably from the cow, the animal sacred to Hindus. "When prepared at the temple, the milky rice, sweetened with sugar and flavored with spices, is ladled out in front of the image of the god, along with fruit, betel leaf, areca nuts, and flowers." After the priest has performed *puja*, the act of worship, and the god has finished inhaling the vapors—the spiritual portion of the offering—the rice is distributed among the rest of the worshipers.

For the offering to be acceptable to the gods, *pukkai*—an offering for health and prosperity that can also be made in the paddy fields, on the threshing floor, or anywhere else—must be prepared in a pure and sacred manner: "A new clay pot garlanded with flowers is placed on an outdoor hearth in front of the temple or the household shrine-room and is decorated with markings of sacred burned cow dung, sandalwood paste, and vermilion powder. The basic idea of a *pongol* is to heat the milk by itself over a brisk fire until it swells up and bubbles over the side of the pot in a messy but nevertheless auspicious and pleasing wave of white froth." Once the milk rises, the rice is stirred in and the recipe is cooked in the normal way.

The best time to perform the ritual, advises Dr. McGilvray, is at dawn, when the bubbling-over can be made to coincide with the first rays of the sun—a ritual with which the berry-gathering Cree of Canada would be perfectly at home. In addition, no menstruating women must approach the pot, and the dish must contain no salt, since salt is essential to the diet of mortal man—symbolizing his dependence on the earth—but not for the gods, who exist on a higher plane.

Ven Pongol rice casserole with mung beans

This is the dish cooked to celebrate the rice harvest in southern India, one of the temple-dishes sacred to Lord Vishnu. The best, says cookery expert Julie Sahni, is the version made to feed their pilgrims by the temple cooks of the Mysore *Brahmins*. In northern India, it's soupier, more like oatmeal, and known as *kichdee*—hence kedgeree, the breakfast dish that tickled the taste buds of the memsahibs of the Raj.

Serves 4–6

6 tablespoons ghee (clarified butter)

¼ lb / 125 g yellow mung beans

1½ cups / 250 g long-grain rice

2¾ cups / 700 ml water

½ tablespoon salt

1 heaped teaspoon cumin seeds

1 heaped teaspoon cracked black pepper

1 tablespoon chopped fresh ginger

3 tablespoons toasted cashew nuts, roughly

❶ Heat 2 tablespoons of the *ghee* in a large pan and fry the beans, stirring, for a couple of minutes. Add the rice and stir briefly over the heat—half a minute, just till the grains turn transparent. Add the water and salt, bring to a boil, stir to break up lumps, turn down the heat, cover loosely, and leave to bubble gently for 10 minutes. Stir again, close the lid tightly, reduce the heat to low, and leave to cook gently for another 10 minutes. Remove from the heat.

❷ Meanwhile, in a small skillet or frying pan, heat the remaining *ghee*. Add the spices, allow to sizzle for a few seconds, and then pour over the rice and beans. Mix lightly, and leave to rest for 5 minutes.

❸ Sprinkle with the toasted cashews.

Serve with *chapattis* for scooping and a couple of *sambals* (fresh chutneys): tomato and onion with chili, green mango with tamarind, or green apple with lemon.

Tamil Rice-harvest Pukkai rice pudding with cinnamon and fruit

Only pure white rice and very fresh milk will do, since this is a Hindu temple offering and must be acceptable to the gods. Although the ritual requires the use of a special pot and the cook to rise well before dawn in order that the first rays of the sun may catch the first bubbling-over of the milk, the dish can be prepared in the ordinary way. The fruit, spices, and sugar—in Sri Lanka, *jaggary*, brown palm sugar—make the dish particularly fragrant and thus more worthy of the deity's attention. The inclusion of green gram—a small, yellow-green, pulse-vegetable also to be found, unhusked, in Asian foodstores as moong beans—is optional, but gives a deliciously nutty flavor. To husk moong beans, roast in a dry pan until lightly browned, spread between two layers of cloth, and crush with a rolling pin to loosen the skins, then toss to separate out the kernels.

Serves 10–12

5 cups / 1.2 liters fresh creamy milk (cow's, buffalo, or coconut) plus extra if necessary

1½ cups / 250 g long-grain rice

¼ cup / 50 g husked green gram (optional)

2 short sticks cinnamon

½ teaspoon cardamom seeds

2–3 handfuls chopped dates or raisins

1–2 ripe bananas, sliced

⅔ cup / 175 g light brown sugar

❶ Place the milk, rice, optional gram, cinnamon, and cardamom in a roomy pot, bring gently to the boil, stirring throughout, then turn the heat right down and simmer gently for an hour or so, until the rice is perfectly tender and has absorbed most of the milk.

❷ Add more hot milk if the mixture looks like it is drying out. When the consistency is thick and gooey, stir in the dried fruit, banana, and sugar. If the sugar is added too soon, the rice will always remain a little crunchy. Leave for about 20 minutes to allow the dried fruit to swell.

Serve warm. Best spooned onto banana leaves, but bowls will do.

Throughout India, when rice is prepared in the home for everyday consumption—or in the normal way in the temple as a religious offering—the method of cooking indicates the religious and ethnic allegiances of the household. The Hindu will cook rice plainly in water and eat it with small quantities of other things—vegetables, pulses, fish—and, if enriching the rice with melted butter, will pour this on after the rice is cooked. Muslim households cook rice as a pilaf—in which the parboiled grains are cooked in the pot with the flavoring ingredients—a dish that did not appear on the tables of India until the Mogul invasions of the thirteenth century. There is, also, a difference in the flavorings. Hindus will tell you that Muslims use far too much onion and garlic, while the Muslim cook will explain that a Hindu sauce is no better than cumin-water. Among the fish-eating Hindu Bengalis, duck and duck eggs were eaten with pleasure, while chicken, a land-based heathen bird imported by the Muslims, was regarded with suspicion. To further complicate the matter, says food writer Chitrita Banerji, a cook from West Bengal will tell you that a Bengali from East Bengal drowns his food in oil and spices, eats his fish half-cooked, and ruins the flavor with bitter vegetables. The easterner will explain that his western counterpart makes everything far too sweet, overcooks the fish, is miserly with the spices, and—worst of all—eats wheat *chapattis* with the meal instead of rice.

If all of this sounds a little frivolous, it must be remembered that the offering of food is the most direct method of communication and exchange between one person and another, requiring neither language nor learning. If honorary membership of a tribe can be granted by the simple act of offering a dish of rice, it can just as easily be declined. In all cultures, without exception, the guest who abuses the hospitality of a host, or the host who puts the welfare of a guest in jeopardy, not only disregards the rules of man, but sins against the laws of God.

left: Setting out the rice bowls within the temple grounds for the celebratory communal meal—a very cheerful affair—after worship in the shrine at Manipur, northeast India.

the grape harvest

No harvest festival can be considered complete without its share of mind-altering refreshments. Of all the substances that, when ingested or otherwise absorbed, have the power to transform men into gods—in mind if not in body—there is none more universally appreciated than the fermented juice of the grape.

Wine, to our ancestors, was a sacred liquid transformed from its natural watery state by some mysterious process that could only be explained as divine. Even today, with the chemical threads unraveled and the biological processes explored, wine is still endowed with more mystical attributes than any other substance, mind-altering or not.

The grapepickers' harvest home is celebrated as soon as the first grapes are trodden, at the moment when the new wine can be drunk. The vineyard owner is honor-bound to serve the best, and the menu, as befits a thanksgiving table, is strictly regional. Among the self-sufficient farming communities in Europe, where each household traditionally tends enough vines to make wine for its own needs, a young animal—lamb or kid—will be roasted over an open fire, and the meal washed down with new wine. Since commercial vineyard work is seasonal, the winemakers (heirs to the monks, whose business was to make sure of a good supply of communion wine) provide employment for itinerant gangs of grapepickers—students, holidaymakers, migrant workers, and gypsies. These days the picking is more usually done by professionals who move from the southern shores of the Mediterranean, where the grapes are harvested in midsummer, to the autumn-ripening vineyards of northern Europe—Austria, Germany, Hungary—where the grapes must be left to catch the last warming rays of the sun.

Farther north where the growing season is shorter, the fruit is left to ripen on the vine till the first frosts (or even, in the case of certain sweet wines, beyond), leaving the pickers to race against time and the closing-in of winter—a matter of days rather than weeks. The vines are strung high on wires to keep the precious fruit out of the mud and particularly in cold winters, vineyard workers fill little iron wheelbarrows with blazing fagots and trundle them up among the frozen vines to chase the icy mists into the valley below. The farmers of the Champagne region in France—smallholders with an average of one hundred and fifty acres apiece—are a hardy breed, managing somehow to wrench a livelihood out of what has long been the battleground of Europe. Their ancient capital, Rheims, had to be rebuilt from scratch with regularity. But the real triumph of the *champagnois*—given the most un-promising of thin-blooded wines and precious little peace in which to enjoy it—is that they managed to produce the world's most favorite celebration tipple.

In the face of all that adversity, it's no surprise that the gastronomy is robust. The grapepickers' feast includes the only dish it is possible to serve at such an occasion in such a place—an Alsatian *choucroute*. The nominate ingredient is sauerkraut, but the main event is stupendous quantities of meat. Pork, to be precise, of every shape and kind—chops, sausages, blood puddings, bacon-joints, loin, leg, hip, flank, brain, tongue, trotter—cooked to sweet perfection in a stock made with the bones, heaped high on a mound of wine-sim-mered, aniseed-flavored, salt-fermented cabbage, sauerkraut, the larder-staple of all those who learned their culinary habit from the Tartar horsemen who rode out to the east. The art of submerging perishable foodstuffs in a salty brine in order to preserve them has been understood by Eastern cooks for thousands of years.

In preparation for the feast, long tables are laid beside the open vats in which the juice of the grapes, pressed but not yet drained, is already beginning to ferment. The accompani-ments for the *choucroute* are set out before the participants take their places. Down the center of the table are set bowls of salt-pickled cucumbers, bunches of radishes, pots of mild mustard, dishes of horseradish grated in slivers and mixed with cream and vinegar, and big slabs of yeasty bread. Once blessed by the local *padre*, the food is ladled into deep plates

Choucroute des Vignerons **winegrowers' sauerkraut**

Sauerkraut (*choucroute*—salt-preserved cabbage) is the winter staple of rural households throughout the lands east of the Rhine, among those who take their culinary lead from Germany. The sauerkraut barrel is to be found throughout the lands of the Slavs, Scandinavia, Russia, and all the way to Mongolia. The preservation of vegetable matter by brining—submerging foods in a solution of water and salt that mimics the saltiness of the sea—is undoubtedly one of the oldest conservation methods known to man. Although usually billed as having originated in China, it would be hard to imagine that the idea might not have emerged spontaneously elsewhere—say, perhaps, in olive-growing areas. The process is actually a light fermentation, a miraculous transformation that not only makes the food more palatable, but preserves the vitamin content while making it easier to digest. The brine is used as a cure-all—from hangovers, to morning sickness, to the aftermath of childbirth. The new-season sauerkraut was traditionally eaten with fresh pork after the autumn pig-killing, which conveniently coincides with the wine-harvest. It is then eaten with salt-pork and smoked sausages throughout winter; reappears with goose for the Christmas festivities; and takes a bow on New Year's Day as an oblation for the year's renewal; the last of the sauerkraut barrel is scraped in Lent, to be eaten with fresh fish as soon as the spring thaw releases the fishing boats from harbor.

Serves 8

4 lbs / 1.8 kg sauerkraut

Salt and pepper

4 thin slices fresh pork fat

1 large carrot, scraped and sliced

1 onion stuck with 2–3 cloves

Bouquet garni of parsley, bay, thyme

1 teaspoon juniper berries, crushed

1 pork knuckle

1 lb / 450 g joint smoked pork loin or bacon

8 thick slices ham

1 large garlic sausage, pricked to avoid bursting

8 large frankfurters

8 tablespoons goose fat or freshly prepared pork lard

2 glasses white wine

About 4 cups / 1 liter bouillon or plain water

❶ Put the sauerkraut in a bowl of cold water, and work it with your fingers to loosen. Drain off the water. Repeat twice, squeezing to remove as much of the liquid as possible. Spread on a clean dishtowel and leave to dry for an hour or two. Season with pepper; it shouldn't need salt.

❷ Line a roomy braising pot with the pork fat. Spread on half the sauerkraut, layer in the rest of the ingredients, except the frankfurters, sprinkle with half the goose fat or lard, add the white wine and enough broth or water to ensure that all the ingredients are moistened. Finish with the remaining goose fat.

❸ Preheat the oven to 325 F / 170 C / Gas 3.

❹ Bring the pot to a boil, lid tightly or cover with foil, transfer to the oven and leave to cook gently for 2 hours, until almost all the liquid has been absorbed. After 30–40 minutes, remove the garlic sausage and keep it warm; after an hour, remove and reserve the bacon; after 1½ hours, remove and reserve the smoked pork loin. 20 minutes before the end of cooking, heat the frankfurters in enough simmering water to cover; don't let the water boil.

❺ Pile the sauerkraut on a large preheated serving dish—long and narrow is traditional—removing and discarding the onion and separating out the meats. Pile the meats, sliced as appropriate, on top of the sauerkraut. The traditional arrangement is a lower layer of sliced ham topped with alternating overlapping slices of bacon, sausage, and pork. Frankfurters should be arranged around the edges.

Serve very hot, on hot plates, accompanied with a big bowl of plain-cooked potatoes, pickled cucumbers, and mild mustard.

along with its aromatic liquor—sauerkraut first, then meat. The grapepickers use their own knives, the soup is drunk from the plate, meat chewed from the bone, and fingers wiped on the bread that serves as a mop for the juices. All these good things are washed down with the first fermentation of the grape juice—no need for daintiness when the jugs can be dipped directly into the vats behind the benches. The wine is made with black grapes, the skins filtered before they have a chance to color the juice, but now, at the time of the feast, the liquor has not yet been drawn from the lees and rises like bubbling lava, cloudy and sweet, with a scent of spring flowers and a fizz on the tongue. But before these fine things can be savored, the priest, solemn in his black *soutane*, seated at the right hand of the host, raises his glass in thanksgiving for the goodness of Almighty God, who gave his people the gift of wine, although not the wisdom to enjoy it wisely. Times change. The wheel turns, and, having turned, will turn again.

While few among us would consider it appropriate to sprinkle the blood of a freshly slaughtered cockerel over the newly dug plough, some of us still sweet-talk our pot-plants—and to good effect. While few of us, when the sap rises, feel a need to dance naked through the woods, and still fewer, when the grain ripens, would consider it appropriate to carry the bones of his ancestors around in a bag, we still feel the urge, as the calendar comes round, to cook the rice, or bake the mooncake, or roast the goat.

And when the year's calendar dictates, we will lay a table in the wilderness and take our ease under the canopy of heaven—though we may no longer remember why. What we do know is that, at such a time in a such a place, we may, if only for the time it takes to watch the sunset, forget who we are and remember from whence we came—the place to which, when the time comes, we surely have no choice but to return.

birth
baptism
initiation

2

The birth of a child, in every culture on earth, unless times are very hard indeed, is a reason for celebration. Ancestral memory dictates the rejoicings are muted at first—we're too close to the days when childbirth could all too easily end in loss—and the welcoming of an infant into the community does not usually take place until a few days, or even weeks or months, after the event.

Amongst wealthy households in pre-revolutionary China, any formal announcement of birth had to wait for a month to make sure of the infant's survival. When it was considered safe to publish the news, visitors were rewarded with a glimpse of the newborn infant, and handed gifts of red-dyed eggs. These were always offered in pairs—in the East, people are very conscious of numbers—taken from pyramids piled high on golden platters. In return, the visitors tucked pairs of silver dollars wrapped in red paper into the infant's clothing. Throughout the house, red and gold candles burned. In every room were scarlet scrolls on which was written, in golden letters, the words "Happiness" and "Longevity." The scrolls were decorated with drawings of the Fairy Immortal—always portrayed as an old man, bearded and stooped—holding a peach in one hand and a staff in the other. "Peaches and noodles together symbolize happiness and long life," explained Hsiang Ju, daughter of writer Lin Yutang, recalling in the 1960s her childhood in Fujian province. "On the birthdays of elderly persons, the little children were ushered in to pay their respects and receive packets of dollars. It was good to grow old and have a glorious seventieth or nineti-eth birthday, with all the smooth-faced grandchildren gathered round. Pyramids of fresh noodles, with cut-outs of red paper placed upon them, and pastries made in the shape of peaches, their pale and doughy surfaces sprinkled with red, stuck with green leaves, stood on stands. All the peaches were put in a mound by the candles. Without this pyramid of pastry peaches, something would be missing."

previous page: *Birth of the Virgin*, c. 1480. The Virgin is presented with sweetmeats—sugary treats to tempt her appetite after giving birth.

right: Ink and watercolor painting of *The Peach Garden* in pre-revolutionary China. Peaches are symbols of longevity, inextricably bound up with birth in a culture in which reverence for ancestors was imbibed with mother's milk.

birth baskets

In eastern European countries, the arrival of a new addition to the community is celebrated by the formal presentation of birth baskets, a kind of edible baby shower. As soon as the drama of the confinement itself has died down, a household blessed with a new baby could expect a stream of visitors bearing food. These ritual gifts, presented by well-wishers to ensure the newborn never goes hungry, are beautifully packed in wicker baskets under snow-white napkins embroidered with images appropriate to a baby. In isolated rural areas where the old ways have survived, the birth-basket bearers wear traditional dress—dark skirts and snowy-white blouses are edged with handmade lace caught at the wrist and breast with bright silk ribbons imported from Paris. Some of these are very beautiful—heirlooms embroidered with flowers and leaves in formal patterns that vary subtly from village to village—passed from mother to daughter, and kept packed away in a painted chest in the living room when not needed.

It is April, 1991, not long after the fall of the Berlin Wall, shortly before Slovakia severed itself politically from the Czechs. Little has changed in Krasna Luka, a village on the edge of the High Tatras, a mountainous region of Slovakia known to Russia's hunting fraternity as the last refuge of a once-plentiful population of black bears. Today, or any other day, the inhabitants of Krasna Luka take no interest in men with guns unless they bring meat for the pot. There are far more important things to be done. Spring is in the air. The hens are coming into lay, the household cow will shortly give birth to her calf, the grass is beginning to grow in the meadow. In short, now is the perfect time for all warm-blooded creatures who take their initial sustenance from the mother, animal or human, to be born.

In an upper room in one of the wood-built houses, a new mother suckles her baby. On the day chosen for the welcome, the baby is already three weeks old, the ceremony of the birth baskets delayed to allow time for the paternal grandparents to travel here from a neighboring village. The senior matron of the village, who has also served as midwife, is in the kitchen preparing food for the guests—*piroshki*, the national dish, dumplings that can be stuffed with savory or sweet. Today, since the *piroshki* are for a special purpose, the stuffing is sweet: black plum jam and fresh, white curd—a subtle message that life is a combination of sharp and soft, sweet and sour, dark and light, old and new; for balance, the crispness and crunchiness of the *piroshki* contrast with the smooth, soft skin of the *pirishki*, a pastry stuffed with poppy seeds and made as a wedding strudel. Set ready beside the feast, are a single glass and a bottle of home-distilled plum brandy—all who share in the joy of the birth must drink from the same source.

The baby's needs are simpler: under his pillow, a soporific herb to soothe his sleep; over his head, a hank of garlic, a precaution against the devil as he dreams. Five visitors, all female, arrive in quick succession. The first, a young girl, the baby's aunt, brings happiness—donuts stuffed with jam. The next, a motherly old lady, brings strength—red-bean soup. The next, a neighbor, brings flour and eggs for a well-stocked larder. The fourth brings a chicken for feast days, and finally, so the child will never go hungry, the fifth brings an everyday dish—a sauerkraut pie.

The purpose of these things needs no explanation, though much is given at the time in verse and song. And all the while, delivered with such discretion that it scarcely interrupts the flow, each visitor, as they pass the cradle, puckers up their lips and makes a spitting motion toward the newborn child. A tiny, but ancient gesture—perhaps a baptismal blessing for health, or luck, or future fertility—who knows? The only certainty is that life is harsh, and the baby needs all three.

next page: Birth scene from a nineteenth-century Hungarian woodcut by Lajos Koloszvary—such scenes often conferred legitimacy where it might be in doubt.

Mushroom Piroshki mushroom dumplings

One man's *piroshki* is another man's ravioli, is someone else's dumpling. The recipe may be as varied as you please, but the principle remains the same: a bit of dough is patted or rolled into a shape suitable for stuffing, stuffed with whatever comes to hand, and cooked by whatever method suits the cook. The stuffing can be flesh, fowl, fish, vegetables, jam, curd cheese, buckwheat, preserves, fruit— or, as here, wild fungi, a late-summer treat. The method of cooking can be frying, baking, steaming, or boiling. The wrapper can be a plain noodle dough, or a pasta dough enriched with egg, a pastry dough (although this is more suitable for baking than boiling or frying), or a yeast-leavened bread dough.

Serves 4

The dough-wrapper:

1½ cups / 225 g all-purpose flour

1 teaspoon salt

2 medium eggs

1 teaspoon oil

About 2 tablespoons cold water

The filling:

1 small onion, peeled and finely chopped

2 tablespoons / 25 g butter or lard

6 oz / 175 g mushrooms, wiped and finely sliced

1 teaspoon chopped parsley

Pinch nutmeg

Salt and pepper

1 egg

4 tablespoons curd cheese

To finish:

1 stick / 100 g melted unsalted butter

❶ First make the wrapper dough. Sieve the flour and salt into a bowl and make a well in the middle with your fist. Crack in the eggs and add the oil. Mix the wet stuff into the dry—easily done in an electric mixer—and add enough water to make a softish dough.

❷ Knead vigorously. Massage it with your knuckles and the flat of your hand until smooth and no longer sticky. Flour lightly, drop into a plastic bag, and set aside to rest for half an hour.

❸ Meanwhile make the filling. Fry the onions gently in the butter, until they soften and take a little color. Stir in the mushrooms and cook them until their moisture has all evaporated. Stir in the herbs and nutmeg, and add salt and pepper. Leave to cool.

❹ When you are ready to stuff the *piroshki*, mix the mushroom with the egg and the curd cheese.

❺ Roll out the dough thinly on a well-floured board, and cut out 2 inch / 5 cm diameter rounds. Put a teaspoon of filling in the middle of each round, wet the edges and fold them in half, pressing the edges together, to enclose the dough. Continue until all is used up.

❻ Bring a large pot of salted water to the boil. Drop in the *piroshki*, a few at a time. Wait till they bob to the surface, let them simmer for 2 minutes, drain and transfer to a warm, deep bowl. Trickle with melted butter and toss lightly as each batch is dropped into the bowl.

❼ Finish with more melted butter.

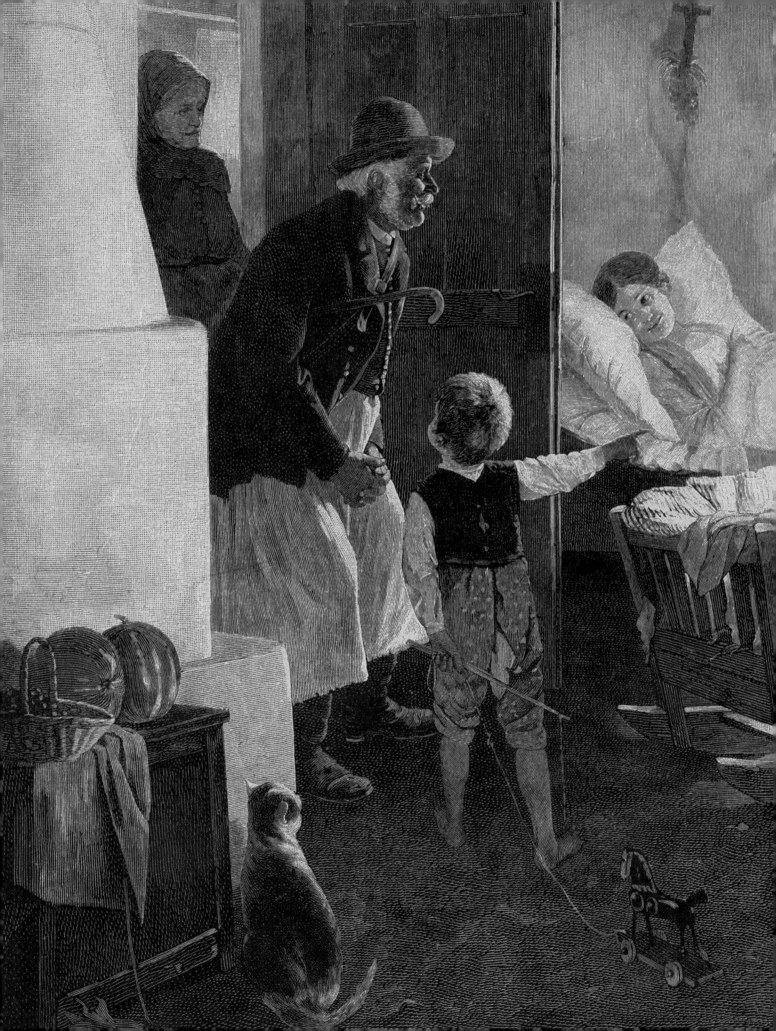

christmas

The festival that commemorates the birth of a historical baby in a real stable some two thousand years ago is the second most important feast day of the Christian year. Only Easter is a holier day, being the anniversary of the day this same baby, grown to manhood, rose from the dead, and did so, according to Christian belief, not as spirit but in the flesh.

The first essential of Christian belief is that this particular baby actually was the Son of God, that he was indeed the savior promised by the prophets of Judaism, and that all was in order according to the Jewish holy book. That the birth date—give or take a year or two—of this particular infant has come to be universally accepted as the date by which all other dates are measured, is a startling tribute to the success of what was, at its inception, a minor variation of a minority religion practiced by a small group of nomadic pastoralists ruled by Rome.

As the only religious festival devoted to commemorating the domestic circumstances surrounding the birth of a historical baby, Christmas holds a particular appeal for families. The

early Church Fathers reinforced the nature of the celebration by linking it firmly to an earlier festival—the midwinter feast of renewal, already an opportunity for those who might never see each other at any other time of year to share a meal and give thanks for whatever the year had brought. Just to confuse the issue a little further, this family gathering is directly mirrored in the feast of Thanksgiving—the annual commemoration of the day that the Pilgrim Fathers first set foot on the shores of their New World home. That the turkey—Thanksgiving's festive roast and a bird native to the Americas—has lately elbowed out more traditional meats on the Christmas table elsewhere around the globe is due mainly to the Jesuits, who introduced the fowl to the old world, and, for several centuries, held a monopoly on turkey husbandry while at the same time giving the practice of eating turkey as a celebratory food some religious approval.

above: *The Adoration of the Shepherds* by Antonio Vassilacchi—a basket of eggs heralds new life and provides an antidote to the symbolism of the cross in the background.

boarshead and pudding

On the tables of old England, the centerpiece of the Christmas feast was the boar's head—thin pickings compared to any other part of the beast—whose gilded tusks and leafy crown reveal it for what it was: a sacrificial offering rather than a serious attempt at dinner. William King, in 1708, penned advice to the Beef Steak Club on how to serve a boar's head:

...if you wou'd send up the Brawner's Head,

Sweet Rosemary and Bays around it spread:

His foaming tusks let some large Pippin grace,

Or" midst these thundering Spears and Orange place,

Sauce like himself, offensive to its Foes,

The Roguish Mustard, dang'rous to the Nose.

Sack and the well-spic'd Hippocras the Wine,

Wassail the Bowl with antient Ribbands fine,

Porridge with Plumbs, and Turkeys with Chine...

Fortunately there was also roast beef, roast venison, and mutton, and stupendous pies filled with roast game. The English love the taste of the fire, while their Celtic cousins lean more toward the boiling pot. On the tables of the Scots, Welsh, and Irish—and, incidentally, among the Galicians in northwest Spain and the Gauls of Gascony, France—the richer the broth, the more festive the food.

Plum pudding, the last survivor on the Anglo-Saxon tables of the Celtic boiling pot, made its first appearance on the Christmas table as a thick potage, or oatmeal, a rich savory meat broth thickened with crumbed bread, spiced with nutmeg and pepper, and sweetened with imported dried plums—*prunes*, as the French called them. So popular was the dried fruit as a winter flavoring that "plum," when associated with "pudding," soon became an indication of the presence of other dried fruits—raisins, currants, and candied peel. By Victorian times, the pudding had lost its meaty content (though retaining the suet), while the addition of liquor—sack or claret—permitted it to be prepared beforehand, stored in earthenware pots, and reheated for the feast. By the time the feast day came around, the mixture had solidified and could be wrapped in a cloth and hung over over a pot of boiling water to be reheated—producing the characteristic round shape of the Victorian Christmas pudding. Brandy-butter—hard sauce—is a modern addition, replacing the custard and cream of the old days.

In Britain, possibly more than anywhere else in the Christian world, the feast that

pictures & text dra

celebrates the birth of Christ has retained its resolutely pagan outlines until the present day. It's hard to know why, unless Oliver Cromwell (scourge of all things Roman Catholic), by removing all but the bare bones of organized Christianity, created a vacuum that, as soon as the old order was somewhat restored, was filled by even older gods. Certainly in England, at least, the Holy Infant is somewhat less in evidence than the Lord of Misrule, overlord of the midwinter feast, whose function was to lift the spirits of men and rouse the gods out of their winter torpor. This was done mainly by over-turning the natural order—permitting the servant to become the master and disguises to be worn: always a signal that bad behavior will be tolerated—seen today in the paper hats of the Christmas table. The presence of the decorated Christmas tree, with its favors of sweets and sugary goodies hung on the branches, and the presents piled beneath, can be ascribed to Queen Victoria's choice of husband. Prince Albert of Saxe-Coburg-Gotha introduced with relish the customs of his native Germany. It is the evergreen holly and the ivy that give the game away, confirming that this is indeed an ancient druidical celebration; and the mistletoe, of course, the Druids' sacred lightning-bush, beneath which many a maiden might expect to receive her first kiss, a relic of the somewhat more robust interactions of pagan times. In other words, the vital elements

Christmas Pudding

This is a Scots version of the great British Christmas pudding as given by Lady Clark of Tillipronie in Aberdeenshire, in the sixteen-volume household manual she compiled between 1839 and 1900. Intended as a *cloutie* dumpling, it is boiled in a well-floured cloth suspended on a wooden spoon placed across the mouth of the cooking cauldron, although the mixture can be steamed in a pudding bowl if you prefer the modern way. Lady Clark does not instruct that the pudding be made ahead of time and left to mature, but you may do so if you wish. To reheat, 2 hours boiling should suffice.

Serves 8–10

2 cups / 350 g pitted and chopped raisins

2 cups / 350 g pitted and chopped golden raisins

²/₃ cup / 125 g mixed candied peel, chopped

²/₃ cup / 175 g sugar, light brown is best

A pinch of salt

1 teaspoon mixed spice or ground allspice

¹/₂ lb / 250 g beef suet, chopped fine, or grated vegetable shortening

5 cups / 250 g day-old breadcrumbs

5 eggs

¹/₂ cup / 125 ml brandy or ale

❶ First mix the fruit, sugar, salt, and spice; then add the suet and crumbs, and keep these ready till wanted.

❷ Next beat up 5 eggs, one at a time, i.e. alone, then add the second, and so on. The 5 eggs to be beaten alone first; then beat in with the brandy; mild table beer or milk can be used, but milk is not so light or good for it as either of the others.

❸ Add these eggs to the fruit and other ingredients, leave the mixture to swell and blend all night.

❹ Next day, boil the pudding in a tightly tied cloth for 8 hours. The water must boil when you put the pudding into it.

left: Dishing up the Christmas plum pudding in a Dickensian household: the pudding's roundness indicates a dumpling boiled in a cloth; a perfect sphere is not an easy trick to master.

of the sacrificial feast are that alcoholic drink must flow, overeating is to be encouraged, and all excess tolerated. Among a people whose inclinations are basically Puritan—perhaps because their nature does not allow much fun to be had at any other time—hair is let down with rather more enthusiasm than it might be elsewhere.

Among the Teutonic nations, throughout what was once called Middle Europe and as far as the central plains of Russia, the Christmas meat is goose. Farther south, on the northern shores of the Mediterranean, the meal is more likely to be pork, the meat that distinguishes the Christian from the Muslim and the Jew. For this reason, perhaps, pork has acquired a special ritual significance where the Moorish presence was strong. In Spain and Portugal, the Christmas feast comes in storable form as salt-cured mountain ham, dense, rich, frilled with golden fat, and tasting of forest-foragings—chestnuts and sweet acorns. Ham, eaten fresh or salted, is also the traditional Christmas meat in Scandinavian countries, although, in an area in which the inhospitable climate made food very hard to come by in the winter months, it is more likely that this is for seasonal reasons rather than due to religious prohibitions.

christmas in germany

In Germany, *Weihnachten*—Christmas Eve—is a night for magic, when mountains burst asunder to reveal hidden treasure, church towers toll their ghostly bells, trees burst into blossom and fruit, and the language of animals can be understood by the pure of heart. But it is the feasting that Hans Karl Adam, writing in *German Cookery* (Wine & Food Society, 1967) recalls most vividly from his own Silesian childhood:

"Christmas was the great moment of the year at table. This is the season for baking *Pfefferkuchen*, honey spice cakes, and *Stollen*, rich fruit breads of which the most famous are those of Dresden. On Christmas Eve, everyone who could possibly eat it ate carp and followed with poppy-seed dumplings. On the first Holy Day, they would eat a noodle soup, followed by a roast goose, crisp on the outside and garnished with red cabbage, and *Klösse*; on the second Holy Day, roast hare larded with bacon fat and served with cream sauce and Sauerkraut. On New Year's Eve, too, there would be carp, but cooked *au bleu* because of the scales which (if you kept them) meant money for a whole year. On New Year's Day, there used to be another goose. On January 2nd, whatever might be left over was warmed up for the last time, and then everyday life resumed its usual rhythm. Nobody grumbled. What was there to grumble about?"

Christstollen   german Christmas cake

Stollen improve with maturity—a Christmas *Stollen* will be nicely aged at carnival time, although some German families keep the last piece to be eaten at Easter.

Makes 4 Stollen

2 lbs / 900 g all-purpose flour

⅔ cup / 100 ml warm milk

3 oz / 75 g fresh yeast

½ cup / 100 g sugar

Generous 3 cups / 500 g raisins

⅔ cup / 100 g currants

1 cup /150 g mixed finely chopped candied peel

Grated zest of 2 lemons

⅔ cup / 100 g blanched almonds

6 tablespoons dark rum

1 stick / 100 g unsalted butter

To finish:

Unsalted butter to glaze

Vanilla-flavored confectioners' sugar for dusting

❶ Sieve two-thirds of the flour into a warm bowl. Pour a little warm milk over the yeast in a cup, sprinkle in a teaspoon of sugar, and leave it for a moment or two to liquidize.

❷ Make a hollow in the flour and pour in the yeast mix. Sprinkle with flour and leave for 10–15 minutes to start the sponge working. Pour in the rest of the milk and work in the flour, drawing it in gradually from the sides, until you have a soft, smooth dough.

❸ When it no longer sticks to your hands or the bowl, cover it with plastic wrap, and put it in a warm place to rise until doubled in bulk—about an hour should be fine, as you have a high proportion of yeast to flour.

❹ Meanwhile, soak the dried fruit, zest and nuts in the rum. Sift the remaining flour onto the pastry board. Knead the dough for a moment or two to distribute the oxygen bubbles. Melt the butter and work it into the dough, together with the soaked fruit and nuts and the rest of the sugar, drawing in the extra flour to keep the dough firm, but soft. Don't overwork it, or the dough will go gray.

❺ Divide the dough into 4 pieces. Quickly knead each piece into a ball and then flatten it into an oval. Make a dent in the oval with a rolling pin lengthwise, more to one side than the other. Fold the wide side over the other. Repeat with the other pieces and transfer the *stollen* to a buttered tray. Cover and leave in a warm place for 20 minutes to prove. Preheat the oven to 450 F / 230 C / Gas 8.

❻ Bake in the oven for 40-45 minutes. For larger *Stollen*, divide the dough into 2 and bake at the same temperature for 1 hour. The oven has to be hot, or the *stollen* will be speckly because of all the butter.

❼ Take the *Stollen* out of the oven when well risen and firm to the finger. Transfer to a wire rack to cool. Paint them while still warm with melted butter. Dust with confectioners' sugar.

Gänsebraten mit Apfeln und Rotkohl

german christmas roast goose with red cabbage

A goose, an obdurately seasonal bird, weighing between 9 and 12 lbs / 4–5.5 kg, that is fattened up for the Christmas market is enough for 6 people. It'll serve 8 if you stuff the neck and roast it alongside: fill the empty neck skin with a herby minced pork and bread stuffing bound with egg.

Serves 6–8

The bird:

1 goose

2–3 large tart apples, peeled, quartered and cored

2–3 onions, chunked

2–3 cloves, minced

1 stem of wormwood or a sprig of sage

Salt and pepper

The cabbage:

1 small red cabbage, shredded finely

5 cups / 1.25 liters stock or water

½ cup / 125 ml vinegar

3 tablespoons brown sugar

½ teaspoon salt

Pepper

2–3 cloves

1 large onion, chopped

1 large tart apple, peeled and chopped

❶ Wipe the bird and trim off excess fat from the interior cavity. Tie two pieces of this fat over the bird's breast. Preheat the oven to 350 F / 180 C / Gas 4.

❷ Stuff the goose with the apples, onions, and the cloves, tucking the wormwood or the sage in the neck end. Sew up the cavity, and put the bird breast down on a rack in the oven, over a dripping tray. Pour a mug of boiling water over the bird and into the tray.

❸ Roast for 30 minutes, then turn the bird breast up. Prick the skin (not through to the flesh), particularly around the throat and the base of the wings to let the fat run. The goose will need 3½–4 hours total roasting, depending on its weight, which includes the stuffing. Pour out the goose fat regularly—basting the bird when you do so. (Save the fat for frying—goose fat is snowy white and very pure: the Romans held it in higher esteem than butter, and our great-grandmothers used it in face creams and embrocations).

❹ Meanwhile, prepare the red cabbage. Pack all the ingredients in a roomy pan, brown the onions in a little goose fat first and bring to a rolling boil. Lid the pan and turn it down to simmer for an hour or so, until the cabbage is tender. Keep an eye on it, and add extra water if it looks like it's drying out. Taste and adjust the seasoning.

❺ To produce perfectly crisp skin, using your fingertips, sprinkle cold water over the bird 10–15 minutes before the end of the cooking. Test for doneness by thrusting a skewer into the base of the thigh If the juice runs pink, it is not yet done; if it runs clear, it's ready.

❻ Scoop out the apple-onion stuffing, mash well, and stir it into the pan juices (skim off excess fat first) to thicken them. Leave the bird to rest in a turned-off oven for 20 minutes, so the meat firms up.

Serve with the cabbage, mashed apple, and potatoes sauteed in goose fat. Or accompany, Silesian-style, with nutmeg-spiced *kartoffelklösse* (potato dumplings) made by binding grated raw potato with egg and a little cornstarch. Drop them in boiling salted water and allow to cook for 20 minutes at a gentle simmer. Flatten a few and fry them in butter for the children.

juleskink and christmas biscuits

Among the independent peasant farmers of the cold lands of northern Europe, the household pig, salted down for winter, provided the Christmas meal—the hams being the best part and so most suitable for the feast. This is how my friend Margaret Erikson remembers the pleasures of her childhood, growing up on a mountain farm near the village of Bortnan in central Sweden: "The most important part of Christmas was the *juleskink*, the dip-in-the-pot my mother made with the ham we kept for the Christmas feast. Everyone kept a household pig when I was a child, forty years ago. My father killed it and then my mother salted the meat so we always had good bacon and ham in the cellar. In the cellar too, my grandfather kept the *aquavit*, white brandy for the Christmas toasts. He made very good *aquavit* with berries, and my grandmother made rhubarb wine, so the grown-ups were very merry, and even the children had a little taste. The *juleskink* ham was cooked in a big iron cauldron with plenty of water and left on the side of the fire all through a day and a night. The broth was wonderful—clear and with little pools of beautiful golden fat that told how delicious it was. We ate it straight from the pot, with our fingers. You took bits of bread—*knackebrod* or one of the other breads my mother used to bake and store in the rafters to dry—and dipped it in the broth. You had to tuck a clean, white napkin into your collar to stop the juices running down your chin, which was why we called it dip-in-the-pot. It was more than enough for one meal, with potatoes if you were hungry, which we always were.

"On Christmas day, we were allowed to eat the meat, helping ourselves as my father carved it in thick, pink slices onto a big white plate. We could spread the slice with sweet butter and roll it up in *lefse*, soft pancakes made with cooked potato mixed with rye-flour, cooked on top of the wood-burning stove. My grandmother

was from Norway and her *lefse* were famous. And before that, there was the herring, of course. There is always a *smörgåsbord* with caviar and salt meat and cheese, and at least twenty-four different kinds of herring—sweet, sour, with beetroot, onion, tomato, potato, celery, mustard sauces, sour cream, curry sauce with raisins. The vegetables and the fish must be in equal proportions, and most people like a little sugar in the sauce, particularly on feast days. The *smörgåsbord* is always very good at Christmas, and my mother liked it because it was easy to prepare and she didn't have to cook. It was best when the neighbors came. One lady made the best Janssen's Temptation, a very Swedish dish: potatoes cooked with cream and salted sild; not anchovies, but similar. The best of all was the reindeer tongue, salted and smoked, very tender and good, that my father exchanged for cheese with the Lappish reindeer herdsmen. And afterward, there would be a wreath-cake, the Swedish Christmas cake, and special biscuits called reindeer horns, *hjortakke*, and a big bowl of whipped cream with cloudberries, which are a special kind of very delicious berry. They look like yellow raspberries but have a short stalk and only grow on the tops of the mountains. You can keep them in a water barrel all through the winter because they have something in them that stops them going bad. These were the foods for which we gave thanks to God because they were good, and because without them we would not have been able to live until the spring. Until you have lived through a Swedish winter, you cannot possible know how important this was."

Although today, most Scandinavians live in towns, few are more than a couple of generations away from the land. In the old days, farming communities depended on a well-stocked larder to get them through the long, dark winters. Isolated and snow-bound for months at a time, a barrel of salt herrings, and the summer's harvest of potatoes and apples, could mean the difference between survival and starvation. Rolled oats, unleavened rye bread and barley breads baked for storage, whey-cheese, and berry conserves were stockpiled through the summer. Dairy cattle, free to roam the upland pastures in summer, were overwintered along with their fodder in the huge, airy cathedral-like barns, providing a year-round source of milk and cream. Good things—butter, cream, fine white flour, sugar, eggs, *aquavit*, dried fruit, nuts, and imported spices—were all carefully saved for the traditional Christmas baking. Although supermarkets now sell the same cakes and biscuits all year round as a matter of course, Scandinavian housewives still take pride in filling their clean, modern kitchens with the rich scents of grandmother's recipe for Christmas gingerbread, *pepparkakor*, crisp fritters, and iced butter cookies baked in rings and stars and other festive shapes.

Kransekake **christmas wreath cake**

A pyramid of crisp almond-meringue rings, built up rather like the French wedding *croquembouche*, is the favorite Norwegian celebration cake—essential at weddings and confirmations as well as at Christmas. The rings, once baked, keep happily in a tin, ready to be finished and decorated as you please.

Makes an 18-ring tower

1 lb / 450 g whole almonds

(or ground almonds)

I lb / 450 g sugar

3 tablespoons all-purpose flour

3 egg whites

❶ Grind the nuts, not too finely, in the coffee or nut grinder. The wreath is best when made with a mixture of blanched and unblanched almonds. Ground almonds work well enough, but give a smoother, paler meringue.

❷ Preheat the oven to 400 F / 200 C / Gas 6.

❸ Mix the dry ingredients together.

❹ Whisk the egg whites until aerated but still soft. Work them into the nut mixture, and knead until you have a soft but firm dough. This can be done in the electric mixer.

❺ Roll the dough into ropes as thick as your finger. Cut them into 18 lengths, starting with smallest at 5½ inches / 14 cm long. The next should be just under 1 inch / 2.5 cm longer, and so on. Splice the ropes together as rings, smoothing down the join.

❻ Grease 3 baking trays thoroughly and dust with flour.

❼ Arrange the rings on the baking sheets, leaving them plenty of room to expand—one inside the other. The first tray should have rings 1, 4, 7, 10, 13, 16, and so on.

❽ Bake for 8–10 minutes until crisp and golden. Transfer to a wire rack to cool. If you don't want to finish the cake, store the rings in an airtight tin with a piece of fresh bread to maintain the meringue's proper chewiness. Or freeze.

❾ To finish, assemble the rings in a pyramid, using a little caramelized sugar to stick the layers together. Decorate exuberantly with holly, miniature Santas and reindeer, confectioners' sugar snow, and whatever pleases you.

To serve, remove the top rings and tackle the lower levels first, so that the pyramid remains intact. For a little taste of the sun, serve with whipped cream flavored with orange zest and rum.

Festival cooking must be rich and special—that's the pleasure of it. When it's the result not of a commercial process but of discernable, measurable human labor, it acquires a different aura. Why else should a positive answer to the ritual question, "You made it yourself?" give such satisfaction? Homecooking, particularly baking, is the domestic sacrament, the female equivalent of the spell cast by the shaman.

Icicles and sleigh rides, decorated fir trees and red-nosed reindeer—these are the familiar trappings of a modern Christmas. Considering that the event commemorated took place in a part of the world where such things would have been thought of as being as weird and wonderful as a camel in a snowstorm, what are we to make of the annual announcement that Father Christmas is alive and well and living in

above: Swedish Christmas baked goods: crisp little butter cookies made with fine flour. Recipes often include almonds and luxurious imported spices, hard to come by in the old days, doubly valuable in the cold of a northern winter.

Lapland? If the strength of Christianity lies in its willingness to borrow the finery of its predecessors, it is none the less odd that it is the rotund and jolly Santa Claus, a descendant of the mischievous forest gods of the Norsemen, who has claimed the most comfortable chair at the feast. It is Santa, too, who is credited with the gifts found under the fir tree the morning after the night before. All the same, the Norsemen never had the monopoly. Whoever it was who first decorated a fir tree with sugar stars—or honey cookies, or little figures made of

Hjortetakk **norwegian reindeer antlers**

There are variations of these Christmas cookie-fritters all over Europe, known variously as rags-and-tatters, or bits-and-pieces, or buttons-and-bows, or how's-your-father, depending on whom you ask. You can make a simple version by frying snippets of pastry—the trimmings from a pie, perhaps—and dusting them with spiced sugar.

Makes about 3 dozen

Scant 1¼ cups / 175 g all-purpose flour

1 teaspoon ground cinnamon

½ teaspoon ground nutmeg

A pinch of ground cloves

1 teaspoon grated orange zest

½ stick / 50 g softened butter

2 tablespoons sugar

3 egg yolks

A splash of **aquavit** or white brandy

Oil for frying

For dusting:

Sugar and cinnamon

❶ Sift the flour with the spices, and toss in the orange zest.

❷ Beat the butter with the sugar and work in the spiced flour, the yolks, and enough *aquavit* or brandy to make a soft, firm dough. You may need more or less liquid, depending on the size of the yolks. Form the dough into a ball, wrap in plastic wrap, and set in the refrigerator to cool and firm, overnight if possible.

❸ Roll out the dough as thin as you would when making pastry. Using a zigzag cutter, cut into short strips about as wide as your thumb and as long as your hand. Cut a slit in the center parallel to the long side, and pull one end through the gash, to give a characteristic twist in the middle.

❹ Heat the frying oil until a faint blue haze rises—test with a cube of bread, which should sizzle and gild immediately. Slip in the biscuits a few at a time, and fry until crisp and golden. Drain on paper towels.

❺ Allow to cool, and dust with sugar and cinnamon. Stored in an airtight tin, these cookies keep fresh for months.

Santa Lucia's Peppersnaps **swedish Christmas cookies**

The cream-rich dough gives a fine-textured crisp cookie when rolled thin enough—too thick and they'll be jawbreakers. The dough must be allowed its overnight rest to develop the body for rolling and cutting; don't be put off when it looks sticky when first mixed.

Makes around 60 little cookies

½ cup / 150 ml black treacle

½ cup / 125 ml heavy cream, whipped stiff

Scant 1 cup / 225 g light brown sugar

1 teaspoon ground ginger

1 lemon, juice and grated peel

3⅓ cups / 500 g all-purpose flour, sieved

Confectioners' sugar for dusting

❶ Preheat the oven to 350 F / 180 C / Gas 4. Heat the treacle until runny. Mix all the ingredients except the lemon juice, then work in enough juice to form a soft dough. Cover and chill overnight.

❷ Next day, knead the dough lightly, and roll it out as thin as you can, dusting the board and the rolling pin generously with confectioners' sugar to stop the dough from sticking. In Sweden, ladies compete to see who can make the thinnest cookies.

❸ Using cookie-cutters, or your skill with a knife, cut out pretty Christmas shapes—stars, trees, hearts, gingerbread men. Transfer the cookies to a baking sheet rinsed with cold water.

❹ Bake the biscuits for 5–6 minutes, until crisp and brown. Slip them carefully onto a rack to cool. Store in an airtight tin to serve with mulled wine or *glogg*—the ferociously strong Swedish hot wine fortified with *aquavit* that has been poured over burning sugar cubes.

The same dough can be baked as flat sheets to make into a gingerbread house—two straight-sided, two topped with a triangle for the walls, and a pair for the roof, with the leftovers to shape into a chimney. Stick it together with melted sugar caramel. Draw on the windows, door, and roof tiles with finely piped fondant. Finish with Scandinavian-style curls and hearts.

gingerbread—was simply retelling an old tale. In the hills of Attica, beside the long-tumbled temple of Pallas Athene, there is a gnarled and twisted olive tree as old as any living thing on earth, on whose silvery branches on the day of the winter solstice appear the sacred tributes—freshly-baked honey cakes—once offered to the goddess herself. No one knows who hangs them there. Although this adds to the mystery, it does not explain why we need to believe in the magic.

hanukkah

The Jewish festival of Hanukkah, although not traditionally a major Jewish festival, slots so neatly into the pattern of the Christian festivities that it is now a high point of the Jewish calendar. The eight-day holiday marks the miraculous renewal of the undefiled oil for the sacred *Menorah* at the time when the tyrant Antiochus IV desecrated the Temple in Jerusalem. So, it is proper to light a fresh oil-lamp or candle each night of the festival, adding a new one each evening. Naturally, the holiday must be marked by a feast, which, as with all Jewish festival food, complies with dietary rules but does not ignore the practical. When the exiled nation headed for the hills, they packed up their dietary laws with their cooking pots, but sensibly cut their culinary cloak according to the available cloth. From those who headed East comes a rich heritage of pilaf, kebabs, and spicy stews, all of which conform to the rabbi's rules, but have been adapted to native habits and local ingredients. In this tradition is Mavis Hyman, whose ancestors moved from Baghdad to Calcutta two centuries ago, forming part of a community of Iraqi Jews who had in their time joined the Bene Israel already established on the subcontinent. For her family at the feast of Hanukkah, there must be something sweet to make the banquet special—perhaps a *halva* flavored with rosewater. The food is prepared the day before, set on the table, and passed around in no particular order. Fresh fruit, pineapple, papaya, oranges, are dessert, and, to finish, there should be strong, black coffee and a nibble of marzipan or a sliver of preserved fruit. As a main course, chicken *hurikebab*—chicken cooked in a closed pot with ginger and turmeric—is served with *aloomakalla*, a beautifully arranged platter of winter salads, including potato, beets, cucumber, grated carrot, and boiled eggs. To follow, piled on the best china serving dish, a pilaf, finished with almonds and raisins, accompanied by a tray of *mahasha*—rice-stuffed vegetables baked with plenty of oil. All this, and never a hint of chicken soup or chopped liver, not a sniff of a bagel (specialities of the cooks of the Ashkenazi tradition, the Middle Europeans).

Elsewhere, among the Ashkenazim Jews who settled in the cold lands of the north rather than remaining in and around the lands of the Mediterranean—it became the custom to mark Hanukkah with the flaming-tea ceremony. This small ritual, in which participants set fire to a brandy-soaked sugar lump and drop it in a glass of tea, mirrors the preparation of the Scandinavian Christmas *glogg*, which also involves flaming alcohol and burning sugar; a similar practice can be found in the English habit of setting the Christmas pudding alight before bringing it to table, a practice introduced by Queen Victoria's German husband.

Among both the Sephardim and Ashkenazim, there is a feeling that dairy-based dishes are appropriate to Hanukkah, a choice that plays tribute to a biblical heroine, the beautiful Queen Judith, who saved her city from destruction by plying the enemy leader with cheese of such ferocious saltiness that

which friends and neighbors are welcome. The sacred food, *ajeel*, is a mixture of seven varieties of roasted nuts and dried fruit—pistachios, almonds, chickpeas, melon or pumpkin seeds, apricots, raisins, dried figs. The vigil of watching through the night is known, appropriately enough, as *shab-chera*, night-grazing. To pastoralists such as the ancient Persians, the phrase must have had particular resonance, since it also relates to the time of the full moon when their flocks could graze through the night, fattening up for the slaughter.

One other small ritual is worth noting. Two weeks before the ancient Persian festival of No Rooz, new year, wheat and lentils are planted in little dishes and carefully nurtured to make them sprout. This ritual can also be observed among the more venerable of the Christian cultures in the weeks before Christmas, which, of course, is immediately followed by the celebration of New Year. The old gods take refuge where they may. In my own experience, in a household in Provence among whom I was recently a guest, the dishes of newly sprouted greenery took pride of place beside the little clay Nativity scene and the Christmas candle. My hostess was in no doubt of the pagan purpose of the wheat although she was a little hazy on the lentils. The wheatgrains, she explained, were sprouted to encourage grass to grow in the meadows, while the lentil sprouts, being prettily fuzzy, served to remind all good children of the innocent golden curls of the Holy Infant. Among those such as the Provencaux whose belief systems can be traced back to Ancient Persia, lentil pottages are commonly served at new year—a celebration that has inherited many of the midwinter rituals—while a *soupe des lasagnes* (*see page 91*) is served at the fasting supper of Provence.

a raging thirst persuaded him to drink himself into a stupor—allowing the feisty heroine to hack off his head with a sword and save the city and her people from ruin. In commemoration of this deliverance, the Sephardim eat cheese fritters—*bimuelos*, from the Spanish *buñuelos*—and the Ashkenazim serve cheesecake.

shab-e yaldå

Iran celebrates the midwinter festival at roughly the same time as Christians celebrate Christmas and the Jews Hanukkah; on a date that marks the winter solstice, the longest night of the year. In the days of the ancient Persians, who, under Darius the Great, commanded a vast empire stretching from the valley of the Indus to the delta of the Nile, celebrants stayed awake through the night to greet the sun at the very moment it brought new life to the world—the light of new day. The festival survives in modern Iran as an all-night family party at

Soupe de Lasagnes provençale pasta soup

A thick winter-vegetable soup is the traditional Christmas Eve *souper maigre*—fasting supper—in Upper Provence. When choosing the pasta, look for the Provençale lasagnes—they look like very broad tagliatelli, but have prettily frilled edges to remind participants of the curls of the infant Jesus. The enrichment—oil or *aioli*—is handed separately to allow participants to adhere as strictly to the rules of fasting as they please.

Serves 6

6 oz / 175 g Provençale lasagne
or broad ribbon pasta

3–4 large, mature carrots, scraped
and chopped roughly

3–4 young turnips, peeled
and chopped roughly

3–4 stalks celery, washed and
cut into short lengths

Bay leaf, parsley, thyme

1 clove garlic, minced

8 cups / 2 liters cold water

Salt and pepper

5–6 stalks chard, washed and
cut into short lengths

¼ cabbage, cut into fine strips

3–4 leeks, trimmed, well-washed
and cut into thin rings

To finish:

Olive oil or an aioli

❶ Break the lasagne into bite-sized pieces ready for poaching in the soup.

❷ Drop the root vegetables and aromatics into the cold water (no preliminary frying is necessary), and bring all to a boil with a teaspoon of salt.

❸ Simmer until the vegetables are nearly done, about 10–12 minutes.

❹ Add the pasta and bring all back to a boil. Add the green vegetables in the order given, bringing everything back to a boil in between additions.

❺ When the pasta is tender—about 20 minutes—taste and add salt and pepper.

To serve, ladle into deep soup plates and finish each portion with a swirl of olive oil. Or hand around an *aioli* —a very garlicky mayonnaise—separately.

reveillon

In the uplands of rural Provence, where things do not change as swiftly as in Paris or Lyons, the Christmas feast, the *reveillon*, starts at midnight on the Eve, and is not over until dawn on Christmas morning. Present-giving waits until January 6, Twelfth Night, the day dedicated to the arrival at the Bethlehem stable of the Three Wise Men—Caspar, Melchior, and Balthazar—from whom the Christ-child received his own gifts. This arrangement, traditional wherever the birth is celebrated according to the Roman and Orthodox Catholic rites, allows Christmas to remain a purely religious festival while ensuring that the food held sacred to the feast, in common with all celebrations of birth, is luxurious and of the best. Most important is the baking: cakes and cookies rich with fruit, nuts, spices, sugar, eggs, butter, and all the good things our forefathers rarely tasted at any other time.

Before the feast comes a fast—a short period of abstinence to make everyone grateful for what follows. On the Eve, before the mass at midnight that reassures the Christian world of the birth of a baby who is indeed the Savior, Provençale families sit down to the traditional fasting supper, *souper maigre*, which is plain, meatless, and washed down with water. In the old market town of Vaison-la-Romaine in Upper Provence, where I have spent many a festive season with my family, the meatless dish is a *soupe de lasagnes*, a French version of the Italian *minestrone*, followed by eggs: scrambled or in an omelet. Some prefer *le grand aioli*, a stupendously garlicky mayonnaise traditionally made without eggs, eaten with salt-cod or snails and plain-boiled vegetables. Others begin the meal with bitter herbs—woolly stalks of cardoon, unblanched celery, and chard—for dipping into a bowl of salty anchovies crushed with garlic and the year's first pressing of olive oil.

Halfway through the meal, the celebrants abandon the hearth, in which the pagan Yule log burns, for the sanctity of the church. They are greeted on entry to the street by the strange music of old Provence—the tinkling tambourin and the deep-throated *galoubet*, a primitive drum. Among the many rural congregations who value the spirit as well as the ritual of the festival, the nativity play, a re-enactment of the events of the first Christmas, is de riguer. In modern times, the playlets are light-hearted affairs performed by children, although in the dangerous days when literacy was limited to priests and scholars, morality plays performed at Christmas and Easter were taken very seriously indeed—not only as a method of religious instruction, but also, at a time when the church's preoccupations were overtly secular, as a medium for delivering a political message.

These days, the medium is still used to advertise the message. Local artisans use the playlets to present their wares to the Holy Family in much the same spirit as their ancestors and, incidentally, advertise their worth to potential customers. The goatherd's daughter might present a dish of freshly drained *tommes*, the child of a farmer's wife, a basket of new-laid eggs. The shepherds might be accompanied by live sheep as well as cheese made from their milk.

After Mass, when greetings have been exchanged and the actors congratulated, the congregation returns home for the second phase of the feast. Before it can begin, the youngest child makes sure the pottery image of the Holy Infant—now officially born—is safely tucked into the miniature crib. The meal then continues, this time without restrictions: with a *foie-gras* perhaps, or a rich game paté. Feathered game is the meat of choice, although guinea fowl, a leg of lamb, or a fine fat capon are reckoned perfectly acceptable.

On Christmas Day itself, youth is expected to pay its respects to age. Leaving their parents to sleep off the festivities in peace, children visit elderly relatives and neighbors, bearing gifts of Christmas goodies: the *pompe à huile*, a sweet bread flavored with blossom-water, a *tarte aux pommes*, a chocolate, dusted *buche de noël* —a log-shaped cake filled with chestnut puree that has replaced the yule log in centrally heated modern houses.

Throughout the twelve days of Christmas, every Provençale household sets out

Galette des Rois three kings cake

France has a whole range of these Epiphany Cakes, whose main purpose is to allow a little regression to pagan times. Recipes range from a simple shortbread, bread made in the shape of a crown, or any sweet pastry in which a favor—a figurine, a bean, an almond—can be buried. The lucky recipient is declared King of the Feast and allowed to choose his Queen, or King. The position has the same responsibilities as those enjoyed by the Christmas Lord of Misrule—the encouragement of unruly behavior. As an incarnation of Pan, we all know whither the goat-god led. Old habits die hard. We all need and love a party, particularly when the winter is long and hard, and heaven alone knows if the earth will ever wake up again. The *galette des rois* had a brief career in politics during the French Revolution, when the sour-faced *Tribunes* made known their disapproval of cake-eating by beheading Marie Antoinette and declaring the Kings' Cookie and its bean an affront to the People. The *maître-patissiers* of Paris proved more than a match for the politicians when they rechristened it "Equality Cake," and transformed the lucky token into a miniature Phrygian cap. When life returned to normal, the bakers of Paris continued to bake the cake as a gift to their favored customers at a time when all the world gave gifts. A buttery pastry would not seem to have much to do with the event commemorated—but that will come as no surprise to anyone.

Serves 12 children, 6 adults

The pastry:

Scant 2 cups / 250 g all-purpose flour

½ teaspoon salt

2 sticks / 200 g unsalted butter

About 2 tablespoons iced water

The filling:

⅔ cup / 100 g ground almonds

⅓ cup / 75 g sugar

1 stick / 100 g softened unsalted butter

4 drops almond extract

2 egg yolks

1 tablespoon kirsch or brandy

❶ Preheat the oven to 375 F / 190 C / Gas 5.

❷ Make sure everything, including the utensils, is cool. See that the butter is firm without being hard.

❸ Take a large bowl and sift in the flour with the salt. Cut in a third of the butter with a sharp knife until you have a mixture like fine breadcrumbs. Mix in enough water to make a paste which, when worked a little does not stick to the fingers. Knead lightly. Set the dough aside for 20 minutes, with the rest of the butter beside it so that pastry and butter both reach the same temperature.

❹ Roll out the pastry to the thickness of your little finger. Dot with a third of the remaining butter, and cut into small pieces. Fold the pastry into three, like a napkin, and again into three in the opposite direction. Set aside for 20 minutes. Go through the last process twice more, adding the same amount of butter each time, until all the butter is used. Set the pastry aside for 20 minutes after each process. Then leave another 20 minutes before using it.

❺ Divide in half, and roll the pastry out into a pair of rounds about 10 inches / 25 cm in diameter. Let it rest for the last time while you make the filling.

❻ For the filling, mix the ground almonds with the sugar and the butter cut into little pieces. Work in well with the almond extract, egg yolks, and *kirsch* until you have a smooth paste. Reserve.

❼ Transfer one round of pastry to a baking sheet rinsed under cold water. Spread the reserved almond paste over the pastry, leaving a border around the edge. Bury the lucky token in the middle. Dampen the pastry edge and cover with the second round of pastry. Press both edges together with a fork. With a sharp knife, mark the top with a lattice pattern, without cutting right through to the filling. Paint the top with a little beaten egg.

❽ Bake for 30 minutes until the pastry is crisp, well risen, and deliciously gilded. Transfer to a baking rack to cool.

To serve, break the galette into as many pieces as there are guests around the table. Don't use a knife, for fear of fights. Whoever gets the lucky token is Lord of Misrule. But I expect you knew that already.

Pompe à Huile **provençale christmas bread**

The central bread, that represents Jesus, is the most variable of all the Christmas goodies. But everyone seems to agree that the bread should be richer than everyday bread, and it must be broken, never cut with a knife.

Makes 2 x 12 inch / 30 cm diameter loaves

6 cups / 1 kg white bread flour

4 oz / 100 g fresh yeast

1 cup / 250 ml warm water

Scant 2 cups / 225 g confectioners' sugar

1 cup / 250 ml olive oil

1 tablespoon orange flower water (or 1 teaspoon grated orange zest)

1 tablespoon aniseeds, optional

Sweet black coffee or a yolk of egg for gilding

❶ Sift the flour into a large, warm bowl.

❷ Mix the yeast in a small bowl with half a glass of the warm water. Stir in 5 heaped tablespoons of the flour—enough to work into a dough ball. Cut a deep cross in the ball and put it in a bowl of warm water. Leave it until it swells and bobs to the surface; it may do so immediately, or it may take 10 minutes or so.

❸ Mix the confectioners' sugar into the warm flour. Make a well in the middle. Pour in the oil and drop in the ball of wet yeasty dough, the orange flower water, and a little more warm water. Work well together, adding extra water until you have a soft dough. Cut the dough in half and knead each into a ball.

❹ Oil two large baking sheets and dust them lightly with flour. Roll each ball out on a well-floured board into a flat disk. Transfer the disks to the baking-sheets and pat them out evenly with your hand until they are about 12 inches / 30 cm across. Put them to rise in a warm place under a clean cloth for 5–7 hours. It sounds a long time, but with all that oil, they need it. Be careful there's no draught—they catch cold easily, causing the bubbles to collapse.

❺ Preheat the oven to 300 F / 150 C / Gas 2. Set a roasting pan of boiling water on the base.

❻ Brush the breads with coffee or egg yolk, and put them in the oven. After 10 minutes, raise the heat to 400 F / 200 C / Gas 6. Bake for another 20 minutes, until well risen and brown.

a table loaded with small dishes of nuts, fruit, nougats, and other good things, with a sweet bread or nut-cake as the centerpiece—thirteen in all. The arrangement, constantly renewed, is known as *les treize desserts*—one for each of the disciples and one to symbolize Christ—and serves as a kind of open larder. The choice varies from household to household, but, in spite of the availability of imported goodies, remains obdurately regional. In Vaison, the traditional fruit is muscat grapes rather than the raisins usual in other areas; King William pears, *poires William*, kept juicy by having their stalks dipped in sealing-wax; yellow-fleshed apples, *pommes reinettes*; dried apricots; and quince paste. Added to these, you will find four different winter foods—*les mendients* that represent the four begging orders of monks—almonds for the brown-cassocked Dominicans, figs for the rough-cloaked Franciscans, smooth-skinned hazelnuts for the brown-and-cream Carmelites, little dried currants for the black-clad Augustines. Other possibilities are oranges, tangerines, and dates (reminders of the land of the baby's birth); also possible are walnuts, hazelnuts, and chestnuts, luxurious *marrons glacées*, and *calissons d'Aix*—little oval marzipans slicked with icing.

right: Midnight Mass in Provence in the 1940s features a nativity play with live sheep. Even today, among rural communities, a shepherd might bring a newborn lamb to add a little authenticity.

NIL SIMILIVS INSANO
QVAM · EBRIVS ·

la consoada

In Portugal, the fast that precedes the Christmas feast is known as *la consoada*, the consolation, and the fasting meal is dedicated to the spirits of the dead. Perhaps it is the harshness of the land itself—rivers too swift for easy navigation, valleys too steep for all but the most labor-intensive of terracing, impenetrable forests—that has left the Portuguese people with a deep awareness of their own mortality. To accommodate those who have left their earthly bodies during the previous year, empty chairs are left and places set, as for the ancestor feasts of the East. Although none makes so direct a connection with the hereafter, a similar tradition exists in other parts of the Christian world—but the reason more often given for the empty place is that provision must be made for the stranger who might, after all, be Christ himself. The fasting food, as always where Roman Catholic rules are followed, is salt-cod, *bacalhao*. To say that in Portugal, salt-dried cod is served as the fasting meal of Christmas Eve would simply be stating the obvious. *Bacalhao* is the Portuguese national dish—the soul food of a nation that, for the sake of survival, had no other option but to sail the seven seas.

Of all those brave souls who trawled the oceans, none had more to gain than the merchant-adventurers of Lisbon's sailor-prince Henry, known to his people as The Navigator. The Portuguese, a nation caught between a rock and a hard place —inhospitable mountains behind, the turbulent Atlantic ahead—sought fortune in a new spice route to the East or West, whichever looked most likely. Under the guidance of their prince—not a man for the sea himself, but one who knew how to show the way to others—the fifteenth-century Portuguese became the most adventurous sailors on earth.

It was Portugal's good fortune (or the downfall of others, depending on how you judge colonial intervention) that a colonial appetite led her, in due course, to create an empire the size and economic power of which was to eclipse her own. You'll find salt-cod dishes everywhere the Portuguese made landfall—a permanent reminder of those long-dead sailors always welcome to share the feast of Christmas Eve.

previous page: *The Twelfth Night Feast* by Jacob Jordaens, c.1656, depicts the crowning of the Lord of Misrule at which the usual order is reversed. Whether celebrated on Christmas Day, New Year's Day, or Twelfth Night the festival kept its pagan trappings.

above right: Henry the Navigator and his wife at table, an image carved on a casket made of ivory. This trade item was exchanged for Portuguese salt-cod, the foodstuff that fueled Henry's merchant-sailors on their epic voyages.

Buddim do Bacalhao portuguese baked salt-cod

Portugal's Christmas Eve fasting supper is a dish that not only had the merit of complying with the requirements of the church, but also provided the first taste of an eagerly awaited seasonal delicacy. Portugal—a nation of skilled seamen responsible for the first circumnavigations of the globe—has been the center of the salt-fish trade since Roman times. The traditional Portuguese olive oil that gives the dish character is something of an acquired taste, since it's made from slightly fermented fruit. I love it, although it certainly has its detractors. Use a Greek oil if you cannot get the real thing.

Serves 6, plus the stranger for whom a place is always set

1 lb / 450 g salt-cod

1 large onion, sliced

2 garlic cloves, chopped

2 lbs / 900 g potatoes, peeled and sliced thickly

½ cup / 100 ml Portuguese olive oil

6 eggs, hard-cooked, peeled and sliced

2–3 tablespoons chopped parsley

Freshly milled pepper

❶ Preheat the oven to 180 C / 350 F / Gas 4.

❷ Put the cod to soak in a covered bowl somewhere cool for 24 hours. Change the water as often as you remember. Drain. Cut the fish into manageable pieces and rinse it again. Bring a pan of water to a boil, and slip in the soaked cod. Simmer it gently (don't allow it to boil) for 10–12 minutes, until it flakes easily when nudged with a fork. Drain thoroughly and, using your fingers, gently pull away the skin and any bones.

❸ Warm the oil in a large skillet and, when it is hot, put in the onion rings and the garlic. Cook very gently for 7–8 minutes, until the onion and garlic soften and turn pale golden. Remove and reserve. Add the sliced potatoes and fry the potatoes gently until just soft. Remove them.

❹ Cover the bottom of an ovenproof dish with half the potatoes. Season with pepper and a sprinkle of parsley. Spread on half the sliced hard-cooked eggs, then half the onion, more parsley and pepper, then the salt cod. Finish with a layer of eggs, then onion and potatoes, seasoning with pepper and parsley as you go. Trickle on the remaining oil from the pan. Bake for 35–40 minutes, until well browned and bubbling.

christmas in tuscany

In Italy, among the people of the Garfagnana—a mountainous region of northwest Tuscany that runs from the olive-oil town of Lucca to the marble quarries of Carrerra—the fasting supper is "white" food, hallowed because it contains neither meat nor tomato. The choice must be a baked bread pudding made with unsalted Tuscan bread layered with greens—chard or the fleshy leaves of everlasting spinach—baked under a golden crust of savory custard. Or it might be a bubbling gratin of the bitter vegetables of a Tuscan winter—cardoons, chicory, sprouting broccoli, cavalo nero. Or, my own favorite— whole heads of fennel baked in wine with oil and garlic. Although in other places the centerpiece of the feast might be salt-cod, poached and finished in oil and garlic, in this part of the world, where the pennies are counted before the housewife goes to market, no one in his right mind would pay good money for *baccala*, mountain-fish, when they could have fresh fish straight from the sea. To supply their needs, in the run-up to Christmas, traveling fishmongers do a brisk trade between the coastal settlements and the mountains. Only white-fleshed fish with scales is considered suitable, mirroring the Jewish prohibitions against eating fish without scales. All others—crustaceans, shellfish, cephalopods, and those with a reddish tinge about the flesh or gills—are unhallowed fish, suitable for pagan new year, but not for the Christmas fast. For those of a more traditional turn of mind, *baccala* can be bought ready-soaked from the delicatessen, along with cheese and ham and all the other salt-preserved larder goods that liven the Christmas storecupboard.

On Christmas Day, the fast is broken with a banquet: the full five courses, the minimum expected by any self-respecting Italian epicure. To placate the gods—and there is no doubt that the feast of Christmas draws its resonances from a darker past—the food must not only be delicious, it must be plentiful. First comes the *antipasti*, the little dishes that allowed the mistress of the house to demonstrate the depth of her larder. From the brine-pot come caper fruits and baby cucumbers, the first of the year's home-cured olives—a little bitter, fragrant with oregano and garlic; from the storecupboard, summer's glut preserved for winter—eggplants, peppers, flavorsome sun-dried tomatoes, spears of fat white asparagus, and porcini mushrooms submerged in golden oil; a *caponata* perhaps, and there is sure to be a dish of baby onions in *agrodolce*—the medieval pickling sauce that combines the sweetness of raisins with the sourness of vinegar, and most luxurious, draped elegantly over a dish of white beans or slivered onto wedges of saltless Tuscan bread: *botarga*, salt-cured mullet roe, the caviar of the Mediterranean. There must be *salumi*, of course—*prosciutto*, *bresaola*, *culatello*, *salami*, *mortadella*—and cheese: expensive Parmesan and pecorino. Then comes the pasta: ravioli dressed with sage and melted butter, gnocchi sauced with Parmesan and cream; dumplings no bigger than a thumbnail poached in broth. Boiled meats, *bollito misto*, provide a moment's pause before the arrival of the *arrosti*. The *arrosti* of Christmas are truly stupendous: a crackle-skinned piglet deliciously stuffed with rice, capons broiled with thyme and rosemary, a goose. Finally the table is cleared for dessert. On come the nut-cakes, lemon tarts, chocolate sponges; ice creams, creamy cassattas, sorbets; fruits in syrup, meringues, macaroons and sabayons, vanilla-scented custards.

The housewives of Barga, principal market town of the Garfagnana, take advantage of modern prosperity to order their roast meats from the *rosticceria*. In Italy, the domestic oven is rarely used for roasting, being considered suitable for bread and bean bakes, but not for meat. When roasting is required, come winter or summer, the Italian male will light the charcoal grill. This, in itself, is a ritual that would have been perfectly familiar to those who celebrated the feast of Pan, the priapic god whose presence assured the land's fertility.

right: Salting cod to make *bacalhao*—a process that converts an Atlantic-caught fish into the traditional fasting food of Mediterranean Europe—served at the fasting supper that precedes the Christmas Midnight Mass.

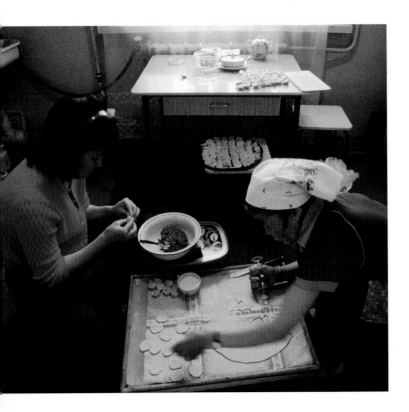

properly be included in the marinade, and advised me firmly against serving anything else at the same time. The Italians have had enough experience of foreigners to know that they have a most disagreeable habit of piling their plates with different kinds of food, when no self-respecting Italian would dream of accompanying a fine roast with anything but bread.

As for the Garfagnana's baking, neither *panettone* nor any of the other nut-and-fruit breads common in the cities of the plain are recognized as native—nor is the *castagnaccio*, a thin cake of pounded chestnuts flavored with rosemary, that marks the festive season in the bakeries of Florence. No, the speciality of the Garfagnana is the *biscotti di befana*, the witch's cookies—crisp little cookies to be eaten not for Christmas itself, but on January 6, the day when all virtuous Italian children receive their presents.

La befana, though she rides on a broomstick and shares the soot-black garments and conical hat of her Celtic sister, is neither bad nor good, but simply willful; one of that merry gang of minor gods—goblins, satyrs, centaurs—left over from pagan times, who, in their homeless state, cause trouble on the eves of holy days. In emulation of their activities, on the day before Epiphany, children dress themselves up as devils, ghosts, monsters, and go around the towns and villages, demanding treats for fear of tricks. In anticipation of these unruly visitors, the prudent housewife bakes a batch of *biscotti di befana*, although it's doubtful if the children of today would be so easily bought off. My informant told me the cookies do not have to be in any particular shape, although fishes, stars, and hearts are the most usual. There is also a cutter that produces an elongated oval, a shape that, had we been in Muslim lands, would have been recognized as the eye of Fatima—the talisman that averts the Evil Eye.

Down on the plain, in the walled city of Lucca where much of Italy's commercial olive oil is canned, I ordered my festive pasta from the local pasta-maker, an artisan of legendary skill. The Christmas speciality, as is only to be expected of the area, was *ravioli di castagna*, plump little pasta cushions stuffed with a medieval mixture of *prosciutto* and pounded chestnuts, each as big as a baby's fist—a single mouthful, if you were hungry. Around the corner in the poultry store—tiny, crowded, marked out from all others by the length of its queue—I chose a muscular little guinea fowl and a fat young gosling. The butcher inquired whether I was going to eat Italian or whether I have the English habit. When reassured of my Italian intentions, he split and flattened the birds ready for the charcoal. The queue of housewives to whom I appealed for culinary instruction offered opinions on whether sage and mint should

Panettone italian christmas bread

Originally North Italian, this Christmas bread is now a popular addition to the festive table throughout Italy. Very light and delicious, a good keeper, it makes a great bread-and-butter pudding and delectable French toast. What more could you ask?

Serves a dozen, more or less

½ oz / 15 g fresh yeast (half quantity if dried)

About a wineglassful warm water

½ cup / 100 g sugar

12 egg yolks (make meringues with the whites)

1½ sticks / 150 g unsalted butter, melted

A pinch salt

3 cups / 450 g white bread flour

Grated zest of 2 lemons and 2 oranges

⅔ cup / 100 g golden raisins, soaked overnight

in grappa or brandy

To finish:

1 egg yolk

❶ Dissolve the yeast in a couple of tablespoons of the warm water and a pinch of sugar. Put the egg yolks, the rest of the water, and the yeasty mixture into the bowl of a mixer, and combine. Add the remaining sugar, the melted butter, salt, and half the flour. Work it to a paste. Add the remaining flour, and work until it forms a ball. Turn out onto a floured board and work it by hand, adding more flour if necessary (or extra water, if not soft enough), until you have a smooth, elastic dough.

❷ Settle the dough ball in a floured bowl, cover with plastic wrap, and set in a warm place to rise for several hours, until doubled in bulk—the richer the dough, the longer it takes to rise; be patient.

❸ Meanwhile, line the sides of a 12 inch / 30 cm springform cake pan with a baking paper collar to increase its height by a hand's width. The higher it rises the better. Punch down the risen dough and work in the orange and lemon zest and the golden raisins (drain off spare liquor and dry with a dusting of flour). Press the dough into the pan. Leave to rise a second time, until doubled in volume.

❹ Preheat the oven to 325 F / 160 C / Gas 3.

❺ Brush the top of the loaf with a little forked-up egg yolk. Bake for 45–60 minutes, until well-risen and glamorously gilded. Check it's ready by tipping the loaf from the pan and tapping the base to see if it sounds hollow.

Biscotti di Befana epiphany cookies

The housewives of the Garfagnana valley above the oil-producing city of Lucca in northwest Italy bake these crisp little cookies for January 6, the Feast of Epiphany, the day when Mediterranean children receive their presents from *la befana*, the Epiphany witch. On the eve of the feast, children go around in disguise and masked—dressed as witches, wolves, devils, and other monsters—and knock on doors to ask for a treat. *Befana* cookies are not of any particular shape, although stars, hearts, and fishes are preferred.

Makes about 3 dozen cookies

The dough:

6 cups / 1 kg all-purpose flour

Generous 3 cups / 800 g sugar

1 level teaspoon baking soda

6 eggs

1½ sticks / 150 g softened unsalted butter

Marzipan topping:

1⅓ cups / 200 g ground almonds

2 egg whites, lightly beaten

Scant 1 cup / 200 g sugar

2–3 drops cochineal or red food coloring

❶ Preheat the oven to 350 F / 180 C / Gas 4.

❷ Make the cookie dough as if you were making pasta: tip the flour mixed with the sugar and baking soda onto the table and work in the forked-up eggs and softened butter—it should be soft but still firm. Roll or pat the dough out to a thickness of about ¼ inch / 5 cm, and cut into shapes with cookie cutters. Transfer to baking parchment laid on a baking tray. Pat the trimmings together lightly and re-roll so that you can cut out as many as possible. Save the remaining trimmings.

❸ To make the marzipan, work all the ingredients together to make a softish pink paste (red is the color of celebration all around the Mediterranean). Top each cookie with a scrap of marzipan paste and decorate with a little strip or cross of leftover trimmings, held down by a dab of water. Fork up the surface of the paste to form little, sharp peaks. Bake for 15–20 minutes, until pale gold. Transfer carefully to a baking rack. They'll crisp as they cool.

irish christmas beef

In Roman Catholic Ireland, the market in the victualling port of Cork is particularly busy in the run up to Christmas. Here, as elsewhere in the lands of the Celts, the midwinter feast still retains many of the trappings of the festival of Samhain that marked the winter solstice. Among the Celts, it seems that the fasting supper of Christmas Eve was never developed as part of the festivities as it was in Mediterranean Europe, although, in Ireland as in the other Celtic lands, the devout observed the usual rules of fast before feast. Instead, the birth of the Christ child is celebrated on Christmas Day itself, with the feasting, drinking, and rumbustious behavior common to all those who endure the long months of darkness—a period of gloom and uncertainty in which no one was really sure the sun would resume his ascent into the heavens and bring lifegiving warmth to the earth.

In winter, the harvest of creel and shoreline—oysters, lobsters, crabs, shrimp—became available, when the ocean-going trawlers are safely tucked inshore, and the ships that came into Cork to be victualled for their transatlantic voyages were berthed elsewhere. Storecupboard fish for the Friday dinner, as well as Lent and the eves of feast days, was salt-cured codling (hard as a plank, known as backboard fish) and salmon, salted and smoked—a method of conservation that added smoke to the salting process as an extra precaution in those places in which the climate was particularly damp.

Until the 1830s, when pork-barrelling for the ships became the main source of income, the business of Cork market was based on the butter trade. All of dairy-farming Ireland sent its butter to be salted and barreled in what was, for at least a century, the largest butter market in the world.

At Christmastide, certain stalls offered buttered eggs for sale—newly laid eggs from hens kept in lay all through the winter, whose warm shells had been rubbed with butter to exclude the air. Another spin-off from the dairy was the whey from buttermaking, which went to fatten the sty-pig. Even when reserved for domestic consumption, pork was never eaten fresh, but salted down as winter stores. Bacon-and-cabbage formed the usual Sunday dinner of Ireland's rural peasantry, with potatoes eaten with buttermilk for everyday. Although goose was considered the appropriate festive bird, reared in the barnyard, it was an obdurately seasonal creature, and the real treat was beef, the traditional centerpiece of the Christmas dinner table. Not, it must be said, the rare-cooked roast beef that turned on the spit of old England, but rather, mature beef that needed the boiling pot—three-toed, set in a corner of the fireplace—to make it tender. The joint of Christmas beef was kept in the winter larder beneath a protective jacket of spices for two or three months, till the festivities came around. The extended shelf-life suited the needs of the Irish people, since elderly milk animals were sent to market in the autumn to avoid the need to feed them through the long winter months.

In the aftermath of the festivities, when those who have celebrated well, but not wisely, might expect to find themselves on the wrong end of a whiskey headache, prodigious quantities of pig's trotters, *crabeens*, are consumed. These, along with the tripes and innards the pork-barrelers of Cork received in part-payment for their labors, are traditionally considered the only effective cure for a *potsheen* hangover—a ritual that binds the participants in brotherhood as surely as the blood-mingling ceremonies of other cultures.

Irish Christmas Beef

This is not at all like regular spiced beef, as the spices are quite dry and form a thick crust that keeps out the air. The meat can be kept in a cool place or in the refrigerator for 4–5 months while uncooked, or a month after cooking. The longer you keep it, the more it shrinks, and the denser the texture.

Serves a family party

6 lbs / 2.7 kg boned joint salt beef

12 tablespoons ground allspice

6 tablespoons ground cinnamon

4 tablespoons grated nutmeg

2 tablespoons ground cloves

❶ Dry the meat thoroughly. Mix the spices together and rub the mixture all over the cut surfaces.

❷ Put the joint in an earthenware dish and pile on the loose spices. Turn it every day or so, and pat down the spices. The beef will soon develop a thick crust.

❸ When you are ready to cook it—say 2–3 days before Christmas—tie the joint up neatly and bring it to a boil in plain water. Lid loosely and simmer for 2–3 hours until the meat is tender.

It can be eaten hot or cold—if the latter, press the meat beneath a weight for 12 hours as it cools. The leftover spices are lovely in an oxtail stew.

Irish Christmas Soda Bread

The mother of all Christmas cakes—an everyday soda bread made special with imported fruit and spices. Irish soda breads, plain or fruity, are traditionally baked in a *bastable,* a three-toed iron pot that sat on the hearth and was converted into a miniature baking oven by heaping glowing peat sods on the lid. The bread is not intended for storage. To keep it soft, wrap it in a cloth. Eat within a day.

Makes 1 large cake

1½ lbs / 750 g all-purpose flour

1 teaspoon salt

1 teaspoon baking soda

1 teaspoon mixed spice

1 generous handful mixed dried fruit

About 1½ cups / 375 ml buttermilk (or skim

milk with ½ teaspoon cream of tartar)

2 tablespoons molasses melted in

a little of the milk

❶ Preheat the oven to 400 F / 200 C / Gas 6.

❷ Mix all the dry ingredients together in a bowl. Mix in the melted molasses and enough milk to make a very soft dough. Work quickly, using your hands. Form into a ball and drop onto a floured baking tray, flatten to a thickness of 1½ inches / 4 cm.

❸ Using a floured knife, mark the top with a large cross.

❹ Bake for about 40 minutes, till perfectly well-risen and golden.

❺ Remove to a baking rack to cool. Break into the marked quarters and eat with salty Irish butter washed down with a nip of *usquebaugh*—the water of life—slipped into a mug of strong, sweet tea.

baptism in italy

Among all cultures, there remains a belief that meat—flesh or fowl—should be consumed to mark the birth of a child, and that the infant's head should be wetted, symbolically or actually, with generous libations of fermented liquor. Common to all is the need to achieve legitimacy—the group's acceptance of the new member as one of their own—most easily done by invoking the approval of a higher power. Whether this takes place at birth, at the moment when survival can be assumed, or during or after the initiation ceremonies through which can be achieved full membership of the cultural tribe, the primary purpose of the feast—the sharing of meat and the passing round of the communal cup—is to ensure that, by partaking of the same foods, eaten from the same dish, the tribe will know and recognize its own.

Among the *contadini*, Italy's independent peasantry, the newborn infant is presented at the font with very little delay, and all are welcome at the baptismal feast. For the smallholders who stock their storecupboards from the fruit of their own labors, the preparation of feast-day food is an act of reverence, a thanksgiving in itself.

Preliminaries are an all-important part of the ritual. Before the celebrations can begin, tables must be scrubbed, furniture polished, floors swept, curtains washed, sideboards dusted, kitchen implements rinsed and polished—a ritual cleansing that, although domestic, would have been as familiar to the priests of the temple of Osiris in Ancient Egypt as it is to the modern housewife.

The date is 1985. I am, as usual, looking for someone to show me the old ways, the cooking that comes from the soil rather than the supermarket. Rural Italy knows what's good,

and it knows who does it best. My enquiries lead to the door of a whitewashed farmhouse in the valley beneath the hilltop village of Monteguidi in the hills to the west of Florence, where Signora Santa Ripudini is preparing the baptismal feast for her new grandson Guido. On the menu, as always at family festivals when the hens are in lay, is a dish of pasta; it is homemade, of course, or it would not be worthy of so auspicious an occasion.

Santa, though her household is somewhat smaller than it was when her children were still growing, keeps hens for eggs and a sty-pig to eat the household scraps. Most of the neighbors no longer bother with keeping animals. In July, when the tomato plants are so laden with the scarlet globes that it seems the branches must break under the weight, Santa packs the ripe fruits in jars and sends them to the baker's oven to take the last of the heat. In January, when the olives on her trees are at precisely the right stage of ripeness, she takes the fruit to the mill and makes sure the oil she receives from the miller is all her own. On these good things, her culinary reputation rests. She has no secrets but these.

Santa's pasta is always made just before it is to be eaten. For everyday, she keeps a stack of store-bought dried pasta: to buy fresh pasta in a shop would be unthinkable. When her children were still at home, Santa used to make fresh pasta every day, but now, she only makes it for festive occasions—betrothals, weddings, and christenings; but never for funerals. For funerals, there is only cold food, as a sign of respect.

Among the *contadini*, there is a very deep awareness of what and what is not appropriate behavior. To such as Santa, whose family has lived in the same place for more centuries than the Pope has reigned in Rome, public acknowledgment

of lines of descent is of very real significance. The baptismal font confers the blessing of the Church; the baptismal feast confers legitimacy. By this not inconsiderable token, reinforced by approval of his maternal grandmother, the world will know that this child is not just any child, but a child to be reckoned with, a true son of the soil.

The pasta is nothing grand. Just pasta made with eggs still warm from the hen, and flour milled that very morning to the correct degree of fineness. These two ingredients are worked to a silky smoothness, cut by hand with a knife reserved for the purpose into ribbons of a precise size and thickness. The ribbons are then dropped from a certain height into more than ten times their volume of boiling water, allowed to cook for exactly the right amount of time before they are drained and dressed with a simple *sugo* (sauce) of tomatoes and oil. That same oil that Santa took to the miller to be pressed from fruit harvested at exactly the right moment from olive trees that are as carefully coddled as her very own baby grandson, now gurgling by the fireside, fully recovered from his alarming ordeal at the font.

All these things can be inspected at a glance from where the baby's mother sits, beside the formica-topped table that occupies the vine-shaded terrace, which, in all but the wettest of winters serves as an annex to the kitchen. Today, the terrace-table is loaded with what appears to be the complete contents of Santa's storecupboard, which is what it may well be, since Easter has come and gone, and there is no longer any need for winter stores. These are the *antipasti*. They only need to be decanted into dishes and finished with the appropriate tricklings of olive oil and sprinklings of fresh herbs.

Guests are received in the front parlor, a gloomy room with dark drapes, heavy furniture, patterned wallpaper, and family photos. Today, the curtains are drawn and all the family, except the grandmother, is entertaining the guests to a little refreshment—a glass of *vin santo*, dark and sweet, made with the grapes from the vine that shades the terrace.

In the kitchen, Santa rolls her sleeves above the elbow and spreads the table with a clean, white cloth. On the cloth she sets a wooden board. The board, a single piece of wood without a seam, ivory-white and as smooth as silk, belonged to her mother, and her mother before her, God rest her soul. On regular days, Santa rolls her pasta directly on the table, but on days such as this, for the sake of the association, it is more fitting to use the board. Beside it she sets a large, plain, white china bowl. This, too, belonged to her mother and is never brought out at any other time. By these seemingly ordinary gestures—no less ordinary, it might be said, than the sprinkling of a baby's head with water—the blessing of the ancestors is invoked. Mary, the Mother of God, in Santa's view, was never averse to helping out with pasta.

There is also a jar of salt, the eggs, and the oil. From the flour bin set ready beneath the table, Santa fills the bowl with flour. She sifts the flour through her fingers, and then presses down with her fists to make a dip. She adds eggs, two for each person, cracking each egg against the next. The deep orange yolks and crystal-clear whites drop in the well. Santa never weighs the ingredients. Proportions depend on the weather and the size of the eggs; today, since the hens are mature, their eggs are large. No water goes into Santa's pasta, although, in a bad year when they were poor, or the war had made things hard, there might be an eggshellful, but nobody liked to admit it—not from pride, but from the fear that those times might return. There are many such small domestic proprieties to be observed; there is never a reason to upset the household gods by lack of gratitude, or insufficient care, or idle talk.

Next, a little olive oil, greeny-gold and viscous is added—as much as can be cupped in the palm of the hand, and as much salt as will not run through the fingers of a closed fist. If you stand in the doorway and look down the valley—says Santa, working the dough steadily with the hook of her hand—you can see in the distance the old salt-road where it runs through the olive groves toward the village, although, she remarks, few people here are aware of this any more.

Curving her fingers, she draws flour from the edges to form an ever-growing dough-ball. When this is perfectly smooth and pliable, she shakes a little flour onto the board and immediately begins to roll it. Close examination of the rolling pin reveals it to be a new broom handle. The dough-sheet widens swiftly under her strokes, the color a brilliant yellow. The board is a little too small and the sheet soon laps over the edges; an imperfection that causes her some momentary irritation. No matter, her mother is present in spirit, if not in the flesh.

She dusts the dough with flour from her fingertips, and rolls the fine sheet of pasta around the broom handle, stretching it against the board, flicking the flap each time with a sharp smack. Very soon, the sheet is paper thin, translucent when held to the light. Santa rolls, slices, piles in handfuls, picks up each handful, and tosses it with her fingers—just enough to dry the strands a little and stop them forming lumps.

Meanwhile, the water to be heated for the cooking is fetched directly from the well. This, too, is part of the ritual. For this particular boiling pot, only well-water will do. The water boils. Salt is added, then the pasta, a handful at a time. Two minutes and it's ready to be drained. Now for the *sugo*, a little for each batch—not too much or too little, just enough to tint and shine the pasta. Thirty minutes after Santa began, the ritual is complete.

A pile of pasta may not immediately declare itself a sacred food. But if the definition of sacredness is that which nourishes the soul as well as the body, there's no doubt that that's exactly what it is.

right: First communion—the Christian sacrament that confirms that
a child is capable of making his or her own moral decisions—
demands an abundance of sweet things.

initiation

The acceptance of young adults as fully fledged tribal members, whether
sophisticated or primitive, follow more or less the same pattern. Anyone who has
ever been inducted into a college fraternity will recognize the ritual common to all
initiation ceremonies—in the course of the initiation, things happen. Most of them
are unpleasant, usually involving some method of branding or otherwise marking the
initiate in order that he or she will ever afterward be instantly recognizable to their fel-
lows. Primitive stuff, but it serves the purpose. The ceremony, naturally, is followed
by the sharing of a meal—the easiest, quickest way to declare blood-brotherhood.
Whether the menu is freshly slaughtered antelope washed down with fermented
cassava juice under a banyan tree, or roast beef and Beaujolais in a smart city water-
ing-hole, the purpose is the same. Although the warrior *morans* of the plains of
Africa and the young bloods of the Western university campus do not, by any means,
share the same lifestyle, they all have the same idea—the formation of a bond that
ensures the support of the peer group at the most important time of their lives.

The same purpose is served among Christian congregations by the ceremony
of confirmation, an official laying-on of hands by which children baptized as infants
have their membership confirmed when judged mature enough to make decisions
for themselves. This conferring of privilege allows the initiate to claim a place at the

Lord's table and partake for the first time of the sacramental bread and wine. While baptism is a sacrament that can be administered at any time in any place and requires no witnesses, confirmation involves the entire peer group, takes place in the presence of as many of the congregation as possible, and needs the presence of a senior priest—a bishop at least—whose authority can be traced back to the laying on of hands by Christ himself of his disciple Peter, first Bishop of Rome.

It is usual among devout Roman Catholics that the children who are to receive the sacrament for the first time—an annual event in each parish—process together to the church dressed all in white, the color of innocence, and that afterward they receive the felicitations of family and friends at a feast.

Among communities such as those of Malta, strongly Roman Catholic and home to the crusader Knights of Malta, the splendor and extravagance with which a child's first communion is celebrated reflects the prosperity and generosity of the family. As with a wedding, it is a public declaration of success—past, present, and future—and an element of competitiveness creeps in. While no particular dish can be said to belong exclusively to a first-communion feast, it is expected that the dishes will be both traditional and luxurious.

Every Maltese feast, explain sisters Anne and Helen Caurana Galizia in *The Food and Cookery of Malta*, must start with a fortifying *timpana*, a succulent macaroni pie of Sicilian origin. For a festive occasion, the Galizia family replaces the pasta with a saffron-flavored risotto rice cooked in a rich chicken broth. Spit roast meats of the domestic kind—pork, chicken, beef, veal—follow. In the old days, as a subtle way

of declaring independence from the Knights—the universal landlords who held exclusive hunting rights throughout the island—game, and particularly rabbit, joined the domestic meats on the spit. For the children who have just received first communion, all manner of sweet things load the table: candied peel; little christening cookies swirled with pink and white icing; pastries stuffed with chopped spiced dates (*mquaret*); hollow pastry horns stuffed with a fresh ricotta and beaten with chopped candied oranges; and toasted hazelnuts. In a good year, when the family feels prosperous, beautifully-decorated candies—realistically painted marzipan fruit, brightly colored ice cream bombes sprinkled with colored sugar—are ordered from the confectioner rather than being made at home. Professionally prepared cakes are always more valued than home-cooked ones, since bought-in food costs money, the hardest of all commodities to acquire.

Among tribal peoples, initiation ceremonies concentrate on the onset of puberty, the time when life partners are chosen and consideration is given to the next generation. For the San people of the Kalahari, the last of the true hunter-gatherers, an unacceptable increase in population was avoided by segregating the sexes as soon as puberty was reached. When the young men came of age to join the hunters and thus were able to provide for others, trial unions were permitted. It was, however, not until young people reached their early twenties, a time when their parents' parents were reaching the end of their life, that any offspring were allowed to survive. The reason was purely practical: hunter-gathering communities cannot afford to expand beyond the natural limitations of their territory as dictated by food sources available to both gatherers and

Kugelhupf **yeast-raised butter cake**

This is a particularly rich bread dough with a high proportion of egg and butter to flour; you'll have to work at it to get it to accept all the butter, but it'll be well worth the effort. Variations on the same theme include Italy's Christmas *panettone* (*see page 103*) as well as many of the Mediterranean's Easter breads.

Makes 1 bread

2⅓ cups / 350 g white bread flour

1 oz / 25 g fresh yeast (half the amount if dried)

3–4 tablespoons warm milk

1 tablespoon sugar

1½ sticks /150 g unsalted butter, melted

3 medium eggs

Make sure all the ingredients are at room temperature before you begin.

❶ Butter and line with parchment a round high-sided cake pan about 8 inches / 20 cm in diameter, preferably one with hinged sides. You're aiming for a tall cylinder of cake about twice the height of its diameter.

❷ Sift the flour into a large, warm bowl, and make a well in it with your fist.

❸ Liquidize the yeast with a pinch of the sugar. Whisk in 2 tablespoons of warm milk, and pour into the well in the flour. Sprinkle the surface with a little flour, and leave for 10 minutes for the yeast to bubble up and begin to work—a process known, for reasons that soon become obvious, as setting the sponge.

❹ Whisk the eggs together till light and white, and whisk in the remaining sugar. Work the fluffy eggs and melted butter into the flour, using the palm of your hand or the dough-hook on the processor, until you have a soft, sticky dough. Tip it out onto a well-floured board and knead. Work with your closed fist and the palm of your hand until you have a smooth, buttery dough-ball. You may need a little more flour, but don't overdo it. Pop the kneaded dough back in the bowl and cover with a damp cloth or plastic wrap, and leave to rise in a warm place for an hour or two, until the dough has doubled in bulk. A rich dough takes longer to rise than a plain dough.

❺ Preheat the oven to 350 F / 180 C / Gas 5.

❻ Work the dough to distribute the air bubbles, knead it into a neat cushion, and settle it into the pan. Set it to rise again for another 30 minutes or so, until it has once again doubled in bulk.

❼ Bake for 30–40 minutes, until well risen and brown, and shrunk from the sides of the pan.

❽ Tip it out and tap the base; it should sound hollow. If it doesn't, return the bread to the oven for another 5-10 minutes.

hunters. The San share with other tribal groups a belief that the preparation of initiation feasts—spit-roast meats is men's business, a rite in which women are not expected to intervene.

The Aga nation of Bali, another tribal group has managed to conserve its identity by discouraging the attentions of outsiders. Enforced isolation, observed ethnologist David Burton after a sojourn in one of the more tolerant villages, imposes severe limitations on the gene pool, making puberty a particularly dangerous time. Unlike the mainstream Balinese, who, he noted, have a relaxed attitude to sexual mores, the Aga segregate the sexes at adolescence, thereafter allowing mingling once a year and under strict supervision. At this annual meeting of the virgins, decorous dances are performed by the girls who are then equally decorously wooed by the young men; this preliminary courtship ritual is followed by a feast that is cooked and served by the men. The main dish—a spicy stew of pork and chili cooked with coconut milk—is ladled with coconut shells onto palm fronds and set in front of the ladies. The ritual, notes Mr. Burton, does not necessarily lead to betrothal, but, as the only moment of the year when a man might demonstrate his culinary skills to win a maid, it helps.

Whenever, and for whatever reason, transition moments are celebrated, these are, in my experience, without exception sanctified by sharing food. Pre-eminent among these celebratory feasts is the Jewish bar mitzvah, the gathering through which a young Jewish boy graduates to manhood. The festive dishes considered proper to *bar mitzvah*—although always obeying religious prohibitions—vary widely, reflecting the raw materials and culinary habits of those among whom the celebrants find themselves. For this reason, even dishes directly related to tribal memory, whose purpose is to feed the soul rather than the body, are by no means universal. To cover even a few, it would be necessary to examine each grouping individually—an impossible task in a book of this size.

Nevertheless, certain groups have been more influential than others—among these the Jews of Germany. For the Ashkenazi Jews, the essential recipes for the

rite-of-passage feasts were born from the food of the *shtetl*—the townships established by landowners who employed Jews to manage their vast estates, from the eastern borders of Germany to the steppes of Tzarist Russia. These were essentially rural ghettos, with muddy streets and cramped wooden houses. The discipline imposed by whole families living in one or two rooms heated by a single cooking source dictated the way of life, which was restrained, domestically austere, but generous to strangers, with an emphasis on anticipation of a better world to come. In an enclosed world, food was of paramount importance. While the men prayed, the women cooked. In a Jewish household, the mother takes all domestic decisions, including what food shall be consumed and when. Within certain constraints—financial, practical, geographical—the celebration menu never varied, unless necessity dictated otherwise. Goose in all its parts—flesh, fat, and chopped liver; sweet-and-sour fish; noodles or pinch-finger dumplings cooked in chicken or pigeon broth; boiled beef; sugar-sweetened carrots. For dessert, there would be a *kugel*, a dish of noodles baked with sugar, raisins, and cinnamon; or pancakes; or a spicy gingerbread.

Celebrations of the earliest rites of passage—birth, initiation that confirm a child as a full member of a group, the rituals of tribal folk and others who follow ancestral habit (often secret and shocking to the modern way of thinking)—all are designed to introduce a new member to the community, officially acknowledging his or her presence in the sight of God and man. The underlying purpose is confirmation of legitimacy so that the group will recognize and protect its own; this is achieved by invoking the blessing of a higher power. Foods assure the future of the newborn, or adolescent, by gathering the community to witness his or her admission, whether as a fledgling member or full adult of the tribe. By ensuring that all break bread together and share food from the same pot, senior members of the community confer their blessing on their juniors—a two-way traffic, since those who are now the supplicants before long will become the providers.

courtship
betrothal
marriage

3

Society, however sophisticated or primitive it may be, recognizes three steps in the mating rituals whose ultimate aim is the reproduction of its own kind, an aim shared, science tells us, by all life on the planet. Among humankind, the generally accepted norm is a period of courtship followed by an interval of betrothal that leads to the wedding.

Ritual foods associated with courtship, a private affair, are those most likely to earn the cooperation of the love-object—edibles chosen for their power to seduce—among these, naturally enough, aphrodisiacs. Ritual foods associated with betrothal—a more public matter but still kept within the circle of close family and friends—take a similar form to those served at weddings, being special, but without the complex ritual significance and lavishness of the wedding feast. Ritual foods associated with weddings, the public occasions at which the intentions of the couple are brought to the attention of the presiding higher being as well as the community, are primarily concerned with fertility, the acknowledged purpose of the union.

On a practical level, most, although not all, warm-blooded creatures—rodents, rabbits, and humans being notable exceptions—give birth in the spring, at a time when nature is at her most fecund. Courtship, the process of selection undertaken by all creatures whose reproductive habit requires the cooperation of another of their kind, takes place in anticipation of conception at a time dictated by the availability of the food source. The human female can bear children at any time of the year. For this to work within the system, a nine-month cycle of reproduction requires a winter courtship, a spring betrothal, and a summer wedding—leading in turn to a spring birth. Perfect timing provides a social answer to a practical problem. It is tempting to imagine that this obvious reality has been superseded by the ability of the human race to feed itself throughout the year, yet modern medical research shows that spring babies thrive where babies born at other times hold back. Food source remains the primary trigger for our reproductive habit—small wonder we celebrate the preliminaries with a feast.

Most, if not all, of our courtship, betrothal, and marriage rituals, including the acceptance of female virginity as a desirable prenuptial state, are designed to ensure that the male can be in no doubt whatsoever that any offspring is of his own making, and will, therefore, be willing to

previous page: Bride and groom at a traditional Japanese wedding.

top right: Love candies—sweet thoughts written in sugar.

take responsibility for their care. The first sign of acceptance of a suitor is the invitation to share a meal with the loved one's family. The simple fact of falling in love—that delicate blend of mutual attraction, mood, and magic that leads to courtship—is not necessarily accepted as a basis for matrimony by those who feel responsible for the family and the extended community. There was not, is not, and probably never will be, an explanation for a process that, being entirely irrational, is often against the interests of organized society. Mythology is full of star-crossed lovers whose stories end tragically because they lack society's blessing—cautionary tales that, though undeniably romantic, served as a warning to others. Such liaisons must remain without public acknowledgment since they cannot earn the approval of society.

Among "primitive" societies, the rules of courtship and marriage might have been different, but alliances were no less strictly regulated. Courtships that were, and in some cases still are, not simply a prelude to an arranged marriage, required a period of licensed privacy during which the couple might get to know each other, or the unattached might have the opportunity to choose a mate. Most obvious of these are the Roman saturnalias, periods of permitted bad behavior during which lots might be drawn and mates chosen at random—a tradition from which springs many of our less-governable courtship habits, including the traditional rituals of Saint Valentine's Day. Stern old Bishop Valentine must have spun in his grave when he inherited the mantle of Bacchus. Gifts of champagne and chocolates, and anonymous love notes would have not been at all to the taste of the saintly ascetic crucified for his faith on the road to Rome.

Festivities that, for one reason or another, involved young people staying overnight in the countryside—which could be as loosely or tightly supervised as suited society's purpose—had an important role to play in the courtship process.

Some of the attendant rituals show their colors quite clearly—a troupe of young women dancing around a maypole, the oldest phallic symbol in the world—others have been given a more elegant gloss. May Day food is as frivolous and seductive as possible—sugary cookies, marzipan fruit, scented infusions, and perfumed syrups. Other courtship

above: *"Sleepeth or waketh thou jolly shepherd?*
Thy sheep be in the corn
And for one blast of thy nimikin mouth
Thy sheep shall take no harm."
The subject of William Holman Hunt's *The Hireling Shepherd* pays court to the beautiful shepherdess: in her lap lies the lamb, universal symbol of sacrifice, and the apple of desire.

traditions simply grew out of natural circumstances, such as the summer transhumance, the moving of flocks or herds

Galician Empanadillas mini meat—stuffed pasties

The spicy meat filling is typically Galician, as is the oil pastry, a hot-water crust that doesn't soak up the juices and stays crisp for days. Delicious on a picnic, particularly with a dipping sauce of yogurt and mint.

Serves 6–8 (makes 20 fist-sized pasties)

The filling:

2 tablespoons olive oil

1 small onion, finely chopped

1 garlic clove, finely chopped

2 red peppers, deseeded and diced

¼ lb / 100 g chorizo or lean bacon, finely chopped

½ lb / 225 g shoulder pork, diced small (or minced)

1 teaspoon Spanish pimiento or paprika

1 teaspoon chopped oregano

Salt and freshly milled pepper

About ½ cup / 125 ml white wine or dry sherry

6–8 saffron threads

½ teaspoon thyme

The pastry:

Scant 2 cups / 275 g all-purpose flour

½ teaspoon salt

4 tablespoons olive oil

2 tablespoons white wine or dry sherry

About ½ cup / 150 ml boiling water

❶ Heat the oil in a skillet and gently fry the onion, garlic, and peppers until soft. Push them to one side (or remove and reserve) and fry the *chorizo* or bacon till the fat runs. Add the pork, and fry until it takes a little color. Sprinkle with paprika and oregano, season with salt and pepper, and turn it over the heat for a moment. Add the wine, saffron with its water, and the thyme. Bubble up, cover loosely, and simmer until most of the liquid has evaporated and the meat is tender. Taste, and add salt and freshly milled pepper. Leave aside to cool while you make the pastry.

❷ Preheat the oven to 400 F / 200 C / Gas 6.

❸ Sift the flour with the salt into a bowl, and make a well in the middle. Mix the oil and wine with the boiling water in a jug. Pour the warm liquid into the well in the flour. Using the hook of your hand, knead into a soft dough. Work it some more until it is smooth and elastic, then tip it onto a lightly floured board, form the dough into a roll, and cut it into 20 small pieces. Knead each piece into a little ball, and roll into thin disks about 5 inches / 12.5 cm in diameter. This is a very elastic dough that can be rolled very thin and is best worked while still warm.

❹ Drop a spoonful of the filling onto one side of each round, wet the edges and fold the other half over to enclose, marking the edges with a fork to seal. Transfer to an oiled baking sheet and bake for 10–15 minutes, until golden and crisp. Transfer to a baking rack and allow to cool to room temperature. The pastry will stay crisp for a couple of days.

To make a single large pie for cutting—an *empanada*—enclose the filling between two disks of pastry, lower the oven temperature to 350 F / 180 C / Gas 4, and allow an extra 20 minutes for baking.

which have overwintered on the plains, to their summer mountain pastures. This was a time when young men and maids (mostly segregated, but loosely so) took advantage of a little privacy to choose a mate, although the main purpose of the exercise—an absence of months—was to provide the community with milk in the storable form of cheese and butter.

Still other traditions, such as the Whitsun pilgrimages *romerias*—overnight visits to the all-important water sources of the Mediterranean—received the tacit blessing of the Church, since the Virgin Mary replaced the earlier goddesses in the grotto. Food for rural outings was carefully prepared and elegantly packed so all might see what a good and thrifty housekeeper the young woman who prepared it would make. For a young man to accept an invitation to share a young woman's picnic could be taken as a declaration of romantic interest. In Spain, the picnic would certainly include a perfectly made *tortilla*—the thick egg-and-potato cake every young girl learns to make at her mother's knee; and, tied in a white napkin, a half-dozen spicy *empanadillas* guaranteed to win the heart of all but the most reluctant swain.

right: *Primavera* c.1478 by Sandro Botticelli. This symbolic figure of spring traditionally associated with renewal and fertility is depicted as a beautiful young woman. Beside her, Flora showers her with flowers. This painting was intended to hang outside Lorenzo de Medici's nuptial chamber.

may queens and midsummer madness

Opportunities for courtship present themselves at the midsummer picnics of Saint Jean—the feast of John the Baptist—the date of which coincides in the northern hemisphere with the summer solstice, the year's longest day. Most obviously pagan of these celebrations are the bonfires of Walpurgis Night, the May Day celebration of those who came within the Teutonic sphere of influence—in Sweden known as Valborg, in Finland as Vapunaato—offering equal opportunity for courtship and the expelling of witches. In Sweden, students wear white caps and misbehave in all the ways that youth has misbehaved since the beginning of time. In Finland, the young light huge bonfires while being warned by their elders to keep their white caps clean. Since white is the color of purity no less for the virgin than for the bride, everyone knows exactly what this means. The proper food for the Saint Jean is anything that can be carried out into the countryside and consumed under the stars. In some traditions, crumbs are scattered for the birds and beasts, while a libation is poured on the earth to appease Flora or Eostre, or the goddess of the moon, or some other female deity who took an interest in the love of man for woman, or even the Virgin Mary herself who, in the absence of holy females among the senior members of the Christian hierarchy, inherited many of the duties of her predecessors.

The seventeenth-century Greek historian Leo Allatius, writing about Chios, the Aegean island famous for mastic, an aromatic gum much valued for culinary purposes—makes the link between the May Queen and the virgin goddess Artemis, patroness of childbirth: "On the first of May, the good women are obliged to make crosses on their doors, saying that the goddess of their mountains is due to come and visit them in their houses, and that without this mark she would not come in." If anyone had earned her wrath, the goddess might be appeased with a gift of honey and other sweetmeats offered at the place where her displeasure had been incurred.

Prior to the courtship rituals of May Day, it was advisable to chase away all malevolent influences—devils, witches, and those who might otherwise blight the proceedings. The quickest way to achieve this was by lighting fires and making loud noises. Such proceedings are the direct heirs to the sacrificial flames of much earlier times.

Ethnologist James Frazer, author of *The Golden Bough*, examined the robust rituals of his Celtic ancestors from the safe distance of the 1920s: "Upon the first day of May, according to a custom still in vogue towards the end of the eighteenth century, all the boys in the township of Callendar meet in the moors. They cut a table in the green sod, of a round figure, by casting a trench in the ground of such circumference as to hold the whole company. They kindle a fire and dress a repast of eggs and milk in the consistency of a custard. They knead a cake of oatmeal, which is toasted at the embers against a stone. After the custard is eaten, they divide the cake into so many portions as similar as possible, as there are persons in the company. They daub one of these portions all over with charcoal, put it in a bonnet and each one blindfold draws out a portion." It will come as no surprise to students of such things that the recipient of the black portion, although the matter was not by then pursued to its logical conclusion, was considered "devoted" and obliged to jump over the flames three times, a rather more acceptable alternative to being burned as a sacrifice to Baal.

The underlying theme of May Day—the need to choose a suitable mate—is reinforced by the traditional battles between gangs, with the young women demonstrating, through their domestic skills, their suitability for matrimony by baking or providing the contents of a picnic; and the young men doing the same through hunting and survival skills. In Portugal in the 1890s, ethnologist Rodney Gallop reported that the frequent and rowdy fights between the supporters of rival queens led to the prohibition of the May Day customs in Portugal in the 1890s. "Before that time, but continuing well into the twentieth century in the rural districts of the Alenteho and the Algarve, the *Maia* or May Queen, adorned with flowers, was set in a decorated chair by the kitchen door, in front of which stood a tall pole twined with sweet-scented flowers and leaves. Meanwhile, her admirers, singing songs in praise of her beauty and virtue, demanded money, none too gently, from all the passersby." Hungarian historian Gyula Illyes also offered, in 1967, a reminiscence of the May day rituals of the poverty-stricken village where he was born: "In May, the maypole was danced out. It was a strong, slender poplar with all the branches stripped from its long trunk except for a little foliage left at the very top, about the size of an umbrella. It was brought down on Whit Saturday, when its real decoration began. Now every unmarried girl had to tie a ribbon to it. And it was also the duty of every craftsman on the *puszta* to put something on it. The cooper made a little wooden tub, the smith a horseshoe decorated with brass, the vinedresser a raffia garland, the shepherds each gave a piece of cheese. After lunch on White Monday, the festival began. Then came the tree-climbing. Everybody except the children had the right to climb to the top of the tree and bring down whatever he wanted…"

Although the traditions of Old England were largely lost in Puritan times, the Victorians went to some length to reinstate them. George Long, a keen student of the folklore of England in the 1920s, identifies the hobby-horse dance performed by the morris men—an all-male troupe of dancers who wear bells, ribbons, and, in pagan times, animal skins and stag's antlers on their heads—as a hunting ritual. "On May day in certain parts of the country…simple rites were performed to ensure the safety of the harvest, the fertility of the flocks and herds, or the success of tribal hunting. Hence the prevalence in nearly all pagan religions of the male and female deity, identified with the sun and earth or moon—the former requiring to be propitiated by human or animal sacri-

left: In *The Village Kermesse* by Pieter Brueghel the Younger, Dutch villagers celebrate May Day with the traditional maypole dance.

fices, and the festivals of the latter being associated with the removal of sexual inhibitions." Quite so. A similar and even more primitive event was recorded by George Gomme, observing the folkways of old England at a Whitsun Ram Fair in Cornwall in the 1890s: "In the center of the field stands a granite pillar or menhir, six or seven feet high. On May morning, before daybreak the young men of the village used to assemble there, and then proceed to the moor, where they selected a ram lamb, and after running it down brought it in triumph to the field, fastened it to the pillar, cut its throat, and then roasted it whole, skin, wool and all. At midday a struggle took place for a slice, it being supposed to confer luck for the ensuing year on the fortunate devourer. As an act of gallantry, the young men sometimes fought to get a slice for their chosen young women, all of whom, in their best dresses, attended the Ram Feast. Dancing, wrestling and other games, assisted by copious libations of cider, prolonged the festivity until midnight." Mr. Gomme recorded that custom had latterly given way to a somewhat less barbaric parading of a live ram decked with ribbons through the streets, although the conclusion was the same.

Similar customs are recorded elsewhere, and are more or less barbaric depending on the point of view of the observer. The *mechoie*, the ram-roast served at Berber wedding feasts and throughout the Middle East, also appears at the lavish wedding celebrations of India. A young male, rather than female, animal is considered the appropriate sacrificial meat at those rituals that lead to matrimony, holy or otherwise—a practical shepherding decision, since rams are of rather less use to the community than ewes. No doubt the deity to whom the animals were offered knew the difference, and approved the people's thrifty habits. Methods of cooking the meat vary—although roasting or earth-oven baking is preferred since the cooking is usually done in the open air by men (further proof of their hunting skills), while the women's culinary skills are deployed more skillfully in the home.

When the early Church Fathers, mindful of the need for compromise with older gods, declared June 26 the feast day of Saint John the Baptist, they added to the general confusion. It is surely no accident that Baptist John (or Jean, or Ivan, or Juan) seems, with his matted hair and hairy cloak, more a wild man of the woods than Christian saint. Perhaps it was no accident that the man charged with the responsibility of baptizing Christ inherited many of the trappings as well as the responsibilities of the goat god Pan.

In Provence, the herbs gathered on the night of the Saint Jean were (and among the devout, still are) considered more efficacious than those gathered at any other time. Every herbalist in a Provencal market will know precisely which of the aromatics—five in all: rosemary, thyme, marjoram, hyssop, and sage—are needed to make an *infusion aux herbes de Saint Jean*.

In Eastern Europe during the 1930s, Hungarian ethnologist Karoly Viski observed the rituals of Flowery Saint Ivan's Day: "The day of the summer solstice is at the time when Hungarian wheat, Saint Ivan's apples, and cherries ripen. The day on which the calendar of the church fixed Saint Ivan's day used to be the feast of love in the calendar of ancient man. The old pagan feast, held at the same time as the Christian festival of Pentecost, is the feast of the internal fire, which burns forever in man. A tall tree trunk is set up on top of the nearest hill, a number of old baskets are placed on it, and a girl's wreath is laid on top of them. When this is done,

the tree is set on fire at sunset. Sometimes a number of Saint Ivan's fires flame up at a smaller or greater distance from each other. If the wreath also catches fire, it is a good sign: its owner will soon be married!"

Many of the rituals of Saint John's Eve have to do with attempting to discover which girl will marry whom in the coming year. More practical steps to achieve this aim were taken by those who attended the bride-fairs held on the plains of what was once called Middle Europe. These were cheerful gatherings, sometimes of many thousands, in which eating, drinking, singing, and ring-dancing facilitated the main business—the pairing up of marriageable young women with young men in search of a bride. These unions required tactful supervision and negotiation by middlemen (mostly elderly and female) during the course of many a campfire meal in which much bread was broken and many toasts drunk. Negotiations included the young woman's dowry—bed linen, milk-cows, domestic utensils—and proof of the young man's ability to bring home the meat. Social standing included a discreet run-through of family history, to avoid cousin marrying non-kissing cousin, a disaster that could be averted by those negotiators who knew their customers, their family history, and their lineage. Contemporary accounts indicate that the bargains struck usually had the approval of all the interested parties, and that young women—and, indeed, young men—had the right to veto their family's choice, provided they had good reason.

the romerias of spain

Of all the summer pilgrimages that afford the young people of Latin lands the opportunity for a little courting, the most romantic is surely the romerias of Spain. Traditionally, these pilgrimages take place at Whitsun, or White Sunday, the Christian festival held on the seventh Sunday after Easter. While the inhabitants of the cold lands of northern Europe needed fire festivals to encourage the sun, those who lived in the dry lands of the south were concerned with water sources. Among the most remarkable of the Whitsun pilgrimages is the long trek across the delta of the Guadalquivir, southwest Spain, to the sanctuary of the Virgin of the Dew, buried deep in the sage brush and cistus scrub of a watery wilderness. These week-long picnics—requiring eating and sleeping under the stars—are a happy compromise between pagan and Christian preoccupations. In earlier times, the objects of veneration, statues of the Virgin Mary, would have been of Artemis, the goddess Diana, or, in even earlier days, the little fertility goddesses, all curves and fecund wombs, who watched over the same ancestral springs. The images are always invested with some mystical provenance—in Andalusia in Spain it is a miraculous escape from the Moors. After the fall of Granada, there were a great many discoveries of Christian images hidden away in rural hiding-places. The belief is that the Mother of God usually managed to insist—by supernatural intervention of one kind or another—on staying exactly where she was, with responsibilities inherited from earlier guardians of the well-springs.

The grave-faced little wooden Virgin of Rocio is unusual in that she was found under a damp thicket in the middle of a wetland, and that she has no well-spring to protect, but is instead in charge of the nightly renewal of the water-source that keeps the marshland alive. The discovery of the little statue, naturally enough, was at Whitsun—at a time when miracles are only to be expected. The rest of her legend is familiar enough: when her discoverers tried to carry her home to their village of Almonte, the statue stubbornly refused to be moved—returning without assistance to her chosen spot. In despair, the men of Almonte decided to build their patroness her very own sanctuary in the middle of the marsh, a place so desolate that only those who were prepared to undertake the hazardous journey across the marshes might worship at her shrine. Her reputation spread, and brotherhoods of pilgrims from far-flung places began to visit her on the anniversary of her discovery.

These days, her festival—once the privilege of horsemen and foot pilgrims who took as long as seven days and nights to ford the rivers and cross the dunes—is open to all who care to take the new road from Seville. The pilgrimage is a merry one, as well it might be, being well watered with sherry from Sanlúcar de Barrameda and Jerez. In the thronged bridleways of Rocio itself, guitars strum and drums beat day and night to accompany the dancing and singing of the *rocieros*, special songs rewritten every year that tell of the hazards and pleasures of the delta crossing. Gypsy frills for the ladies, and the elegant short black jackets, sombreros, and heavy leather chaps of the Andalusian horsemen are still required dress for those who wish to honor the Mother of God, in whatever guise they see her. In the view of the *Andaluz*, whether saint or sinner, there's no more certain absolution for the year's sins than keeping the Whitsun vigil with Our Lady of the Dew.

Although the communion wafer is all that passes the lips

left: Whitsun revelers trace the formal patterns of a *sevillana*, Andalusia's traditional dance-form, in El Rocio, at the shrine of Our Lady of the Dew, guardian of the water-source of the Guadalquivir.

above: *The Pilgrimage to the Miraculous Fountain of San Isidro,*
1820–23, by Francisco José de Goya.

of those who pay their respects to the doll-like image of perfect motherhood in the sanctuary at El Rocío, the sacrificial feast is to be found elsewhere—in the dusty streets of the little town, that only come to life at this one moment of the year.

Pilgrimage food is either that which can be carried in the pocket—bread and ham—or that which can be cooked using water from the stream over an open fire on one of the raw-iron, flat-bottomed pans a horseman might strap to his saddle. A *paella* perhaps, or a *perol*—a soupy paella popular in the mountains—or anything that takes a minimum amount of fuss and very little displacement. Although the marshes are now the great nature reserve of the Coto Doñana, and no wild-gathering is permitted, in the old days—twenty years ago, when I made the pilgrimage across the dunes with my children on a mule-cart—people took nothing with them but rice and oil (well, maybe saffron and salt) in the confident expectation

that the Lord would provide the rest. Indeed He did. Anyone with a gun could be sure to pick up a rabbit, or a brace of duck. A horseman might even manage to ride down a *jabali*—one of the tough little pigs of the wild breed that survive in the dunes. The children would be able to gather the exquisitely patterned snails, no bigger than a thumbnail, that clung to the spiny skeletons of dried-out thistles; or search out under the prickly bushes the spindly but delicious shoots of wild asparagus. You could always count on a variety of herbs—feathery tufts of fennel, thyme, and rosemary—and also various sour-stalked or peppery-leaved plants.

Paella de Campo andalusian country paella

The *paella* is one of those amiable one-pot dishes that take their name from the pan in which they are cooked. If you have a proper *paella* pan—each comes in a size appropriate to the number to be fed—and the necessary wide-based heat source—a brush-fire that has been allowed to die down to charcoal or a barbecue pit—so much the better. If not, a flat-bottomed wok or a large skillet will do, although, strictly speaking, the true *paella* must be prepared over an open fire, and only by a man. As for the ingredients, these are as variable as you please. The only essentials are rice—round grain that soaks up the juices while still retaining a firmness at heart—saffron, and olive oil. The rest is whatever comes to hand in the countryside and will serve to flavor the rice—wild asparagus, wild garlic, crayfish from the stream, snails gathered from the dried stalks of tall thistles, shore-gathered shellfish, pigeon, partridge, rabbit, frogs (hind-legs only) from the marshes, fresh water from the spring. Failing these wild gatherings, you will need to flavor the rice with market ingredients: a chicken, a handful of diced pork, something tasty from the fishmonger—shrimp, squid, mussels; in addition there might be a couple of links of softish *chorizo*, a handful of peas or beans, diced capsicum pepper, a chopped tomato or two. Don't be tempted to use stock as the cooking liquid: plain water is all you need.

A true *paella* is eaten straight from the pan with the first three fingers of the right hand, Moorish-style, by a group sitting around the pan in a ring, each person tackling the portion directly in front of him. Failing this, provide forks, bread chunks, and romaine lettuce leaves for scooping, but insist that your guests share from the same pan.

Serves 6

1 wild rabbit or a couple of pigeons or a small chicken, jointed small

About a dozen live freshwater crayfish

2–3 handfuls fresh live snails (gathered from dry thistle stalks)

A pinch of saffron threads, about a dozen

About 4 tablespoons olive oil

A handful shredded fresh garlic leaves or 2 cloves garlic, chopped

About 2½ cups / 450 g round rice (risotto or pudding rice)

About 6 cups / 1.5 liters water

A handful wild asparagus (thin green shoots), chopped small

A handful young fennel fronds (the shoots that grow on wild fennel)

❶ Chop the bird or rabbit into 20–24 bite-sized pieces. I use a hammer to tap the knife through the bones. Pick over whatever fishy things you have and clean or scrub as appropriate.

❷ Set the saffron to soak in a splash of boiling water—some people toast it first.

❸ Heat the oil in the pan. When lightly hazed with blue, add the garlic and all those rice-flavoring ingredients that require a thorough cooking—meats, snails, *chorizo*, etc., and leave to cook gently until the meat juices no longer run pink.

❹ When it's all frying nicely, sprinkle in the rice—the layer should be thin (ideally, a single layer) and fry for 2–3 minutes, till the grains turn opaque. If using tomatoes, add them now and let them bubble up. Add the saffron and its soaking liquid. Pour in enough water to submerge all the rice grains completely to a depth of one finger—or, if using a proper *paella* pan, up to the bottom of the round-headed screws that fix the handles to the pan. Sprinkle with salt and let it all bubble up fiercely for a moment, then turn down the heat (or lift the pan away from the coals a little) and leave to cook for 15 minutes without stirring. Add more water if and when it looks like it's drying out—at the end the rice should be very juicy, with little bite left in the heart of the grain, and the surface should be pitted with little craters. If you are using a narrow spread of heat, such as the flame of a gas burner, you will have to move the rice around as it cooks so that the heat can get at all the grains.

❺ After 10 minutes, add the green vegetables. Add the crayfish or shrimp or shellfish 5 minutes before the end of cooking, so that they cook in the steam. When the rice is tender and juicy but still retains a nutty kernel, remove the pan from the heat, cover the whole thing with a clean cloth, and let it rest for 20 minutes.

a taste of honey

In the Middle East, among the followers of the Prophet, water takes the place of wine as the drink for which the deity must be thanked. To those who follow a strict moral code, a trip to the water-source offers young people an opportunity— possibly the only one available—for a little gentle courting. In the hot lands of the Mediterranean, the beach is left to the tourists. In the lands where the sun sucks the moisture from the people and the land, white skin is a sign of a leisurely life, tanned skin the badge of the fieldworker. On a summer weekend in Istanbul, whole families of city dwellers head for the hills to spend the holy day wandering through the cool canyons where the water-springs rise. Nor do they need to trouble themselves to pack a picnic, since each water-source is as busy as a hive full of bees with hawkers of every kind, and little tables and cushions set ready for customers, on pon-toons built out over the waters. Small boys offer slices of watermelon, freshly squeezed orange juice, baskets of figs, strawberries, cherries, fresh walnuts. There's always a broiler of kebabs, a roaster of fish. Here and there along the way, an enterprising cook has set up a domed bakestone for the making of *gözleme*—rolled-out flatbreads, sprinkled with herbs, pungent scraps of chilli, and snowy flakes of fresh curd cheese. And everywhere there are sweetmeats—wrapped, boxed, in baskets—homemade or shop-bought, but always in profusion.

There's a saying that to be an Arab and lack a sweet tooth is to be a Muslim and not believe in Paradise. In Arabia, courtship is no courtship at all without a taste of honey. The Ottoman Sultans and the Moorish Caliphs taught all with whom they came into contact—whether through conquest or trade—the hot art of sugar-work, the cool skill of the pastry chef. To the unaccustomed palate, Arab sweetmeats are very sweet indeed—just for good measure, they come drenched in sugar-syrup or honey, or both. In addition to the nut-stuffed phyllo-wrapped *baklavas* and shredded-pastry *künefe*, which today even skilled domestic cooks purchase from specialist

bakers, there's a vast range of fritters, donuts, and nut cookies that are made at home. They are eaten at any time, for celebrations of every kind, including religious festivals and even funerals, but most especially at the semi-formal Sabbath picnics that form such an important part of Arab courtship. The origins of these sweetmeats are so ancient they cannot be claimed by any single group. *Halvas*, *loukum*, fruit preserved in syrup, rice puddings flavored with orange-blos-som, thickened creams—these are the sybaritic sweetmeats beloved by the beauties of the harem. One of the most deli-cious of all Arab sweetmeats is *haytallah*, a dish composed of small squares of a softly set gelatin-like dessert, *balouza* (a kind of *loukum*), slipped into rosewater syrup, scattered with bright green pistachios and pale pink rose petals: very pretty, much appreciated by lovers and children.

Turkish Gözleme pancakes with greens and cheese

Simple to make and good to eat, Turkish street-food flatbreads are cooked to order for the summer pilgrims who make their way to where the cool springs rise in the mountains of Asian Turkey. A specialty of Turkish village women, this is not a bread you're likely to find in a bakery, although you might find a lady preparing them to order in the corner of the market square. *Gözleme* are easy to make, even if few of us can achieve the sleight of hand with the broom handle that seems to be the birthright of every Turkish cook.

Serves 3–4

²/₃ cup / 100 g white bread flour

¹/₂ teaspoon salt

1 tablespoon olive oil or melted butter

About 5 tablespoons warm water

The topping:

4–5 scallions, trimmed and finely chopped

1–2 garlic cloves, finely chopped

A big handful (about 200 g) fresh

spinach, shredded

¹/₂ teaspoon Turkish mild chili flakes (kirmizi

biber) or paprika with a little cayenne

About ¹/₂ cup / 100 g cottage cheese

Optional extras for sprinkling:

Hard cheese (Cheddar or Parmesan), grated

Parsley, chopped

❶ Sift the flour and salt into a bowl. Work in the water and oil until you have a nice smooth dough. Knead it some more. Divide into 4 and work each piece into a ball. Cover with a cloth and leave for 20 minutes or so, to rest.

❷ On a floured board with a thin, well-floured rolling pin (a broom handle is the preferred instrument in Turkey), roll each piece out into a very thin disk, 12 inches / 30 cm in diameter.

❸ Heat and lightly grease a heavy skillet or griddle and slap on one of the disks. Use your fingers to move it about so it blisters and browns. Brush the top with more oil or butter and flip it over.

❹ Sprinkle the cooked side with a quarter of the topping while the underside is cooking. When the underside is done, lift the *gözleme* onto a piece of waxed paper and roll it up into a cone.

❺ Continue with the other three, and eat hot, straight from the griddle.

above left: Rolling *gözleme* dough—unleavened bread—for good eating at a midsummer picnic.

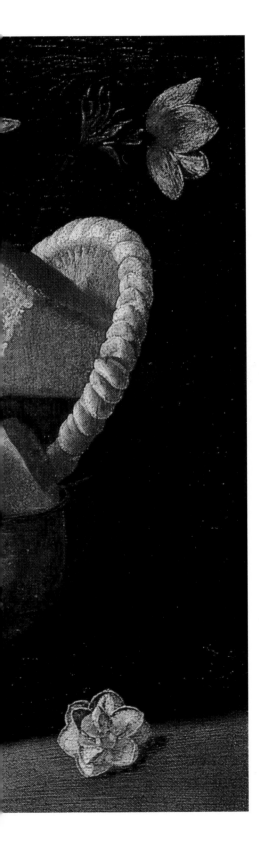

left: *Still Life: Sweets and Flowers,* c.1660–70. An affectionate painting of convent sweetmeats by Josefa de Obidos—a delicious endorsement of the Holy Sisters' skills.

Sugar confections feature in the courtship rituals of all those nations that came under the Arab sphere of influence. Portugal, a subject nation of the Berber dynasties for many centuries, has hundreds of egg-and-sugar confections. These, collectively known as *doces de ovos*, egg-sweets, although undoubtedly introduced by the Moors, found their true home after the conquerors departed. To the enclosed communities of the convents, the confectioner's art provided not merely a source of income, but a way of demonstrating individuality. Each time a new abbess was appointed—effectively, a marriage ceremony, since the Mother Superior became the senior bride of Christ—the sisters invented a new and ever more exquisite variation on the sweetmeats they loved to cook. To underline the matrimonial aspect of the feast, the confections have names that might be considered more appropriate to Venus than the Virgin Mother of God: nuns' bellies (cinnamon-dusted balls of cake-crumbs bound with custard), virgin's nipples, young girls' kisses. Many of these confections are based on *fios de oves* (egg-threads), fine noodle-like strands of egg yolk pushed through needle holes in an egg shell directly into a boiling pan of sugar syrup—a curious confection, but delicious. *Fios* provide the filling for *Dom Rodrigo*, a confection named for a wealthy patron of a convent in the Algarve, appropriately slipped into a silver envelope. *Oves mole*—soft eggs— a thick custard of sugar and egg yolks cooked to the consistency of lemon curd is used lavishly in virtually every Portuguese *doce*, spread between layers of pastry or sponge cake, stuffed in little choux buns, or providing a foundation for a fresh fruit dish.

These days, the populations of the convents are much depleted, and the nuns are hard-pressed to meet the demands of their customers. With the cost of raw materials rising all the time—in the old days, the eggs came free—combined with the need to make ends meet in other less labor-intensive ways, the making of the convent sweetmeats has largely been taken over by commercial enterprise, usually under license, although not always—the ways of commerce not being as scrupulous as the ways of God. So, if what you find in the local patisserie disappoints, blame the secular interpretation of divine intent. Convent recipes, though usually handed from sister to novice sister, were also recorded as margin notes or observations in the journals kept by the holy women. If God—as the irascible reformer Saint Teresa of Ávila (1515–82) was fond of pointing out—is to be found in the pots and pipkins, how much more present must He be in the miraculous transformation of base ingredients into the most exquisite of earthly pleasures; the only one permitted.

In 1747, Juan de Mata, in his *Arte de Reposteria*, records a convent-learned recipe for *yemas*, little custards perfumed with orange-flower water enclosed in a shell of translucent caramel. From seventeenth-century Mexico, Sor Juana Ines del la Cruz—a national heroine in much the same mold as Saint Teresa of Ávila—sent a gift of walnut cookies to her friend, the wife of the Viceroy, with a little note of chaste endearment. At the same time, in the old world, Sor Maria Vittoria della Verde of the Dominican Order of San Tommaso of Perugia in Italy kept notebooks in which she not only recorded holy thoughts but also one hundred and seventy recipes. These came with the kind of asides that indicate a working cook who knows what she's doing: "Give it a right good boil-up," and "This'll need so-and-so's baking dish."

Among Spain's hundreds of convent sweetmeats are many with recognizablly Moorish names such as *alfojaras* and *hojaldrinas* as well as others which, though prepared to Moorish recipes bear Spanish names—*roscas* (ring biscuits), *magdalenas* (little sponge cakes), *buñuelos* (sugar-dusted donuts), *tortas de aceite* (oil crackers). Others such as the deliciously crumbly *polverones* (melt-in-the-mouth cookies known as dusty biscuits) are crossbred, being flavored with Moorish cinnamon and shortened with the purest Christian lard. *Tocino de cielo* (celestial fatback), is another delicious recipe of mixed parentage. Still other varieties of sugary works— *ojuelos*, *pestiños*, *meringues*, *natillas*, *rosquillas*—were the speciality of a single sisterhood, making recipes so treasured that each novice was sworn never to divulge what she knew. The nuns chose their occupation wisely; the gentle art of preparing sweetmeats provided an outlet for creative energies for which the devil might otherwise have found other work to do. Such culinary secrets, it must be said, are not likely to be of much use to the uninitiated, since the trick lies not in the ingredients— which are of the simplest—but in the knowledge and the skill, and this can only be acquired by observation and experience. What matters is the ability to recognize the precise moment that the yolks for the *yemas* are ready to accept the syrup, or that the flour has been ground to the precise degree of fineness for the *polverones*, or the exact degree of heat needed to toast the perfect almond. These are things that cannot be learned from books but are passed on in silence in the enclosed tranquillity of a convent kitchen, secure in the knowledge that whatever is done has been done before, will be done again, and will continue to be done until all are called to the table of the Lord to share in the sweetness of Heaven.

Tocino de Cielo **celestial fatback**

In rural Portugal in the 1970s, Susan Plant Dos Santos found the traditions of the convents alive and well. The nuns were taking advantage of the apparently endless supplies of cheap Brazilian sugar that had replaced the cane sugar introduced by the Arabs. In the middle ages, the convents, notorious centers of gastronomic luxury, manufactured enormous quantities of sweet delicacies from the basic ingredients of egg-yolks and sugar. These were sold, and many became customary foods at religious festivals. Only a limited number of these are still made, but the *docaria* of Portugal represents the most extensive repertoire of homemade sweets in the world. The ingredients are still mainly egg-yolks and sugar combined in an infinity of different ways and varied by the addition of almonds, coconut, walnuts, bean curd, and sugared pumpkin, flower essences and liquors, vanilla and cinnamon, and delicate pastry cases and wrappers. Convent sweets of Arab extraction are still to be found in all the cake shops of the Mediterranean, identified by erotic names such as 'nuns' bellies,' 'angels' crops,' 'maiden's spital.'

Serves a dozen

For the caramel:

2 tablespoons sugar

2 teaspoons water

Juice of half a lemon

For the custard:

1⅓ cups / 350 g granulated sugar

Thinly pared peel from the half lemon

Generous 1 cup / 300 ml cold water

12 large egg yolks (another 2
if the eggs are small)

You will need an 8 inch / 20 cm square cake-pan, and another somewhat larger pan to act as a bain-marie

❶ Make the caramel in the cake pan. Melt the ingredients together in the pan, turning it over a high flame until the sugar caramelizes into a rich golden brown. This will take only a moment or two. Tip to coat the base. Set aside to cool. Preheat the oven to 350 F / 180 C / Gas 4.

❷ Put the sugar with the lemon peel and the water in a heavy pan, and heat over a medium flame until the sugar is dissolved. Boil for about 20 minutes. Stir with a wooden spoon: if the syrup trails a transparent string when you lift the spoon out, it is cooked enough. Remove the lemon peel.

❸ Meanwhile, whisk the egg yolks thoroughly. Pour the hot syrup into the eggs, beating as you do so. This will begin the thickening process. Pour the mixture into the caramel-lined baking pan. Cover with foil.

❹ Set the cake pan in the roasting pan, and pour boiling water all around. Bake for about 30 minutes. It should be firm and solid when it is done. Allow to cool.

❺ Cut into squares: sticky, rich, and golden as the sun. Serve in the Moorish style, with a glass of ice water.

betrothal in afghanistan

By agreeing to a period of betrothal, the process by which mutual interest is established without taking the final irrevocable step that leads to the social and economic consequences of matrimony, a betrothed couple buys time. Whether or not this acts as a period of trial marriage depend on what is considered socially acceptable. Among communities whose marriages are arranged, particularly those in which property, wealth, or title (or all three) are involved, and which are brokered by third parties when children are very young, a betrothal acts as a down payment, a first installment on the transfer of wealth—often quite literally. Among those for whom divorce—the dissolution of the ties of marriage—is not an option, a period of exclusivity, a time to allow the betrothed to get to know each other before taking the final step, is an important time.

The business of betrothal, among those who follow the social code of the West, is usually kept low-key, involving no more than close family and friends. However, among eastern civilizations whose social inclination is to see marriage as a contract between families rather than a love-match between two people, public acknowledgment of intention to wed is considered almost as feast-worthy as the marriage itself.

Among the Afghans, explains Helen Saberi, writing in *Afghan Food and Cookery*, betrothal is (or was, in pre-*Taliban* days) a time for sweetness, literally as well as figuratively, since the word for betrothal, *shirnee khoree*, translates as sweetness-eating. At the time of her own betrothal, says Ms. Saberi, an Englishwoman who served at the Embassy in Kabul in the 1970s and married an Afghan, the Afghans welcomed any excuse for a party. Rites of passage—birth, circumcision, marriage, and, most particularly, betrothal—required much feasting and merrymaking involving as many members of the community as possible.

Afghanistan has long been a victim of its own geography, serving as the crossroads for the main trade routes between the Far East, Central Asia, the subcontinent of India, and the Middle East, and hence to Western Europe. Where there are trade routes, there are armies on the march. No nation can indefinitely sustain the tides of war without itself becoming warlike. While constant contact with outsiders, both friend and foe, has produced a cuisine that draws its inspiration from many sources, Afghan cooks have adapted rather than surrendered. While customs and food vary between the different ethnic groups, and between rural peasantry and town dwellers, neighboring villages and even individual households, certain foods are considered appropriate to specific occasions. For instance, the birth of a firstborn son merits a ten-day orgy of meat eating by the menfolk while the women care for the new mother, who rises from her bed on the tenth day to take a ceremonial bath and eat a special meal of *orshola-e-olba*, sweetened rice flavored with fenugreek. Meat, mostly in the form of kebabs prepared from the meat of a formally sacrificed lamb is also eaten in quantity on the day of the infant's circumcision, while the ladies enjoy a daintier meal of *aush*, a soupy dish of homemade pasta with delicately spiced meatballs and yogurt.

A betrothal, above all, must be celebrated with sweet things. As soon as both families are in agreement on practical matters, the groom's family brings gifts of sweetmeats (*goash-e-feel*) to the family of the bride. In return, the bride's family cooks and presents the betrothal banquet. The richer and more lavish the food, the more opulent the setting, the greater the number of guests, the higher the honor, and the nobler the union.

To mark a betrothal of rank, professional male cooks are engaged and outdoor kitchens set up to cope with the lengthy business of preparing the huge amounts of food required to feed all comers. The menu is not the rough roast meats that remind participants of a nomadic ancestry, but more sophisticated dishes—pastas, *pilafs,* and the like—that require skill and patience, and are a richer version of what emerges

Ashak afghan betrothal ravioli

The Italian ravioli meets and marries the Chinese dumpling—very appropriate, under the circumstances. *Gandana*, Chinese chives, are the usual filling, but leeks will do very well. The traditional cooking fat of the Afghan kitchen—used as a frying medium, as well as to enrich a dough—is a soft, white lard rendered from the rear appendage of the fat-tail sheep, but don't let it worry you.

Serves 6-8

The dough:

3⅓ cups / 500 g white bread flour

1 teaspoon salt

1 large egg

1 tablespoon vegetable oil

About ½ cup / 150 ml water

1 teaspoon vinegar

The filling:

1 lb / 450 g leeks, finely chopped

1 teaspoon chili pepper flakes

1 teaspoon salt

1 tablespoon vegetable oil

To finish:

Generous 1 cup / 300 ml thick strained sheeps' milk yogurt

2–3 garlic cloves, finely chopped

1 tablespoon dried mint, crumbled

❶ Sift the flour with a teaspoon of salt into a bowl, make a well in the middle, and drop in the egg and oil. Work together with your hands, adding enough water to make a soft dough. Knead thoroughly for 5–10 minutes, until smooth and elastic. Wrap in plastic wrap and rest for an hour or so.

❷ Meanwhile, make the filling. Work the chopped leeks with the chili flakes and salt, rubbing vigorously till the fibers soften a little. Work in the oil. Reserve. Mix the finishing yogurt with the garlic and mint, spread half in a shallow serving dish and set in a warm place.

❸ Cut the dough in two, and knead each piece into a ball. Roll each ball out on a lightly floured board with a rolling pin; it should be very thin, almost transparent. Cut into 2½ inches / 6 cm rounds.

❹ Drop a teaspoonful of filling on half of the rounds, wet the edges, and cover with the remaining rounds. Continue until the dough and filling are all used up.

❺ Bring a large pan of salted water to a rolling boil, add vinegar, and slip in as many of the *ashak* as will comfortably cover the surface. Cook for 4–5 minutes, till they bob back to the surface. Remove with a draining spoon and drop them into their bed of warm, garlicky yogurt.

❻ Cover with the rest of the yogurt and serve with a basic meat sauce made with ground lamb, flavored with well-browned onions, generously peppered, and moistened with tomato juice or water.

To make *boulanee*—crisp little deep-fried savory pastries served as an appetizer at festive occasions such as betrothals—prepare a batch of *ashak*, but cut the dough into rounds the size of your palm and enclose the filling by flipping one side over the other to make a semicircular pastry.

daily from the domestic kitchen. Slow-simmered stews, *qorma*, delicately spiced and made with meat or poultry are served with *chelau*, plain boiled rice enriched with oil, the most prized part being the crisp crust that sticks to the base of the pan; Afghan ravioli, *ashak* (*see above*) and *boulanee*, plump dough-pillows stuffed with green onions and bathed in a rich meat sauce—,one boiled, the other fried; saffron-tinted *pilafs* sweetened with raisins in whose fragrant hearts are buried whole roast chickens. In the absence of table furniture, all these good things are scooped from the dish with a piece of snowy-crumbed and black-blistered *nann* hot from the *tandoor*, the traditional clay-walled bread oven.

In spite of all this culinary splendor, it is the desserts that mark this out as a betrothal banquet. Pride of place goes to jelly puddings perfumed with rosewater; sugary *halvas*; *baklavas* filled with pistachios and walnuts drenched in a saffron-perfumed syrup. Perhaps less familiar are *jelabi*, deliciously crisp little fritters soaked in syrup; *firni*, a cardamom-flavored milk custard thickened with cornstarch rather than eggs; *shola shireen*—rice pudding scented with rosewater and colored with saffron (*see page 145*). There must be fruit, of course, in abundance, particularly the sweet-juiced melons and the plump red and white grapes that make the sweetest of frost-shriveled raisins; and in winter only, there will *besheer yakh*, ice cream frozen with snow water.

For liquid refreshment, there is pure water—always a special pleasure where alcohol is forbidden—and endless rivers of *qymaq chai*, a festive tea flavored with cardamom and enriched with clotted cream. It is very strong and made by boiling and reboiling green tea leaves till the brew turns brick red. At other times, black tea—brewed with black or green leaves and heavily sugared—is taken in the Chinese way, in little porcelain cups that must be reversed when the guest has drunk his fill.

The presentation of the festive meal—often eaten in the open air, even in winter—is informal. Guests are accommodated on cushions placed on the beautiful carpets that are every family's most prized possession. The dishes, sweet and savory together, are placed on a fine cloth in the center of each circle of guests, allowing everyone to choose what, and in which order, they eat, although it is usual to reserve the desserts till last. The host is obliged to make sure no dish is ever left empty, and guests are expected to eat a little more than their fill. To refuse a second helping would be most unmannerly. It is also the custom among both rich and poor to give thanks for special joys by handing out gifts of food to passersby in the street, a custom known as *nazer*. *Nazer* can be a modest offering of *nann*, sweet *halva*, or succulent slices of roast lamb if the event and means of the giver stretch to such richness. Food, freely given in the name of God, must always be accepted with grace, as must the invitation to a feast. To refuse either would be to deny the bounty of Allah—something no follower of the Prophet would countenance.

Since betrothal is a declaration of commitment by two people to proceed to marriage, invitations must be issued, food must be shared in the sight of God by the two groups most intimately involved—and it is this, the formal nature of the gathering, the drinking of toasts, the pronouncings of blessings, that elevates the spirit and sanctifies the feast.

Firni afghan betrothal custard

Quick and easy, a milk custard made without eggs and a minimum of fuss, also served at weddings and for Eid-e-Ramazan, the feast that marks the end of Ramadan. Children love it.

Serves 6–8

4 cups / 1 liter whole milk

Generous 1 cup / 275 g sugar

8 level tablespoons cornstarch

½ teaspoon freshly ground cardamom seeds

1 heaped tablespoon finely chopped pistachios

1 heaped tablespoon finely chopped almonds

❶ Heat the milk gently in a heavy pan with the sugar.

❷ Meanwhile, mix the cornstarch with a little water, enough to make a thin paste.

❸ When the milk is hot, but before it boils, whisk in the cornstarch. Add the cardamom and whisk over the heat till the mixture thickens. Pour into a shallow dish, leave to cool, and sprinkle with the chopped nuts.

Delicious served with little wood strawberries, cherries, and peaches.

Shola Shireen afghan betrothal rice pudding

Rosewater and saffron make this as seductive a dessert as is found anywhere on the planet. Also served at new year and for *nazer*, a form of alms-giving that gives thanks for prayers answered or marks an occasion for special celebration such as betrothal, marriage, or the safe return of loved ones from the *Haj*, the once-in-a-lifetime visit to the holy city of Mecca to which all devout Muslims aspire. Short-grain rice is used for sweet dishes, long-grain for savory.

Serves 4–6

1½ cups / 250 g short-grain rice

4 tablespoons milk

⅔ cup / 175 g sugar

12 saffron threads, soaked in a little boiling water

1 tablespoon rosewater

Pinch freshly ground cardamom seeds

1 tablespoon ground pistachios

1 tablespoon ground almonds

Optional to decorate:

Rose petals

Blanched almonds

❶ Rinse the rice in cold water, drain, and put it in a roomy pan with enough cold water to cover the grains to a depth of 2 finger-widths. Bring to the boil, turn down the heat, cover loosely, and simmer, stirring frequently to avoid sticking, until all the water has been absorbed—about 20 minutes.

❷ Stir in the milk, the sugar, and the saffron with its soaking water. Return to the boil, reduce the heat again, cover tightly, and leave to simmer gently for another 20–30 minutes; this can be done in the oven if you prefer.

❸ Stir in the rosewater, cardamom, and nuts. Simmer for another minute or so, and pour onto a flat dish to cool.

Finish, if you like, with fresh rose petals and whole blanched almonds.

the marriage feast

Wedding menus, as with the ritual foods of spring planting, are of the variety whose purpose is to encourage new life: seeds, nuts, fruit, and all manner of round foods, symbols of the sun as well as—it is to be hoped—the merrily fertile belly of the bride. The universal symbol of the marriage feast, the elaborately decorated white-iced wedding cake, covers both categories, being full of nuts and fruit, round and well-endowed with sugar. In less sophisticated culinary cultures, there will be more modest roundnesses, such as nut-stuffed dumplings or donuts rolled in seeds. The popularity of the wedding cake—a bit of a hybrid, frankly—simply confirms that we all want the same thing.

If roundness is desirable as a reminder of fecundity, sweetness reminds all to speak well of each other—not an inconsiderable task at a wedding feast, notorious for family feuding. The French *croquembouche*, "crack-in-the-mouth"—a pyramid of little round *choux* buns held together with caramel—covers all eventualities with the added advantage of there being no need to cut it with a knife (an unlucky gesture for practical as well as ritual reasons). A tap with a hammer will send the little balls flying among the guests, a kind of edible bridal bouquet, bringing good fortune to the couple and joy to all.

At the marriage feast, when all has been done to ensure long life, good health, and many children, precautions must be taken against fortune's reverses. For this reason, no foods that might harbor or draw malevolent spirits are served. There's a prejudice, for instance, in Celtic cultures, against serving vegetables at weddings, since green is the color of goblins; at Hindu marriage feasts, dishes include neither onion nor garlic, the food if not of the devil, of the Muslim invaders; there is a feeling, too, that wedding food should be prepared in such a way as to be eaten easily in the fingers without a knife—weapons, as always, being the cause of strife. Last, but most important of all among societies that tolerate intoxicating liquor, a toast to the health of the newlyweds must be drunk in wine, conferring a blessing whose source is acknowledged by raising the glass toward the heavens: small gesture, strong magic.

There must, above all, be sweet things, a tradition common to all cultures. Sweet talk—sweetheart, sugar-plum, honey-lamb—translates without explanation into every language. Sugar—sweetness in all its forms, whether as

left: *Croquembouche*, the French bridal cake—a tower of cream-stuffed *choux* pastry buns secured in place with caramel—is easily broken in pieces without the use of a knife, thus avoiding the necessity of disarming the guests.

cakes, ices, preserves, syrups, honey, ripe fruit, dried fruit, cookies, candies, honey-pastries—is the element that transforms a meal into a feast. Our taste buds crave sweetness. The form by which we plight our troth may vary, but a marriage celebration without sweet things is, well, not really a marriage celebration at all. We confirm this every time we cannot resist another little crumb of cake; or when, satiated with good things, we hide our portion, knowing that to refuse a slice would somehow bring ill fortune.

Addictive foods such as sugar, substances that help us see the world in a different light, already have a spiritual dimension, making them worthy as a sacrificial offering. Although sugar cannot confer the technicolor dreams of natural mind-altering substances, it makes us happy—whether the reasons are chemical, emotional, or simply because consuming them

above: Malaysian wedding guests prepare gifts of brightly wrapped eggs. Presented to the bride, they remind the happy couple of the purpose of their union—the birth of babies within the security of wedlock.

endows us with extra energy. In tropical lands where sugar cane flourishes, guests are often greeted with a peeled stick of sugar cane to suck. The Ottoman Turks, whose empire once stretched from Rabat to Vienna, were accustomed to offering visitors sweet, sticky preserves on a silver tray with a little glass of water for sipping. This welcome had the express intention of sweetening the encounter should the visitor have hostile intentions. The habit continues to this day throughout the lands of the Ottomans, perhaps because the gesture is so universally understood.

The *soupe de mariage* traditionally served at a peasant wedding in Provence is a classic *pot-au-feu* of particularly lavish composition. Nonetheless, it was in Paris, in the far north of France, that I first encountered the traditional dish of the south. I was just sixteen when, fresh from incarceration in an English boarding school, I was sent abroad to learn French and acquire a slick of Gallic polish.

The supper of welcome prepared for her young English guests by Madame Heughins, our widowed landlady, was a magnificent *pot-au-feu*, one of those slow-simmered, all-in soups that contains all a man or woman might need to brave matrimony. The broth, a sunny gold, clear and pale, had the incomparable flavor that, our hostess swiftly explained, can only come from hours of patient simmering. *Mijoter* was the word she used, waving her hands like a conductor quieting an unruly orchestra.

All the ingredients had been specially ordered from her village. The chicken had feathers, the beef had bones, the

above: Painting by Albert-Auguste Fourie, c. 1900—*A Country Wedding at Yport* in northwest France. The presence of the child on the nursemaid's lap might indicate that Easter has been celebrated before Palm Sunday.

carrots were covered in earth. Our instructor demonstrated the basic necessities of the broth: shin-beef, marrow-bone, and a boiling-fowl of the blue-legged breed whose stringy sinews had acquired their strength from a lifetime scratching in the yard. When the meats were tender enough to be eaten with a spoon, the broth was finished with fresh vegetables—leeks, carrots, creamy-fleshed potatoes, and thick, green wedges of cabbage. The finishing touch, she explained proudly as she showed us how to blend egg yolks into thick golden oil, was an *aioli*, made with farmyard eggs and the finest olive oil.

This, the *soupe de mariage*, was the very same soup she had helped her mother prepare for her own wedding feast,

Soupe de Mariage **provençale marriage broth with saffron**

The French, as might be expected of a nation that takes such a passionate interest in all matters gastronomic, probably have more *pot-au-feu* recipes than Napoleon had nights with Josephine—this, in essence, is one such. At the end, you might like to *faire chabrot* by pouring a little of the red wine from your glass into a final ladleful of the hot soup, and drink the health of your companions just as it comes, straight from the bowl.

Serves 6–8
2 lbs / 900 g beef shin
2 lbs / 900 g rolled boned shoulder of lamb
1 chicken, cleaned but not jointed
4–5 carrots
2–3 turnips
6 fine fat leeks
1 head green unblanched celery
1 onion stuck with 6 cloves
2–3 tomatoes, skinned and roughly chopped
6 peppercorns and 1 teaspoon salt
Small bunch of herbs: bay leaf, rosemary, thyme, and marjoram
3 tablespoons rice
12 strands saffron

❶ Put all the meats in a stew pot with the vegetables, well washed and roughly chopped, plus the cloved onion, tomatoes, the peppercorns, the salt, and the herbs. Cover with water.

❷ Bring the water to a boil, cover the pan, and turn down to simmer. Leave to cook gently (no large bubbles should break the surface) for 3–4 hours, until all the meats are tender. If some are soft before the others, remove them when they are done. When all the meats are cooked, arrange them on a large platter with the vegetables. You can replace the vegetables with new ones (plus a few potatoes) toward the end of the cooking time if you feel the old ones look too soggy. Keep the meat and vegetables warm.

❸ Strain out 9½ cups / 2.4 liters of the stock, return it to the stew pot, bring it back to a boil, and add the rice and the saffron. Simmer for 20 minutes, until the rice is soft. Taste and adjust the seasoning, and serve the saffron soup first in deep bowls.

The meats and vegetables follow, and are to be eaten from the same bowls. Accompany them with a vinaigrette made with olive oil and wine vinegar, into which you have stirred plenty of chopped fresh herbs—chives, parsley, and fennel fronds.

many years ago. The meal was in the nature of a memorial and, as was proper on such an occasion, accompanied by reminiscences of happier times in the sunshine of the south. We might be sure the recipe was authentic, she added, since the wedding soup never varied, although in other areas, such as the village in the Auvergne where her father was born, they served the *aligot*, a stupendous dish of potatoes mashed with a great deal of garlic—even more than there was in the *aioli* and which, to our English palates, was a very great deal indeed—enriched with cream, butter, and cheese. But that was because in the Auvergne they had butter and cream in plentiful supply, whereas, in her village, they had olives that went to the mill to be pressed for oil. The garlic was a pre-caution against malevolent spirits—rural wedding foods, as far as she knew, always had garlic somewhere in the recipe. Apart from this—explained our hostess—the vital ingredient that made a *soup de mariage* different from the *pot-au-feu* was the addition of saffron, an expensive item for a poor household, but which made all the difference to a groom's performance on the wedding night. However, she continued, fixing us with a stern, blue eye, we could be sure that none of us, whose virtue she was sworn to protect, were likely to have an opportunity to verify the truth of what she said. That, she added, shaking her finger, would be what was known in her village as celebrating Easter before Palm Sunday. And that, as everyone knew, would never do.

eastern european wedding

Although in western Europe, the more robust of the ancestral wedding rituals (visible briefly in stag parties) have long been veiled by sentimentality, the truth is that hearts, flowers, and wedding veils hide the realities of what would now be considered thoroughly antisocial behavior. The outlines of such rituals can still be traced in the customs of ethnic minorities that fell, for more than half a century, under the control of Soviet Russia.

For ethnologists, the isolation imposed on Soviet satellite nations was a blessing and a curse. On the one hand, the old ways were discouraged by central government—whose policy was dictated by Moscow—as likely to lead to inconvenient manifestations of national consciousness. On the other hand, many traditions survived among rural communities precisely because they were isolated from the mainstream.

I had occasion to observe this firsthand some years ago, soon after the fall of the Berlin Wall, when I was filming a documentary on the foodways of rural Europe. We had the good fortune to be invited to a wedding among the Ruthenes, a small population of Ukrainians marooned in Slovakia by war and the politician's pencil. The wedding couple, Marcela and Josef, born and bred in the little village of Rukovini near the Polish border, were childhood sweethearts whose union was the culmination of a long courtship. Among such communities at that time, traditional costume was worn for weddings, relieving everyone of a great deal of anxiety and expense. For the women, there were many layers of snowy petticoats, brightly colored overskirts, cinched-in waists, embroidered velvet aprons, and little waistcoats that show off a creamy bosom to perfection. For the men—tall and handsome with blue eyes and curly blond hair—there were dark trousers tucked into black leather boots, and embroidered waistcoats worn over full-sleeved white shirts.

Before the ceremony, Marcela and Josef had responsibilities to discharge: a visit to the cemetery to seek the blessing of their ancestors. In Marcela's case, this was doubly impor-

tant since her mother was a widow and her father's approval could not have been sought in any other way. After this, the women took charge of the preparations at the communal house—neutral territory—that was also the venue for the bride-dressing, a formal occasion involving all the ladies of the community. To the senior matron fell the responsibility of informing the bride, through the rituals of song and dance, of her duties and obligations as a married woman. In preparation for her new estate, Marcela's long golden tresses had been braided into a thick plait, ready to be cropped in time for the ceremony. While maidens may wear their hair long, matrons must cut their hair short and hide it under a scarf. The cropped braid is kept in the bride-chest along with all the other household treasures, to be restored to its owner on the day of her death.

The communal house—a single large room with a kitchen and other facilities attached—is used for weddings and other gatherings in which the whole community is involved, providing facilities for public entertaining not available in private households. Preparing the wedding food is also a communal effort—a way to spread the workload and share the expense, as well as allowing the young girls to learn from their elders how to prepare the celebration dishes not prepared at any other time, whose secrets would otherwise be lost. The recipes, though richer and more luxurious than everyday food, nonetheless reflect the culinary skills every young woman might be expected to bring to her new household. Chicken and meat, much esteemed since rarely tasted, are richly sauced, vigorously spiced, and brightly colored. Ingredients, too, are special. Eggs are used in quantity, as is butter, sugar, and spice. The kitchen in the communal house, equipped with a wood-fired stove, two large tables, a sink, and running water, has all that is needed to prepare even the most elaborate of the wedding foods.

First to be cooked are the pancakes. Nothing dainty, they are as big as dinner-plates and are made by pouring a yeast-raised rye-flour batter enriched with eggs directly onto the top

above: Russian wedding at which newlyweds share the ritual bread and salt prepared by their families: an edible lesson for life, the bread provides the sustenance while the salt provides the savor.

of the stove, expertly flipped as soon as puffed, finished, and piled in a snow-white cloth. Meanwhile a batch of all-egg pasta is being hand-rolled with a broom handle and cut with astonishing dexterity into neat little shapes—squares, matchsticks, diamonds— each appropriate to its dressing. The little pastas, no bigger than a thumbnail, are tossed into a huge cauldron of boiling water, allowed to rise to the surface, then swiftly removed with a draining spoon. Each batch is tossed with hot butter as soon as it is drained, and then finished with

three different dressings: the first, with sugar and cinnamon; the second, with poppy seeds tossed in sugar; and the third, mixed with curd cheese.

For practical reasons rather than from any lack of faith, Marcela and her groom had decided on a secular ceremony. The blessing of the state had to be secured before that of the church, with the result that only the very rich could afford the luxury of a double ceremony. On the steps of the town hall, the colorfully costumed groomsmen barred entrance to the bridal party, rowdily demanding money before they would permit the marriage to proceed. Traditionally, the price of a bride was her ransom value if kidnapped—a rather barbaric method of courtship that had the merits of ensuring any

Wedding *Babka* **wedding cake**

Yeast-raised doughs enriched with egg and butter are eastern Europe's equivalent of western Europe's rich fruit cakes, replacing extravagant white-iced, many-tiered wedding cakes as the centerpiece of the wedding feast.

Makes 1 *babka*
5 cups / 750 g white bread flour
1 teaspoon salt
Walnut-sized nugget fresh yeast
1 teaspoon sugar
1 egg
Generous 1 cup / 300 ml warm whole milk
4 tablespoons / 50 g unsalted butter, melted

❶ Preheat the oven to 400 F / 200 C / Gas 6.

❷ Sift the flour and salt into a warm bowl. Cream the yeast with the sugar, and fork it up with the egg and milk and melted butter (reserve a little of the egg-and-milk to brush the top of the braid later).

❸ Pour the yeast mixture into a well in the flour and work it all well together. Knead thoroughly until you have a soft smooth dough—you may need more or less flour.

❹ Set the dough to rise for about an hour in its bowl in a warm place under a damp cloth, until doubled in size. Punch it down, and cut it into three equal pieces. Roll each piece into a rope. Pinch the ends with a damp finger and plait neatly. Coil into a tall round, buttered cake pan. Brush with the reserved milk mixture and set to rise for another 30 minutes, until doubled in size again.

❺ Bake for 35–40 minutes, until well risen and golden. Transfer to a wire rack to cool.

degree of kinship was very distant indeed. When the Orthodox Church, struggling to survive under communism, refused to countenance such overtly pagan traditions, the playacting was simply transferred to the town hall, where the secular authorities, having nothing to lose, were perfectly happy to tolerate the antics—providing another reason for the young couple to prefer the secular ceremony. In all other matters—the few solemn words, the exchange of rings, the signing of the register—the ritual was no different from that enacted in other town halls elsewhere.

Thereafter, the celebrations took a distinctly pagan turn. As soon as the bride arrived back at the communal house, the senior matrons circled her in a stately ring dance, pausing at intervals to land a few not entirely gentle punches—treatment designed to ensure the couple's firstborn is a son. All participants except the bridal party then took their places , admiring the splendor of the table, the bottles set ready, the sparkling glasses. The playacting then continued, amid much laughter, with a guessing game. One at a time, the bridal

party entered, each muffled in a cloak and wearing the bridal headdress—a middle-aged matron, an old man, the bride's brother—obliging the bridegroom to guess which was the real bride. In this ritual, my informant among the bridal party explained, could be observed a rather more ancient preoccupation—the need to outwit malevolent spirits who might otherwise be tempted to carry off the bride and keep her for their own. Last to enter, unmistakable in her beauty, was the bride. Marcela and Josef, having found each other at last, made their peace, as befits a virgin bride torn from the bosom of her family. Then, kneeling in front of both sets of parents, they asked forgiveness and a blessing on their union. This being freely—if a little tearfully—granted, the guests are free to demolish the feast and continue the fun. On the table, sweet things are there to mark a festival of joy—in the old days, honey from wild bees. The wedding soup—lamb, onions,

right: Hungarian wedding party: music and multicolored eggs are both essential to the proper celebration of the match.

left: Wedding ring dance in Hungary—a troupe of young women form a circle around an elderly couple charged with instructing the bridal pair in the duties and obligations of married life.

potatoes, and garlic—is stirred with plenty of paprika to fortify the young couple for their wedding night. Finally, there are feather-light donuts, and the wedding babka—a buttery yeast cake.

Meanwhile, at the hands of his rowdy groomsmen, the bridegroom gets a shave; no beardless boy without responsibilities, he's now ready to take on the duties of matrimony. Meanwhile, in return, the bride permits the farrier to mime the nailing of horseshoes onto her slender-heeled black boots—the obligations of wedlock mean there'll be no more light feet in the spring grass. Suddenly, without warning, the senior matron fills her mouth with water and sprays it over the happy couple. This explains my blushing informant, is to fertilize the marriage bed. Of course; what else?

The musicians take their places and the dancing begins—decorous waltzes at first, and then, as the wine flows and the dancers become more bold and more of the elders take to the floor, the ancient ring dances whose irregular rhythms are accompanied not by popular tunes approved by the thoroughly modern young persons gathered to celebrate a ritual as old as the hills, but by the haunting music of the steppes. As the music fades, tears are shed, absent friends remembered, the dead mourned, and meanwhile, two by two, the lovers—betrothed, courting, and married—slip out in the darkness to find each other in the moonlight.

Similar bride-bartering rituals were recorded by ethnologist Kåroly Viski, studying the folkways of his native Hungary during the 1930s:

"Innumerable symbolic memories of the purchase of women are still alive in Hungarian weddings. The purchase price of a woman was as much as her *were-geld* (the fee of compensation in ancient teutonic law) in case she was kidnapped. They attempt to kidnap, or, for fun, actually kidnap, the bride; they besiege her house, all kinds of obstacles are placed before the wedding procession, even shots are fired…" At the same time, Gyula Illyes described the rowdy weddings on the *puszta*—one of the huge farms worked by Hungary's landless peasantry: "The wedding feasts were prodigally extravagant. On the long bean-shelling tables borrowed from the estate, there were vast quantities of wine and dripping, and, in the pots that had been collected from three *pusztas* there were rows of fried chicken and ducks. This gorging was as indispensable a part of the wedding as the priest's blessing. Indeed, it was even more important, for while there were plenty of couples who got married without the blessing of the church, there was not a single instance of a marriage in church before they had found some way of holding a 'proper' wedding feast."

"The bride," he continues, "was not expected to eat or drink at the banquet but simply pecked at the food, a sign that she was virgin enough to have been married against her will." The bridegroom, fortunate fellow, was expected to eat and drink his fill—stuff himself like a goose—while his famished bride was whirled off her feet by every guest who had brought a present, however great or small—a salt shaker, a jug, a pair of slippers. Every guest who brought an envelope full of money had the right to dance her dizzy…But since the bride-groom's triumphant shouts are along the lines of, "The bride is mine!" it might, perhaps, be wise not to look too deeply into their significance.

berber wedding

A Moroccan wedding is never less than memorable—but a wedding among the Berbers is something to remember for the rest of your life. The Berber, the nomadic people of the Mahgreb—the desert lands to the west of Egypt—have long settled the Moroccan hinterland, where they effectively form the ruling class. When I lived with my young family of four children just across the water from Tangier, on the southern-most tip of Andalusia, in a valley from whose rocky slopes the blue mountains of Africa could be seen, every month or so we would take the ferry across the Strait of Gibraltar. We left in the early morning, returning in the evening, full of the sights and sounds of the *souk* and laden with fragrant packages.

On one such visit, we delayed too long in the *souk* and the afternoon ferry left without us. No matter, said our urchin-of-the-day guide, his sister's wedding was being celebrated that very afternoon, and we would be more than welcome to join the wedding feast—for a small amount in his palm, of course; an introductory fee, but certainly not as payment for any hospitality, which would be entirely without reward on the orders of Allah himself. Hospitality to strangers is an obligation placed by the Prophet on all his followers, and our presence would confer good fortune on his sister's union.

Among the many sophisticated culinary traditions of the Middle East, the reputation of the cooks of Morocco is only matched by that of the cooks of the Lebanon, which is rivalled only by those of Iran who learned their habits from the ancient Persians. At the level of what one might call palace cooking—that includes, for all those who can afford it, the dishes served at a wedding banquet—the cuisine of Morocco is dauntingly labor-intensive. This mattered little in the old days, when the women of the household were many, their labor was free, and the preparations were an important part of the celebration itself. These days, the feathery phyllo-like pastry, *ouaka*, made not by rolling or stretching a dough ball, but, by dabbing it over a hot griddle till it forms a large lacy pancake—can be bought in the market from a specialty stall. And in the cities and towns, it is the confectioner rather than the ladies of the household who supplies the trays of delicate sweetmeats—gazelle-horns, delicious little fried donuts soaked in honey, almond shortbreads, exquisite nut or date-stuffed pastries—that are served as soon as the guests arrive, accompanied by tiny glasses of tooth-achingly sweet mint tea. No Moroccan wedding feast would be complete without its full complement of sweet things.

By now, the guests are seated on cushions at the low, round tables set out in the wedding tent; traditionally, men with men, and women either remaining in the kitchen or with other women. The star of the feast, the first dish to be served to the guests, is the mighty *bistilla*. This dish is the glory of the Moroccan table, never less than two feet in diameter, and at least as thick as a fist, a sweet-savory pie stuffed with whole young pigeons, spiced and enriched with eggs and almonds, that is the glory of Moroccan palace cookery. The pie is

left: Berber wedding pancakes piled with thick cream are topped with preserved cherries—with more honey offered separately to satisfy those with a taste for the truly sweet.

assembled like a huge round *strudel*, with butter brushed between the layers of *ouaka*. This mighty construction is then cooked in a thin iron pan (of similar design to the Spanish *paellera*) on top of the charcoal-burning stove—a method of baking that requires that the whole delicate edifice be reversed and tipped back in the pan to toast the other side. Anyone who has ever watched an Andalusian housewife flip a *tortilla* will understand exactly how it's done, and the muscle power required to do it. The crisp pastry is then finished with a criss-cross pattern of powdered sugar and cinnamon—a touch of sweetness entirely proper to the wedding feast.

above: A Moroccan wedding feast at which male guests enjoy a saffron-spiced *tafaya:* lamb cooked with whole eggs, almonds, and raisins in a *tagine* (a cooking pot with a high, domed lid) in the style of Fez—by which is meant palace cooking, extravagant and rich.

Middle Eastern tradition dictates that fingers are the appropriate tools for conveying food to the mouth. At everyday meals, everyone not only washes their hands but must be observed by others to do so—every restaurant has its washbasin in one corner. At a feast, the hand-washing is more formal. Before any food is set on the table, bowls of rose-

right: A Berber woman prepares ceremonial bread in the High Atlas region of central Morocco: a thin disk of unleavened bread patted out by hand is baked nomad-style on a layer of hot stones with burning twigs on top. This method cooks both sides at once.

scented water and scented towels are brought round by the servants—or, indeed, by the ladies of the household since, traditionally, the women do not join the men at table, but eat their food after the men have finished. Arabs eat their food neatly without knife, fork, or spoon, taking only as much as can conveniently be eaten at one time, using two fingers and the thumb of the right hand only, which means that everything that is set on the table must be soft enough to break apart one-handed.

After everyone has had their fill of *bistilla*, on comes the second dish. Whole roast lambs are carried high over the heads of the guests, a whole beast per table, trailing the delicious scent of well-caramelized meat and crisp crackling. While the *bistilla* is traditionally women's work, the *mechoie*—a whole beast, the plumpest young ram of the shepherd's flock, roasted in the open air over a brushwood fire— is the business of the men. This division of labor is particularly apparent at a wedding feast, since the dishes are served in succession.

The final dish, conforming to the traditional view that no one has feasted who has not feasted to excess, is a *couscous*—the seven-vegetable version that is also served on the Muslim holy day (*see page 163*). At this point, the guests have no option but to protest they cannot eat another thing. The musicians arrive, the tables are cleared, and the dances can begin—decorous at first, but becoming wilder and more Berber as the day wears on and the *raki* begins to flow. The normal prohibitions of the Prophet against the drinking of hard liquor are loosely applied at weddings; only the ladies stay sober.

All these good things are offered up in the name of Allah—a feast for the spirit as well as the body. As for ourselves, the strangers at the banquet, it was dawn before the children, replete with sugary pastries and exhausted by the pleasures, curled up like puppies on the cushions amid the debris of the feast.

The wedding dish prepared to welcome a bride to her new home among the Tiv, a people of Equatorial Africa, is chicken cooked with sesame seeds—delivering in a single dish both the universal celebration—bird and seeds—and the universal symbols of fertility. The Tiv, whose domestic habit was the focus of anthropologist Laura Bohannan's field studies in the 1960s, live communal lives, forming homesteads in which several families live together and are mutually supportive. Nature dictates that, if the group is to thrive, wives must be sought from outside the homestead. As Muslims, the men are permitted more than one wife, although only the first wife rates a wedding feast of chicken. The most significant element of the dish lies, not in the recipe or method of cooking, but, in the acquisition of the raw materials. The birds must be caught by the bridegroom himself or his agents—

mother, brothers, and the young men of his own age—while the sauce ingredients must be provided by the bridegroom's sisters, mother, and her co-wives, and the wives of the friends of the bridegroom's father. The cooking is done by the homestead's married men, who also have the pleasure of eating the finished dish—a kind of consolation prize for not enjoying the favors of the bride. On such a night, Ms. Bohannan records, everyone in the homestead seems to be out chasing chickens, catching chickens, plucking chickens, singeing the feathers off chickens, and cooking chickens. And those who aren't are off on other—somewhat more romantic—business.

below: Elegantly served, a platter of saffron rice is presented to the wedding guests.

Seven-vegetable Couscous

Couscous is the Moroccan family meal for Friday, the Muslim holy day. The seven vegetables—seven being the number that brings good fortune—can be varied according to the season. This recipe suits the early spring, a time of year to give thanks for the safe delivery from winter.

Serves 4–6

The couscous:

1 lb / 450 g couscous grains

4 cups / 1 liter vegetable stock or plain water

1 teaspoon powdered saffron or turmeric

Cilantro/coriander or parsley sprigs

1 short length cinnamon stick

1 garlic clove, crushed with salt

1 teaspoon ground cumin

2 tablespoons olive oil

The vegetables:

14 oz / 400 g can chickpeas, drained

2 tablespoons raisins

2 cupped handfuls new potatoes, scrubbed

1 handful baby white turnips, scrubbed

1 handful new carrots, scrubbed

1 handful fresh young fava beans in the pod, topped and chopped

1 handful young green beans

2 zucchini, sliced lengthwise

1 handful green asparagus spears

Harissa sauce:

1 teaspoon dried red chilies, soaked in hot water

1 clove garlic, skinned

1 teaspoon salt

2 tablespoons olive oil

Juice 1/2 lemon

1/2 teaspoon ground cumin

❶ Soak the couscous grains in cold water for 10 minutes, and then drain off excess water. Work the grains with your fingers to get rid of lumps.

❷ Bring the stock or water to the boil with its flavorings in a roomy saucepan that has a steamer to go over the top. Line the steamer with a piece of clean muslin or linen, and put in the couscous. Set it over the boiling stock and steam for 20 minutes, uncovered. Remove and tip the couscous out onto a wide surface. Sprinkle with cold water and work out any lumps.

❸ Drop the chickpeas, raisins, potatoes, turnips, and carrots into the boiling stock, and return the couscous to the steamer. Bring everything back to the boil and cook for another 10 minutes. Slip in the green vegetables and continue to cook for the final 10 minutes, or until the vegetables are perfectly tender.

❹ Meanwhile, drop the *harissa* sauce ingredients in the liquidizer with a ladleful of the vegetable broth, and process to a puree.

Reheat to serve. In Morocco, you can get a tiny earthenware brazier to keep the sauce hot. Serve the *couscous* piled high on a hot serving dish, with the vegetables prettily arranged on top and plenty of liquor to moisten. Serve the *harissa* sauce separately.

chinese wedding banquet

In pre-revolutionary China, wedding banquets—at least among those who could afford public displays of wealth—were as extravagant as possible so that the groom's family might demonstrate a proper degree of prosperity to the bride's family, who had, in any event, already put their matrimonial cards on the table by agreeing on an appropriate dowry. The principal vehicle for this public declaration of marriage-worthiness was the wedding banquet, observed in the splendor of the setting, the delicacy of the china, the number of dishes served, the costliness and rarity of the ingredients, and the skill of the cooks. All these great things were done not only to honor those directly involved, but could be expected to please the ancestral spirits watching over the household, who, it was to be hoped, would intervene with higher authority on behalf of their relatives.

Hsiang Ju, daughter of writer Lin Yutang, describes the ceremony of bride-fetching: "Several decades ago, when there was a wedding in Fukien, the groom would go to the bride's house to fetch her, taking with him fresh flowers. He himself made the journey there and back in a blue and yellow teak sedan chair. For the journey to the bride's house, the place under the bridal chair was occupied by a quarter of a freshly slaughtered pig, and on the footstool on which she was to place her feet was placed the 'drum' of firecrackers."

Hsiang Ju doesn't elaborate on the significance of the firecrackers, but explains that the placing of the meat under the bride's feet symbolized the groom's agreement that life at home was under the control of the women. Meanwhile, the ladies of the bridal household had their own ways of judging the worthiness of the groom. The chair and its occupant were greeted at the gate with a tray on which was arranged various foods: a basket of lychees, a pot of tea, a dish with two hard-boiled eggs cooked in syrup, a bowl of rice noodles cooked in a rich broth. Having deposited their offering, the ladies withdrew to a decorous distance, waited and watched. While the offering must be admired and acknowledged, eating it would have been a great disgrace, and if any suitor had been unwise or greedy enough to do so, his mistake was never forgotten.

The bride and groom were then free to depart, serenaded by the firecrackers that exploded one by one, but leaving behind the pork, which was then cooked and given to the beggars who, being forewarned, had already gathered at the gate, and whose acceptance of this bounty would confer good fortune on the marriage.

Meanwhile, on her arrival at her new home, the bride might expect to be

right: A reconstruction of a Chinese traditional wedding of the Sung Dynasty: the bride waits unseen in a sedan chair until the groom has completed all the arrangements.

greeted by the groom's family and all members of the household lined up in their separate groups: women with women, and men with men. At this time in China, explains Hsiang Ju, the women did not share the lives of the men, but, nonetheless, once they had borne children, the power they wielded was absolute. Even at the feast, men and women occupied different tables.

The setting was as splendid as possible. The room in which the marriage feast took place was decorated in scarlet and gold, the colors of happiness and prosperity; to the Chinese, a practical people, the first is unlikely without the second. All the guests were expected to wear their most splendid jewels and most exquisite silks. The tables were covered in damask and laid with the most delicate porcelain. The formal Chinese banquet—whatever the occasion—consists of a minimum of thirty-two dishes, not including rice and *congee*, the staple foods throughout the region. Awaiting them on the table when they take their places, guests can expect to find twelve dishes of cold food—*wuy deep*—foods that, although serving as appetizers, are also symbolic, conferring health and prosperity on all who participate. The arrangement, season permitting, consists of a dish each of oranges, mandarins, candied fruit, nuts, grapes, hundred-year-old eggs, pickled vegetables, one of cold, sliced chicken, and one of ham. These, the secondary dishes, are moved to one side to allow the eight principal dishes to arrive one by one, each taking its turn in the limelight. Meanwhile, throughout the meal, hot tea is served in exquisite little porcelain cups—the delicacy of the china being as important as the quality of the tea.

All dishes must be delicious, but care must also be taken to appeal to all the senses. Nothing must be overlooked, nothing neglected—particularly at a wedding banquet, where all things must be experienced at the highest possible level. Hsiang Ju explains the philosophy: "It is the texture-foods which provide the most vital elements of the feast. These foods are what one might call the absurdities, not for general daily use, which, in order to become palatable, are completely dependent on the flavor of other ingredients. They are the gastronome's pets, the cook's burden, the host's pride, and the guest's joy."

For this reason, the first of the principal platters is almost always a shark's-fin dish. Very much a rarity, shark's fin is prepared for storage by skinning, boiling, and drying—a mucilaginous cartilage that has to be soaked in many changes of water, and repeatedly reboiled to soften it to the desired smoothness. The aim is a consistency of unctuousness and resilience. The prepared shark's fin is then packed in a bowl with broth and wine, and steamed until perfectly tender.

Next to arrive on the table is another texture-filled dish served when much honor is due to a guest: the famous (or notorious) bird's-nest soup. The raw material is not, as might be imagined, a handful of tangled grasses, but the gluey secretions of a species of swift that builds its precarious nests on the cliffs of the islands of the South Pacific. The best quality birds' nest is sold with the twigs and down still embedded, and has to be soaked and thoroughly cleaned before it receives an hour-long simmering and sweetening with rock-sugar. Since supplies of bird's nests are somewhat limited and unpredictable, a soup of similar composition and sweetness can be made with silver tree-fungus, a rare ingredient not to be confused with the common black tree-fungus sold in Asian supermarkets.

Among the other important dishes might be a dish made with fish maw, the air bladder that controls a fish's ability to withstand water pressure that is purchased as a dry, stiff yellowish leaf. It puffs when fried, and when cooked in a broth, it becomes light and soft, soaking up flavor like a sponge. Included in the pantheon of texture foods is jellyfish which, when dried and pressed into a thin sheet, needs to be soaked overnight in several changes of water. When cut into narrow ribbons and scalded with boiling water, the strips form elegant curls, whose virtues are tenderness, crunchiness, and elasticity.

At a wedding banquet, each dish has to have an element of sweetness. Among recipes considered appropriate in the maritime province of Fujian, Hsiang Ju lists, in addition to a succession of fish dishes, various soups sweetened with rock-sugar, red dates, and a sweet soup made with pigeon's eggs. All these things had to be served in extraordinary abundance. The last dish was always a fish—real or in effigy—brought on at a moment when all the guests had already declared they couldn't eat another morsel. To send a wedding guest home hungry would be a terrible disgrace. In Fujian, however, the last of the important dishes was always duck because seafood had already played its part in the banquet.

In addition to paying attention to aesthetics—serving platters should always be round or oval, never square or oblong, and utensils must be of a color chosen to complement the food—Chinese cooks see their professional responsibilities as reaching beyond the mere obligation to satisfy hunger. This, a priestly task worthy of the attention of the most subtle and exalted minds, is made easier by following the nutritional rules based on the principals of *yin* and *yang* developed by the Taoist school of philosophy. In essence, *yang* is the bright side of the hill and has to do with sunlight, maleness, fire, creative thought. *Yin* means the side of the hill in

shadow, and has to do with the moon, femaleness, darkness, coolness, and stead-fastness. *Yin* is cool while *yang* is hot. When these two forces are not in balance, the body becomes unwell and can only be brought back in balance by the eating of certain foods, and the avoidance of others. Nevertheless, it is far better not to become ill at all. The maintenance of good health through a balance of the essential elements of life is fundamental to Chinese tradition and philosophy. For this reason, a Chinese cook will maintain the balance of *yin* and *yang* in every meal, simple or complex. To achieve this, all dishes must be perfectly harmonious in all their parts, providing a balance of color, flavor, scent, and texture. Seasonings are automatically balanced in pairs—salt (*yin*) with pepper (*yang*), sugar with vinegar, spring onion with ginger, soy with wine. In the composition of dishes, since there are no strict rules, the cook must rely on instinct and the application of a knowledge of the Five Elements or Powers of Nature—metal, wood, water, fire, and earth—as expressed in the five traditional flavors—sweet, sour, bitter, hot, and salty. In nutritional terms, the principals of *yin* and *yang* are used to provide a diet that cures as well as maintains. Call it the culinary application of *feng shui*—that peculiarly Chinese mixture of practicality and superstition which provides a means for men and women to exist in harmony and good fortune with both the natural and the supernatural world.

Every Chinese cook, whether professional or amateur, is expected to work according to these principles, making the preparation of food, even as an everyday activity, a complex philosophical statement, an expression of man's awareness of his place in the universe. At an auspicious occasion such as a wedding celebration, the banquet—its rarity and complexity in the composition of dishes served, its splendor, the manner and order in which it is served, the attitude and appearance of the principal participants, and the importance of the guests—has a spiritual significance that profoundly affects not only the happy couple (who, in the old days, might never have set eyes on each other before), but also the welfare of all who witness their union, most particularly the two families involved, who are soon to be joined by the irrevocable ties of blood.

in art as in life

Among the affluent traditionalists of Japan, wedding banquets follow the courtly Kyoto tradition—a gastronomic style that has its origins in the ninth century, when the Chinese influence was strong. As in China, there is an awareness that, since nature has provided all good things, her bounty must be acknowledged in both the composition and presentation of the meal. Each dish is treated as a work of art, themed to reflect the beauty of landscape and the changing season. However, rather than dipping into the same dish, each diner has his own helping served in separate containers, with all dishes arriving in front of the guest at the same time. The usual composition is three important dishes, each cooked by a different method—party time can feature many dishes, but always an uneven number. Tableware is carefully chosen to suit a particular dish, and certain rules dictate the arrangement of the food on the plate.

The arrangement of the food gives it a spiritual context. Japanese society is very formal. A meal served without order would not bring satisfaction, let alone pleasure. A fish laid on a flat dish should face to the left and at a slight angle with its tail away from the diner. A fillet of fish is always placed with the skin underside. Simmered foods should be arranged in dishes with the most important item placed at the back of the bowl, the second most important food is placed in front and to the left, the third to the right. Salads should not touch the side of the plate, but be piled in the center. The rice bowl is placed in front of the diner, to the left, with the chopsticks pointing toward the bowl. The soup bowl is placed to the right, and other dishes are arranged behind. The handless cup and teapot, constantly renewed with green tea, is in the far right-hand corner. Now you know—so make no mistake.

At a less formal wedding banquet—one at which the guests are not served collectively—the appetizers, *zensai*, are placed on the table at the beginning, and the rest of the dishes arrive in sequence. First, *suimono*—a clear soup; then *sashim*—raw fish; next *yakimono*—grilled food; then *mushimono*—steamed food; after this, there will be *agemono*—deep-fried foods; then *sunomono*—foods dressed with vinegar; and finally, *aemono*—cooked salads. Soup and a hot savory custard are served during the meal. Last to be set on the table, though not to be eaten there, but taken away to fortify guests on their way home, comes grain-food, rice, in portable bundles—*sushi*, rice and fish in a seaweed wrapper; or *sekihan*, rice with beans. The provision of journey food, though part of Eastern hospitality, is reminiscent of the Greek custom of providing mourners with *koliva*, a wheatgrain oatmeal finished with raisins, pomegranate seeds, and almonds.

right: The arrangement of a Japanese banquet follows strict rules of court etiquette. Formality of presentation enhances the atmosphere and confirms the care taken with every detail—in art as in life.

right: An Indonesian couple, magnificently enthroned, feed each other with wedding delicacies—a promissory note to be redeemed in future happiness.

twin joys of life

In Indonesia, rice is the central dish of the wedding feast—traditionally *nasi kuning*, a delicate *pilaf* colored with turmeric and enriched with coconut. As is by no means uncommon in the East, the combination has significance in several different ways. In Indonesia, there's a saying that civilization is based on four sacred plants—rice, bamboo, banana, and coconut; in addition, since rice is the food of fertility and yellow the color of happiness, when cooked together, they celebrate the twin joys of life—weddings and the birth of children. To cover the future as well as the present, the same dish is also sacred to Saraswati, Hindu goddess of art and learning. The same combination is also to be found in Bengal, among the rural Hindu, to whom rice is the food sacred to Lakshmi, goddess of prosperity, and to waste it is a sacrilege. Unhusked rice, *dhan*, the traditional offering to the gods, is also offered to a new bride on her arrival at her husband's house. In addition, a young banana tree is placed outside the husband's front door, together with a green coconut balanced on top of a pottery pitcher.

While the western tradition selects midsummer—June and July—as the most auspicious time for a wedding, in subtropical India, the calendar dances to a different tune. The holy *Vedic* books identify March to June as the right time for a Hindu wedding. Not only is this convenient, since it can be expected that the Lord Vishnu's attentions are not required elsewhere—in the Himalayas, say, attending to the sacrificial rituals of the monks—but March to June are the hottest months of the year, the fallow time that follows harvest and precedes the monsoon season. For a people whose preoccupations are largely agricultural, it makes good sense to hold a party when the storecupboards are full, at a time when no work can be done in the fields, not least because a Hindu feast is likely to be vegetarian.

Food writer Julie Sahni, assisting, a few years ago, at the gentle rituals of her sister's wedding in southern India, outlines the principals behind the preparations for a Brahmin Hindu wedding. First comes *puja*, the preparation of the temple, the altar,

left: Preparations for the wedding banquet of the fabulously wealthy Maharajah of Jodphur—an alliance between two high caste Brahmin Hindu families, celebrated with legendary splendor.

Sacrificial butter—*usli ghee*, the sacred food of the Hindu Brahmin ancestors, the *Vedic* Aryans—is poured into a holy flame on the altar.

Meanwhile, in the garden behind, the temple chefs, bare-chested and wrapped from the waist down in magnificent gold-embroidered white cotton cloths, prepare the wedding feast. Bubbling in vast copper cauldrons are rich stews of lentils, chickpeas, all manner of vegetables, some finished with fried spices, and some stirred with yogurt and herbs, to be served with relishes made with coconut and green chili. In addition, there are vast piles of almonds to be pounded for *halvas* and sweetmeats. *Vedic* cooks must prepare all food fresh on the day so that the gods can bless it.

The ceremony serves to remind the participants of their Aryan ancestry. For this reason, the bride's foot is placed on a stone symbolizing the mountains crossed by the *Vedic* Aryans, after which the bride and groom circle the holy fire seven times while their families shower them with rice— symbol of fertility and prosperity. Later comes the banquet, at which twenty-two courses is not considered excessive. A vast array of dishes—savory stews, great bowls of snow-white rice, and yellow *dal* rich with butter, innumerable kinds of bread for scooping and wrapping and dipping, chutneys, pick-les, sweetmeats—are all presented togther on the long tables set out in the temple precincts. The bride and groom don't participate in the meal—not a crumb of food can pass their lips. Instead, they are given toys with which to amuse them-selves: little lentil wafers to break over each other's heads— maybe, says Ms. Sahni, a throwback to when children were betrothed at four years old, as soon as they reached an age at which they might be expected to survive to adulthood.

and the banquet that is offered to the presiding deity, Lord Vishnu. This must include eleven sacred elements—rice, san-dalwood, betel nuts and leaves, turmeric, coconut, bananas, sweets, fruit, holy grass, and holy water to ensure the good-will of the Aryan gods of earth, water, wind, thunder, and sun.

Kerala Wedding Coconut Curry

A delicately spiced dish of mixed vegetables colored with turmeric and enriched with yogurt, as prepared by the wedding cooks of Kerala, a southwestern coastal state. Many Indian vegetables, as might be expected of a nation so dependent on the fruits of the earth, are gloriously unfamiliar outside the region. Among them are all manner of gourds both bitter and mild, drumstick beans, jack-plum seeds (a little like chestnuts), mangos and bananas eaten green, weirdly shaped and oddly flavored leaves, roots, and tubers of every shape and size. More familiar, but also in unusual shapes and sizes come onions, tomatoes, potatoes, carrot, eggplants, zucchini, celery, pumpkin, squash, peppers, beans, okra—any or all of which can find themselves in a wedding curry.

Serves 8–10

2 cups / 500 g freshly grated coconut

2 teaspoons cumin seeds

3–4 garlic cloves, roughly chopped

2–3 green chilies, deseeded and chopped

Salt

4 lbs / 1.8 kg mixed root vegetables, chopped

6 curry leaves or 2 teaspoons curry powder

2 teaspoons ground turmeric

4 lbs / 1.8 kg mixed green vegetables, chopped

2 large plantains or 4 unripe bananas, peeled and chunked

2 green mangos, peeled and cubed

To finish:

2 cups / 500 ml plain yogurt

2 tablespoons vegetable oil (coconut, for preference)

Generous handful cilantro/coriander, chopped

❶ Drop the grated coconut in the food processor with the cumin, garlic, chilies, and a little salt, and process to a paste. Or pound everything up in the mortar with a pestle. Reserve.

❷ Put the root vegetables in a pot with the curry leaves (or powder), stir in the turmeric, add 1 teaspoon salt, bring to boil, turn down the heat, and simmer gently for about 15 minutes.

❸ Add the remaining vegetables in the order of how long each needs to cook. Lastly, add the plantain and mango, and allow to bubble up, and simmer for a few more minutes to soften the fruit.

❹ Just before serving, stir in the pounded coconut paste and the yogurt. Reheat gently (don't let it boil), and finish with a swirl of oil and a sprinkle of cilantro/coriander.

right: Traditional Indian wedding banquet: the food is laid out on banana leaves and guests are served in relays, the better to accommodate as many witnesses to the nuptials as possible.

above: Rice-throwing at a wedding in India: a sacrifice to propitiate the gods—a pre-Hindu ritual that has survived to the present.

In Bengal, says cookery writer Chitrita Banerji, describing the marriage of her mother and father in the 1940s, the wedding food was served on banana leaves and guests took their places at the table in succession to be fed in relays—very practical, since it saved not only the washing-up, but also solved logistical problems, such as how to accommodate hundreds of guests all at the same time. Placed first on the table were *luchis*, thin, golden disks of rolled-out dough fried in *ghee,* to be eaten with fried greens and some other fried vegetable, such as eggplant or *patol*, small green gourds not unlike little round zucchini. Next came the famous Bengali *chanchra*—a dish of vegetables cooked with fish oil and innards, followed by a rich *dal*. Once all this had been mopped up, there would be a luxurious dish of fish, meat, or vegetables (depending on the degree of devoutness of the guests) cooked with a great deal of oil and *ghee* in a sauce based on ground ginger and pounded onion. One essential was that only the best quality rice, Basmati or some other fragrant variety, be used while the huge quantities of *ghee* it required for three or four hundred people had to be absolutely pure with not a hint of modern vegetable shortenings. When preparing the *pilaf*, the broth that is added to the rice after its preliminary frying in *ghee* is perfumed with mace, nutmeg, saffron, and *sajira* (a kind of cumin). Additional dishes might contain shrimp that are prolific in the rice paddies during monsoon time. For strict vegetarians, there would be curried *channa* or *dhonkas* made of ground *dal*. Next would come various chutneys made with tomatoes, green mangos, green papayas, and prunes, and eaten with crisp *papor* (*pappadums*). Finally, a sweet yogurt, *mishti doi*, is served to accompany the obligatory sweetmeats, and a sweet-spiced *paan* to cleanse the palate.

By the 1960s, the first course of greens had been dropped as too time-consuming. At the modern wedding feast, particularly in a city like Calcutta, even in orthodox Hindu households, meat is often served. The food is no longer cooked at home, as it was in the old days, with the assistance of specialist chefs. Instead, caterers bring in all the dishes ready-prepared, to be reheated and served on smart china plates rather than the traditional banana leaves. Today, too, the *mishti doi* and sweetmeats are ordered from one of Calcutta's many confectioners, thus depriving a new generation of one of the chief joys of childhood—a chance to observe the making of such traditional delicacies first hand. In the old days, the sweetmeats were made at home by hired cooks who, says Ms. Banerji—nostalgic for the taste and fragrance of sweetmeats still hot from the *khari*—never minded when, as a child, she reached out with greedy little fingers and stole a handful.

reciprocal gifts of turkey

A wedding in Mitla in central Mexico, as described by American anthropologist Elsie Parsons in the 1930s, was an elaborate affair. Negotiations opened with reciprocal gifts of turkey, a bird native to Central America, and a tray of sweetmeats like *marquesote*, sponge cakes. The gifts were practical as well as ritual, ensuring no guest went hungry, and allowed rival households to indulge in a little competitive cooking.

Once a suitor had been accepted, relatives and godparents were invited by the bride's mother to drink chocolate, the sacred drink of the Aztec emperors, and eat *tamales de frijoles*—little steam-cooked maize cakes stuffed with soft black beans wrapped in maize husks—round foods to satisfy the universal desire for fertility. On the eve of the ceremony, the bridal couple attended church to make confession, returning to the groom's parents' house to consume the gifts of sponge cakes washed down with chocolate known as *de atole*, that was hand-pounded and sipped from exquisite little porcelain bowls. After the necessary sweetness had been shared, a savory stew was served—a *mole*, whose principal ingredients (a dozen chilies, and as many different kinds of nuts) are peppers, patience, and a thorough pounding. No knives, forks, or spoons are provided, the sauce and the tender scraps of meat being scooped straight into the mouth with *tortillas*—griddle-baked, maize-flour flatbreads—the purpose and preparation of the Mexican *tortilla* is identical to the damper of the indigenous peoples of Australia as well as India's *chapatti*.

The same menu was served again at the bride's house after the ceremony, with a blessing as each course was served. Meanwhile, at the groom's house, twenty women are at work in the cook shed: "There are two fires, one for hot water for the incessant dishwashing, one for the huge cauldron of *higadito* into which twelve turkeys have disappeared. One woman is beating the chocolate to a froth, using a chocolate beater in a green glaze pitcher. The groom's mother presides, passing out the replenished dishes to the young men who serve the table. We all sit on mats, and there is much talk and gaiety. Someone fetches me a leafy necklace and a bouquet. We smoke, and a gourd of *tepache* is passed round…After dinner those who are capable of exertion dance fandango till late in the evening."

The next day was allotted to the formal reception of the bride in her husband's house, with more dancing and feasting. This was followed by two days of feasting at the godparents' house on the *mole* made with the turkeys given by the groom, to be followed by two days at the house of the bride's parents to eat another batch of the groom's turkeys. On each change of venue, the bridal couple carried with them supplies of flowers, soft drinks, *mescal,* and *tortillas*.

It was not always so. For a glimpse of a betrothal feast in pre-Columbian Mexico (here translated by Professor Sophie Coe), there is no better account than that of Hernan Cortez' contemporary, Bernadino de Sahagun, whose *General History of the Things of New Spain* was written in the time of Montezuma, last emperor of the Aztecs: "He who undertook the banquet began what now was to be done in his house. He summoned guests from twelve cities…and then he prepared all the grains of dried maize which would be needed. Chilie she placed in containers of matting; and he laid out salt; and he arranged to buy tomatoes; and then he provided turkeys, perhaps eighty or a hundred of them; then he bought dogs to provide the people as food; at the bottom of the sauce dish, they placed the dog meat, on top, they placed the turkey as required. And then he provided the cacao beans, perhaps twenty sacks of them; and the chocolate beaters, perhaps two or four thousand of them…The old women made tamales and wrapped them in husks. They made tamales of meat. Some cooked the tamales in an olla. Some broke up, ground, and pulverized cacao beans. Some mixed cooked maize with chocolate. Some cooked stews or roasted chilies—different kinds of chilies."

Anyone contemplating such strenuous activity would do well to acquire a set of old-fashioned relations, or, heaven knows, the marriage might never be consummated.

Mole Negro de Boda mexican wedding turkey in black chili sauce

An aromatic chili-spiked stew enriched with chocolate is the Mexican wedding feast. This is a quick version; the authentic recipe uses three different varieties of chilies and takes three days' grinding and simmering.

Serves 6–8

2 lbs / 900 g turkey meat, sliced into thin fillets

(save the bones for broth)

2¼ cups / 600 ml turkey broth

(made with the bones)

3 tablespoons pork drippings or oil

3 garlic cloves, slivered

3 red sweet peppers, deseeded and diced

2–3 fresh red chilies, deseeded and diced

3–4 dried chilies, deseeded and

torn into small pieces

2 slices day-old bread, diced

1 cup / 150 g slivered almonds

3 tablespoons sesame seeds

1 teaspoon ground cloves

1 teaspoon ground cilantro/coriander seeds

½ teaspoon crushed peppercorns

1 teaspoon ground cinnamon

2 tablespoons peanut butter

2 tablespoons vinegar

2 oz / 50 g unsweetened chocolate (at least

70% cocoa solids), broken

Salt

❶ Poach the turkey meat in the turkey stock for 5 minutes or so, till cooked right through. Reserve the meat and the stock.

❷ Melt the drippings or oil in a heavy pan. Add the garlic, peppers, and chilies, and fry until they caramelize a little. Remove and reserve. Fry the bread cubes till golden, remove and reserve. Gently fry the almonds and sesame seeds. As soon as they take a little color, stir in the spices, then add the turkey stock, and let it all bubble up.

❸ Meanwhile, crush the reserved chili mixture with the fried bread and stir it into the sauce. Bring back to the boil and stir in the peanut butter and the vinegar. Simmer gently for 30 minutes, crushing everything together to make a smoothish sauce (you can put it all in the food processor if you prefer).

❹ Stir in the chocolate at the end. Reheat the turkey in the sauce; you may need a little water or extra stock. Taste and add salt.

Serve with *tortillas* for scooping.

My mother married my father with the blessing of the family rabbi—a blessing, no more, since my father was a Christian and my mother was a Jew. Later, my brother and I, the children of the union, now fatherless since our mother was almost immediately a war widow, were baptized and brought up in our father's faith. On the Jewish side of my family, it was always said that it was the females who provided the backbone—a polite way of saying the women took charge. I can't say if this is true, but if it is, I can take a guess at how it might have come about. There is an element in the domestic structure of the religious Jewish family that reverses the usual role of the male. In a traditional Jewish family, particularly those who, like mine, had settled in Middle Europe, the women were supposed to be pink, plump, and practical, while the men were required to be thin, pale, and studious. The boys sat and argued over the holy book; the girls were trained to be the breadwinners with cooking, sewing, market trading, or whatever was necessary to earn the family living. The obligation to leave the shelter of the parental home and operate in the world developed their social skills while favoring an unusual amount of independence.

Contact with the outside world had the inevitable result of encouraging the young women to marry outside the community, while the young men were left behind, prohibited from seeking a bride elsewhere by religious conviction as well as lack of opportunity. Outsider marriages, such as those made by my mother, were more likely to be made by the women than the men, diluting the bloodline and dispersing accumulated wealth. Since the Jewishness of progeny descends through the female line, communities of Jewish origin, including those in Israel, are likely to become more and more secular, and more and more mixed, just like my own.

This willingness to adapt is reflected in what happens in the Jewish kitchen. While religious taboos are never ignored, ingredients and methods change to suit new circumstances. By the time my mother chose a husband, the family had made good in Baltimore and recrossed the ocean to repeat the process in Britain. My grandmother employed a French pastry chef as well as the full complement of kitchen staff. We ate French food cooked according to Jewish laws, with occasional forays into Aunt Sadie's *Settlement Cookbook*. I never discovered the identity of Aunt Sadie, but the *Apfelküchen* was superb. My mother's marriage feast, I was told, featured the usual white wedding cake, but the rest of the food was French. *Poulet de Bresse en demi-deuil* was served, made with truffles specially flown in from Perigord. The bird at least, if not the truffles, followed family tradition, since chicken is the festive bird among the Jewish communities of Middle Europe.

previous page: At a Syrian Jewish wedding feast, the appropriate message is conveyed through the exquisite arrangements of fruit and an abundance of sweetmeats.

At a Jewish wedding in France, I'm told, they serve Andalusian *pastillas*, little pastry turnovers stuffed and spiced in the Spanish manner—a miniature version of the Moroccan *bistilla*. The recipe dates from the Moorish ascendancy in Andalusia, a time of unusual tolerance of the Jews. At a wedding feast among Jews of Moroccan origin, it is customary to serve a *couscous* to the guests and two stuffed pigeons in a sauce of lemon and honey to the newlyweds, to sweeten their night of love while reminding them there will always be sorrow in life. Among Tunisian Jews, says Claudia Roden, on the Saturday before the wedding, it was the custom for the groom's family to present the family of the bride with an elaborately decorated chicken. The bird, boned and stuffed with ground veal, pistachios, and hard-boiled eggs, served as a promise of future happiness and the intention of fulfiling the family's desire for many children.

Among those of the Jewish faith, the symbolic nature of foodstuffs is well recognized and highly developed—more so, perhaps, than in any other culture. The dishes served at any celebration are a subtle language of the table that can be read without words—the message sent by the inclusion of certain foods (and the absence of others) served to communicate those things that could not be spoken out loud for fear of persecution. Even if the food is of the simplest kind, the unification of the family in the sight of God though the serving and sharing of a meal is always a sacred undertaking, recognized in the prayers and rituals of blessing as an opportunity to glorify God and take joy in the gathering. And, of all reasons for gathering, a wedding is the most joyful.

The foods appropriate to the three different phases of humanity's mating game—courtship, betrothal, and marriage—share a common purpose: the giving of pleasure. Everyday foods are set aside in favor of the rare, the imported, the unfamiliar, the exquisite, even if these are in limited supply. Sweetness is always valued, as are foods that have a reputation for enhancing desire: aphrodisiacs and foodstuffs that fortify without sating. Courtship foods are likely to be portable and made in small quantities for the obvious reasons that lovers need privacy and no more than two are invited. Betrothal and wedding feasts, in contrast, are designed to give the maximum pleasure, and to include the maximum number of people—a way of ensuring the community's blessing on the union of two young people. Both ceremonies have a similar purpose and share a similar menu, with chicken or other barnyard fowl taking pride of place and sweet things very much in evidence. While betrothal food concentrates on richness and deliciousness, wedding food takes greater account of the main requirement—procreation—a message delivered through the provision of seed-foods and other reminders of the need for fertility.

death
remembrance
resurrection

4

Confucius, when asked about the possibility of an afterlife, replied: "About life we know nothing—what can we know of death?"

Our ancestors managed to view the final mystery with tranquillity as long as they saw it as a prelude to rebirth. Simple observation of the world around them taught them that out of the cold earth of winter came the new growth of spring. Just as calm follows storm, sun follows rain, winter follows summer, day follows night—so, it might be assumed, life follows death. No doubt it was their shamans and wise women who first discovered it was possible to re-create the cycle artificially by consuming nature's own homemade hallucinogens. Since the effects of these were similar to death and induced a trance-like state that led to out-of-body experiences—it mattered little if the source was *Papaver somnifera*, *Cannabis sativum*, the mescalin derived from the peyote cactus, or even—most potent of all— the Druid's toadstool, *Amanita muscaria*, that, with its shiny scarlet cap sprinkled with little white polka dots, provided the raw material of a thousand fairytales.

Failing the drugs so thoughtfully provided by Mother Nature, it did not escape the sages' notice that it was also possible to induce a mood of euphoria by depriving the body of food. Fasting—refraining from food for short periods, or by limiting consumption for longer periods, or simply eschewing certain luxury foods for a prescribed length of time—is practiced by all organized religions. Among adherents of the Muslim and Judeo-Christian faiths, fasting serves to heighten the pleasures of the feast—Lent, Ramadan, or Yom Kippur, the Jewish Day of Atonement, when candles are lit for remembrance of the dead. In the belief systems of the East, particularly among Hindus and Buddhists, fasting is seen as an end in itself, a means by which to achieve and maintain a state of higher consciousness. A belief that only by escaping the bonds of earthly existence can man reach union with the divine dictates the aesthetic lifestyles of those holy men who have taken vows of poverty on earth in the hope of Paradise hereafter.

Just as the rituals that surround death are inseparable from the expectation of birth, so the "little deaths" induced by other means carry within them the promise of renewal. In a wide range of cultures, this is most easily expressed in the meals consumed in memory of the dead. Funeral and mourning foods—

previous page: Day of the Dead, Bolivia: Amaya Indian women prepare bread figurines and baskets of fruit to take to the churchyard on the night of All Souls.

from the sesame seeds of Indian burial rites, to the wheat-kernel oatmeal of Greek funeral customs, to the egg-hiding rituals of the Christian Easter—all confirm the hope and expectation of rebirth. Allied to this is the custom of taking food to the burial grounds on a particular day, usually in the months when the earth is preparing itself for winter. In the Christian calendar, this is at Halloween, the Eve of All Saints. In Eastern cultures, the dead visit the living at the winter solstice—the time when Christians celebrate Christmas. In China and Japan, the ancestors share another meal with their earth-bound descendants in the early spring, although this time it is the living who visit the dead, lying in their unmarked graves in the fields and rice paddies—Eastern funeral habits and custom leaning, with all due respect, rather more to the functional than the sentimental. In this way, the mortal

above: Women of Karpathos, southeast Greece, preparing individual Easter breads, each embedded with a whole colored egg in its shell, and only eaten after the Mass of Resurrection on Easter Eve.

remains of the departed are in the right place for a little fertilization, both ceremonial and practical.

Even if it was obvious to all who observed the natural world that life springs from death, the process by which a single seed becomes many must have seemed like powerful magic. Even now—when every child knows that a seed planted in the right place at the right time, given sufficient moisture and warmth, will reach maturity—the process has not entirely lost its mystery. The shamans and medicine men who governed the lives of our ancestors—and still hold sway in some corners to this day—encouraged their congregations in the belief that the natural world could somehow be influenced by the behavior of man. For this reason, festivals of the dead never overlook an element of resurrection—a preoccupation clearly visible in the planting rituals associated, for instance, with the Persian Days of the Dead and the Christian Easter—the latter including egg hunts, hanging cookies on trees, water sprinkling, egg cracking, baking and eating of anthropomorphic breads and confectionery, and making loud noises in the fields to scare away mischievous spirits. In the islands and highlands of Greece, the eves of important saints' days are still seen as a time when unreliable minor deities, the centaurs and goat gods of pagan times, might be abroad working mischief, upturning the natural order of the mortal world as immortals are thought bound to do.

An element of topsy-turviness often creeps into our appreciation of the divine,

no doubt because we ourselves are engaged in a permanent struggle to impose order on a disorderly universe. The magical transformation of one substance into another is a recurrent theme in fairy stories. In the folktales of Africa, droplets of blood become seeds when carried on the wind or spilled on the ground. Since every pastoralist knows that grain-food, whether in the form of seeds or leaves, can be transformed into flesh—how much more holy would it be if the process is reversed? The idea of blood sacrifice remains enshrined—sometimes hidden, sometimes obvious—in all forms of worship, from the most evolved to the truly primitive. Whether the sacrificial offering is actual or in effigy, real or replaced with some other substance or creature endowed with the same ritual significance, depends on the degree of sophistication of the celebrants. While humankind, although omnivorous by nature, doesn't approve of eating its own—not even close relations such as monkeys—this is a decision not usually made until food supplies can be assured.

The transition from opportunist to moralist seems to be dependent on the level of success a community has in imposing its collective will on its environment. We can skip daintily around the question of whether or not eating people—or the bits of them considered to contain covetable virtues—is wrong. Nevertheless, it is one that has exercised all of us, and continues to do so whenever civilized persons find themselves hungry and in extremis. Humanity, with few exceptions—mostly in the islands of the South Pacific and the Antipodes, where meat was hard to come by at the best of times—quickly took up a moral position on the matter. A natural aversion to eating anything that reminds us of ourselves manifests itself in the Hindu rejection of meat, the Buddhist reluctance to take life, and—in modern, more secular times—in the worldwide vegetarian movement, though this is to some extent prompted by distaste for modern methods of husbandry as well as dislike for the process of slaughter.

The rituals designed to encourage the eternal cycle of fecundity—particularly those that involve such simple gestures as decorating the dwellingplace with leaves and young shoots—can be witnessed in the customs that surround Passover, the Jewish festival of renewal as well as thanksgiving for deliverance from captivity. And it was the Jewish Pesach ritual that gave shape and form to the Christian Easter festival; which, to further complicate the matter, takes its name and much of its identity from Eostre, the Norse goddess of spring, whose sacred animal, the hare, pops its furry pagan face over the Christian parapet in the guise of the Easter bunny. And so it continues, the ancestral dance that has no beginning and no end.

left: A remembrance service in Romania, celebrated at the graveside with offerings of bread and wine, takes place one year after someone's death. The candles that decorate the bread serve as a reminder of resurrection.

funeral food

It is universally acknowledged that funeral foods should be of a shape which most closely approximates the celestial bodies that can be seen in the round dome of the heavens. Among these foodstuffs are circular breads such as pancakes, *tortillas*, *chapattis*, bagels, dough fritters—even cream-stuffed donuts. In cultures where bread is less important, spherical pulses are preferred—chickpeas, peas, and seeds of any kind, but most particularly sesame and pomegranate.

In the rich ceremonial life of Bali, observed anthropologist Ingela Gerdin, all temple ceremonies, including cremations, are happy and colorful occasions: "There is feasting, of course, and beautiful, elaborate offerings of flowers and fruit. People are seated in groups of eight, and eat communally from the same tray of rice which is constantly replenished and eaten with a number of vegetable and meat side dishes—as a sign of friendship. *Sate*, roasted meat on bamboo sticks, is always served. The preparation of meat dishes for traditional feasts is men's work. The night before the ceremony or early the same morning, the male guests arrive, each armed with a *golok*, a huge knife with a curved handle and a sharp heavy blade, used only on ceremonial occasions for cutting meat and chopping up vegetables and spices. If it is to be a large feast, the male guests may spend all night preparing, interspersed with drinking coffee and palm or rice wine, chatting, joking, and listening to recitations from palm-leaf manuscripts in the classical language. It is an occasion for great enjoyment; the mood is happy and boisterous...."

Among the Iteso of western Kenya, reported Ivan and Patricia Karp during the 1960s, funeral feasts always consisted of roast meats: "What is interesting is the manner in which cooking is tied up with behavior associated with the two sexes. Only women can cook a starch (finger millet being the main foodstuff), and it must be cooked inside the cooking-house on the women's fireplace constructed with three stones. Men, on the other hand, can cook meat but only outside and only by roasting. The primary occasions when roasted, as opposed to boiled, meat is eaten are during funeral sacrifices."

below: Balinese men preparing funeral food—roasting meat is considered to be men's work.

Halloween

Once a year, up they come, rattling their bones, shaking their sheets, and every year we welcome them anew. It would be a dull world indeed if there were never a night when ghosts might wander abroad. The early Church Fathers, battling with devils whose faces their congregations knew all too well, did the best they could to sanctify a purely pagan festival. Hallowmass—the feast day of All Saints—is celebrated on the day allotted to the Celtic festival of Samhain. In England, such goings-on were outlawed by Cromwell as unbecoming in God-fearing Protestants, but popped up again like a bad apple in the commemoration of Guy Fawkes on November 5. The sacrificial victim may have been politicized, but the ritual survived intact. We fear the wolf-man in the woods—maybe because he may well be our ancestor, shambling out of the darkness to haunt our dreams. It's not the creatures of the wild that catch our imagination—wolves, or bears, or even dragons. For all their pointy hats and crow-black cloaks, for all the horns and cloven hooves that they may be possessed of—our chosen demons have human faces.

All Hallow's Eve marks the old turning of the year, give or take a week or two, when the calendar was rearranged by Pope Gregory XIII in 1582. The dishes appropriate to Halloween often have an element of lucky dip. In rural Ireland, the traditional Halloween festival food was *champ*—a bowl of potatoes mashed with buttermilk, made green with leeks, enriched with a pat of fresh butter (luxurious because, at all other times, the butter went to the landlord) and set on the table for all to share. In the creamy green mass, favors had been buried: a coin for wealth, a ring for a wedding, a dried pea for prosperity, and a blackthorn twig to beat an erring spouse.

In Scotland at the beginning of the last century, culinary historian Marion McNeill recalled that the poet Robert Burns recommends buttered *sowans* as the proper food for Halloween. *Sowans* is an oatmeal made with *sids*—the inner husks of the oat grain—soaked in water for three to four days until the liquor sours and ferments. The liquid is then strained into a jar and left to stand until the water at the top clears and the solids drift to the bottom. The clear liquid is the *swats*, and the starchy matter is the *sowans*. The *sowan* sediment is then thinned with water, salted, and boiled until it thickens. It is served with milk, or, alternatively, with a knob of butter to melt and stir into it.

The festivals associated with the end of summer, a time of life and growth, and the beginning of winter, the season of slumber which might be mistaken for death are linked by ethnologists to the traditional practice of transhumance—the moving of flocks and herds between domestic animals on winter and summer pastures. When the flocks returned from the highlands to the home pastures that had been left to lie fallow through the summer, the fields had to be made safe for winter grazing. Malevolent spirits had to be scared away by human trickery: men dressed up in frightening disguises, riding hobbyhorses or striding around on stilts—a habit that survived well into the last century in the uplands of Germany and Austria. To reinforce the general chaos, children went trick-or-treating, while others let off firecrackers and hung lighted turnip lanterns carved into grotesque faces on the gateposts. The New World's pumpkins replaced the old world's turnips as soon as Europeans began to colonize the plains of North America; the pumpkin, quite simply, was larger and more convenient to scoop out and carve.

In the orchards of England, the Halloween lucky dip was more likely to be apple-bobbing—participants held their hands behind their backs while they tried to use their teeth to catch apples bobbing around in a barrel of water, affording much robust amusement to all. The food given to those who called at the door at Halloween was (appropriately enough) a soul cake, and in return, souling songs were sung—or, as in Cheshire, there was a short performance of a Soul-caking play.

Halloween Champ

An Irish dish, special to Bonfire Night because it has favors buried in it, and a festival food because it has butter—a most extravagant luxury in the peasant community, where the butter went to pay the rent. In the old days, everyone usually had buttermilk as a sauce for the potatoes, and if you didn't have the buttermilk, well, you put out the empty bowl and dipped in the potatoes just the same. The potatoes themselves were never peeled before cooking, but shaken over the heat so they split to show their floury insides, and then dumped on the table in the middle of a strong, cotton, flour bag, with the bowl of buttermilk alongside for dipping.

Serves 4–5

2 lbs / 900 g mealy potatoes, scrubbed

Salt and pepper

4 large leeks, trimmed and finely sliced

Scant 1 cup / 200 ml buttermilk or soured milk

The favors:

A ring (for a wedding)

A dried pea (for prosperity)

A blackthorn twig (for a husband or a wife who would beat you)

To finish:

1 stick / 100 g salted butter

❶ Cook the potatoes till tender in plenty of boiling salted water.

❷ Meanwhile, simmer the leeks in another pan with the milk—don't overcook or they'll lose their pretty color. When the potatoes are soft, drain thoroughly. As soon as they're cool enough to handle, slip off the skins, return the snowy innards to the saucepan, and mash thoroughly.

❸ Reheat the mashed potato gently, and beat in the leeks and milk, which will turn it a delicate creamy green. Taste, and add salt and pepper.

❹ Stir in the favors, and tip the potato into a hot bowl. Make a hollow in the middle. Drop the softened butter into the well.

Everyone should eat out of the same bowl, dipping into the melting butter with each mouthful. You'll know when you find a favor what it means. It's like fortunetelling—it all depends what you're after.

Hallowfair Broonie orcadian gingerbread

This is Marion McNeill's own recipe for *broonie*, the Orkney oatmeal gingerbread. As an Orcadian born and bred, Ms. McNeill's recipe can be expected to be the real McCoy. In the old days, favors would have been buried in a dish of *crowdie* or *champit* (mashed) tatties. The charms most commonly used are the ring (foretelling marriage to the recipient), the button (bachelordom), the thimble (spinsterhood), the coin (wealth), the wishbone (the heart's desire), and the swastika (happiness—a poignant wish indeed).

Makes 1 gingerbread

6 heaped tablespoons oatmeal

6 level tablespoons all-purpose flour

1 teaspoon baking soda

1 teaspoon ground ginger

½ stick / 50 g unsalted butter

2 tablespoons dark molasses

1 egg, lightly whisked

Scant 1 cup / 200 ml buttermilk

❶ Mix the oatmeal and the flour, and sift with the baking soda and ginger. Rub in the butter with the tips of your fingers till it looks like fine breadcrumbs, as for pastry.

❷ Melt the molasses and mix it into the flour and butter, together with the egg and enough buttermilk to make the mixture soft enough to drop from the spoon. Mix thoroughly.

❸ Preheat the oven to 350 F / 180 C / Gas 4.

❹ Stir in a few silver or nickel charms or favors, each wrapped in a morsel of waxed paper. Tip into the cake pan, and spread into the corners.

Bake for 1–1½ hours, until well risen and firm in the center.

above: Apple-bobbing at Halloween—a children's game with a serious purpose.

The practice of calling from house to house, ethnologists explain, dates back to the Great Plagues of the Middle Ages, when black-clad men—sometimes accompanied by a figure draped in white and wearing a horse's head—went from house to house collecting money and gifts to pay for masses for the dead. The recipes for soul cake—spice-and-honey gingerbreads—varied from region to region; the uplands made oatcakes or *parkins*; the lowlands made wheat-based cookies. In the English county of Yorkshire, they were known as Harcakes—the food of the Norse god Har (otherwise known as Odin), and, similarly, in the peak districts of Derbyshire, they were known as Thorcakes, from the Norse god Thor.

But it is the Celts, the ancient inhabitants of the fertile lands of Europe, we may thank for our most venerable celebrations—the festivals that mark the eternal ring dance as death follows life follows death. The ancient Celts, a robust tribe, celebrated the solstice with a sacred bone-fire—a fire kindled on open ground, located either at the top of a mountain or in the center of a plain. The intention was to purify the living by burning the bones of the dead. The highlight: the breaking and sharing of a round bread baked on the embers, in Scotland is called the Beltane *bannock*. The distribution of the *bannock* was recorded by the eighteenth-

English Soul Cakes

A gingerbread, or *parkin*, fragrant with spices and rich with butter, baked for distribution to the Soulers when they came to call on All Hallow's Eve.

Soul, soul, for a soul cake!

I pray, good missis, for a soul cake!

An apple or pear, a plum, or a cherry,

Any good thing to make us merry.

One for Peter, two for Paul,

Three for Him who made us all.

Up with the kettle and down with the pan,

Give us good alms and we'll be gone.

Makes 10–12 portions
1¾ cups / 250 g all-purpose flour
2 cups / 500 g oatmeal
1 tablespoon sugar
2 teaspoons ground ginger
6 tablespoons / 75 g butter
6 tablespoons / 75 g drippings or lard
Generous 1 cup / 275 ml honey
½ cup / 125 ml milk
1 teaspoon baking soda

❶ Preheat the oven to 350 F / 180 C / Gas 4.

❷ Mix all the dry ingredients together in a bowl.

❸ Melt the butter and drippings or lard with the honey and the milk over a gentle heat in a small pan. Stir in the baking soda. As soon as it froths, stir the mixture into the dry ingredients. Beat all well till perfectly smooth—it should be soft enough to drop from the spoon—add a little warm water if necessary.

❹ Grease a cake pan and pour in the cake mixture. Bake for about 45 minutes, until deliciously browned and firm to the finger. Let it cool in the pan, and cut it into squares. It's nicest if you keep it in an air tight container for a week, during which it matures and softens.

century traveler Thomas Pennant: "Everyone takes a cake of oatmeal, upon which are raised nine square knobs, each dedicated to some particular being, the supposed preserver of their flocks and herds, or to some animal, the real destroyer of them. Each person turns his face to the fire, breaks off a knob, and, flinging it over his shoulder, says: 'This I give to thee, preserve thou my horse; this to thee, preserve my sheep,' and so on. After that, they use the same ceremony to the noxious animals that threaten their flocks and herds: 'This I give to thee, O Fox, spare thou my lambs; this to thee, O Hooded Crow, this to thee, O Eagle!'"

When the *bannock* was distributed, the last one to receive a portion was also the last to leap the flames and thus most likely to be caught by the devil—"de'il tak' the hindmost" is a colloquial phrase still in common use in the Highlands of Scotland today.

Old ghosts, fears, and superstitions are not easily laid to rest. If all else is barred, they take refuge in the games of children. The spirits of the dead still warm themselves at the fires of Halloween, or rejoice at the flames of Guy Fawkes' night in November, while we—not knowing what we do—roast chestnuts in the embers of the bonfire and share them out, stuffing them greedily into our mouths and burning our tongues on the roasted flesh, if not of our ancestors, on the vegetable matter from which all life springs.

left: A feast laid out in the graveyard on the Day of the Dead in Michoacán state, Mexico; the living share their provender with their departed loved ones.

the mexican day of the dead

My only direct experience of the great Mexican Day of the Dead was some forty years ago when my stepfather, a career diplomat, had been posted to the British Embassy in Mexico and I, equipped with secretarial skills, had managed to twist a few arms and land myself a job in the embassy typing pool.

At the time—the early 1960s—the Catholic Church was in retreat and the wearing of the *soutane*, the priestly garment, was outlawed as likely to cause civil unrest in a post-colonial republic. The Dominican monks charged with converting souls in the post-Columbian world had long since abandoned their posts, leaving their work half done. With the congregations left to their own devices, things were inclined to get out of hand, and the newspapers of the capital regularly carried reports from the outlying districts of crucifixions at Easter and altar-slaughterings on All Souls Day.

I soon noticed that the Spanish I had spoken since childhood was by no means universally understood. The lingua franca of the ordinary people—the smooth-skinned, high-cheekboned villagers who sold their produce in the market, or presided over the steaming vats of chili-spiked *tamales* everyone ate on the way to work, or kneaded and baked the maize-flour *tortillas* that serve as Mexico's daily bread, or took employment in the households of the wealthy—was Nahuatl, the ancient language.

These people seemed to me of far more interest than the semi-colonial dwellers of the capital, and I took every opportunity to explore the hinterland—hitching a lift to outlying villages with the fieldworkers from what was called the Institute of the

Indigenous Peoples. Although superficially Christian, the customs and ways of worship of the Nuahtl-speakers seemed to owe more to that of their ancestors, whose culture and traditions had been buried but not entirely destroyed by the Spanish conquerors.

The Mexican cult of the dead—based on the belief that the gods were thirsty for the blood of the living and that their anger might be appeased through human sacrifice—fitted neatly into the Christian festival of All Souls. No great leap of faith was needed, since the Christian churches had risen on the sites of the pagan temples, and the ancient burial grounds had been conveniently converted into Christian graveyards. It then became a natural progression for the people to follow what had always been their custom, and return to their ancestral boneyards to celebrate a festival that, though pagan

above: An array of gaily painted sugar skulls to take to the cemetery on the Day of the Dead.

in inception, had acquired, however uneasily and owing much to default, the blessing of the Christian Church.

The ceremonies of the Aztec emperors—whose blood-fueled rituals are evident in their artifacts and temple furniture, as well as recorded in the annals of their European conquerors—made the transition in spirit, even if the sacrifices were now in effigy rather than reality. Sugar skulls and marzipan bones replaced the grisly banquet demanded by the belief that ferocious gods required to be fed on human hearts torn from living flesh. The scale of the sacrifice could sometimes amount to the deaths of as many as four or five thousand people at a time.

Bacalao de los Muertos all souls day salt-fish

Esperanza, my mother's housekeeper in Mexico City, came from a village in the Guadalajara region, where there was a tradition of eating the Catholic fasting food on the Day of the Dead.

Serves 6–8 as a dip

1 lb / 450 g salt cod, soaked and cleaned, skinned and deboned

About ½ cup / 125 ml olive oil

1 large onion, one half finely chopped, the other half finely sliced

4 garlic cloves, chopped

1 sweet red pepper, deseeded and chopped

2–3 fresh red chilies, deseeded and chopped

2 lbs / 900 g tomatoes, skinned and chopped

2 tablespoons slivered almonds

2 tablespoons green olives

4 tablespoons chopped parsley

❶ Choose middle-cut salt-cod and give it no more than 18 hours soaking, or you'll lose all the flavor. If it is still too tough to flake, simmer in water for 5 minutes first. Heat 4 tablespoons of the oil in a heavy pan, and add the chopped onion (reserving the sliced) and garlic. Allow to gild lightly before adding the red pepper, chili, and tomatoes. Bubble gently for 20–30 minutes, till thick and rich.

❷ Stir in the flaked fish, and bubble for another 10 minutes.

❸ Meanwhile, in another pan, fry the sliced onion in the remaining oil till soft. Remove and reserve.

❹ Fry the almonds briefly till golden, add the olives and the reserved onion. Reheat, then stir into the tomato. Simmer for another 10 minutes to blend the flavors.

Eat with quartered hard-boiled eggs and the soft maize-flour *tortillas* that are Mexico's daily bread, for scooping.

Mole Negro de Todos Santos mexican black chili pork for all saints

Comfort food for the morning of All Saints, the day after All Souls, left on the back of the stove and reheated on the family's return from the cemetery. Serve with *frijoles refritos*—black beans cooked till soft and then refried in pork fat to give them a dense, smoky flavor.

Serves 4–6

2 lbs / 900 g boneless pork, cubed

1 large onion, diced

6 garlic cloves, crushed

2 bay leaves

2 teaspoons salt

6 tablespoons rendered pork fat or lard

4 large mild dried chilies, deseeded and torn

1 slice dry bread, cubed

1 maize-flour tortilla, torn into small pieces

8 green tomatoes

2–3 oz / 50–75 g unsweetened chocolate

1 teaspoon ground cumin

1 teaspoon dried oregano

1 teaspoon grated orange zest

❶ In a heavy pan, simmer the cubed pork with the onion, 2 garlic cloves, bay leaves and 1 teaspoon salt in enough water to cover generously. The poaching liquid should tremble rather than bubble for 1½–2 hours, until perfectly tender.

❷ Remove the meat with a draining spoon. Reserve the broth. No need to strain.

❸ Melt half the lard in a heavy pan and fry the torn chilies for as long as it takes to say three Hail Marys, then remove and add to the broth.

❹ Fry the bread cubes and *tortilla* till crisp and brown, then add to the broth. Fry the green tomatoes till soft and soupy, and add to the broth. Set aside to soak for 15 minutes.

❺ Meanwhile fry the pork in the remaining lard till well browned. Grate the chocolate.

❻ Using an electric blender or a pestle and mortar, blend the broth with the cumin and chocolate till perfectly smooth.

❼ Return to the pot, reheat, and add the browned pork, oregano, and orange zest, and simmer for 20 minutes till the oily sauce begins to pool a little.

Serve with freshly baked *tortillas* and refried black beans.

My mother's housekeeper Esperanza, who came from a village in the region of Guadalajara, took me home with her for the holiday. As well as the paraphernalia of blood sacrifice—the candy bones and skulls, the puppet skeletons of horses and people, the bright little figurines, the garlands of yellow flowers, the candles, the incense—she prepared special dishes to be shared with the dead. These, as befitted the eve of a holy day, were meatless—the salt-cod and dried shrimp dishes eaten during Lent. On sale by the cemetery gate were *tamales*—steamed maize-flour dumplings, and *mole*—a rich dark stew flavored with chili, great steaming vats of soupy chocolate to be sweetened with honey or sprinkled with chili, according to the taste of the purchaser.

As the centerpiece of the meal, Esperanza ordered from the baker a *pan de muerto* —bread of the dead. This, a yeast-raised, egg-enriched circular bread decorated with stylized bones laid like the spokes of a wheel around a bun to represent the skull, was seen as rich and luxurious, replacing the maize-flour flatbreads of everyday meals. In other villages, the bread was given a human shape, while in the state of Michoacán, from whence came Esperanza's husband, the offering breads were small figures of animals or people—*monos*—made in precisely the same shapes as the ancient pottery figurines that were included in the grave furniture of pre-colonial-Christianized times.

To wash the meal down, the villagers brought quantities of homemade *pulque*, a potent cactus-beer made by cutting the heart from a maguey-cactus and passing the sap through the mouth by means of a straw, and from thence into a storage gourd. This processing—always performed by the women, whose saliva is held to be more efficacious in starting the fermentation (an oddity confirmed by modern chemists)—is complete within a few hours. In the days of blood sacrifice, *pulque* was used to render the large numbers of temple victims insensible to their fate. When combined with *mescal*, the button cactus that induces technicolor dreams, or with one of the hallucinogenic mushrooms that grow in the countryside, its effect could well complete the transition from life to death somewhat prematurely.

Since the general view was that death was by no means the worst that could befall a person—particularly in such a place and on such a night—a few fatalities were accepted as part of the ritual. Although people would travel for hundreds of miles to visit the graves of their departed relatives, if this was impractical, they might set up an altar in the home, dressing it with the same yellow flowers and candles, and sharing the meal, too, in the same way.

left: A descendant of the Mayan people of Mexico preparing *tamales*—maize dumplings steamed in the husk—a round food, traditional to the Day of the Dead.

lost days

The ancient Persians celebrated the five Days of the Dead immediately before the new year, the first day of No Rooz being calculated to be the first day of spring. The solar calendar of the ancient Persians was arranged as twelve months of equal length, leaving five days at the end of the year that could not be allotted to any particular month. These were thus declared God-given, lost days without any purpose, when the dead might visit the living.

Fires were lit on all the roofs to guide the ancestors to their earthly homes, and food laid out to welcome them. In order to reassure the departed that their descendants had prospered, adults and children, master and servant had new clothes, and relatives and friends were invited to join the family at the banquet. The food was as lavish and plentiful as possible. At the end of the God-given days, the ancestors, duly reassured, returned from whence they came, accompanied by the good wishes of their descendants, who spent the evening under the stars to speed them on their way. In modern Iran, although the ancestral flames no longer burn on rooftops to guide the dead back to their earthly dwellings, the people still feel the need to light fires. During the week before the festival, trucks piled high with spiky branches roll into the towns. On the eve, when the sun has set, fires are lit on street corners, drawing all, young and old, to leap across the flames, calling, as they do so, on the fire to heal their winter whiteness and restore their rosy health. The wood of the thornbush burns fast and bright—just as it did for Moses, savior of the Jewish people, when he was summoned to ascend Mount Sinai to receive the laws of God—making the ritual more dramatic and the flames less dangerous.

chingming

A reverence for the old as well as the departed is an integral part of the Chinese way of life. In Fujian province in pre-revolutionary China, Hsiang Ju Lin describes her memories of the Day of the Dead: "Life was a jumble, but there was order in it. The passing of time was marked by weddings, birthdays and funerals…The days swung from the whites of death to the reds of marriage and birthdays. Hemp and yards of white cloth, unhemmed smocks and the wailing of men and women mixed with the smoke from burnt gilded multicolored paper objects, as offerings to the dead. Only the joy of birthdays and weddings could wipe out those horrors." On the coming of spring, as soon the weather turned warm, a day in April was set aside to visit the graves: "There were few cemeteries as such, and graves were placed at sites chosen at will, where the configuration of trees, rivers, and fields was considered fortuitous. Rice fields, which belonged to private families, were dotted with the raised mounds of graves. On the day before Chingming, only cold food was served. One did not light fires. The offerings were composed of cooked bamboo shoots and boiled fish. Dumplings and cooked red lotus root were sold in the streets. The outing to the graves was rather like a solemn picnic. Food was brought to the graves, to which one traveled by boat or on foot. In earlier times a son-in-law and daughter had two visits to make, the day before Chingming for the visit to the daughter's family graves, on the day itself to his family graves. The graves were swept and the incised letters on the stone, worn down by the weather in the past year, once again filled with red ink paste. The food was presented, arranged with the orderly symmetry which one observed on these serious occasions, and then eaten by the

left: In Yunnan Province, southwest China, a Bai memorial ritual brings comfort to the spirits of the dead. Rice bowls are set ready, a cockerel is prepared for sacrifice, and the scent of incense alerts the departed to the feast that awaits them.

relatives. This marked the coming of spring." In China, at least, the dead and the living are perfectly at ease in each other's company—sit at the same table, eat the same food, and share the same preoccupations.

Among devout Buddhists, there is a day dedicated to the soothing of orphaned spirits—those who drowned at sea or have no descendants to remember them—when a deep-toned bell is struck every minute to reassure them they have not been forgotten. Paper offerings of useful gifts—horses, servants, money, clothes, favorite food, and drink—are ceremonially burned and wafted heavenward as smoke, a wish list to be consumed in spirit.

In Japan, ancestors are honored much as they were among the ancient Persians. The official day of the dead, Shoro Nagashi, is traditionally marked by a visit to the graveyard and a performance of the bone dance—slow circular dances performed around specially erected towers festooned with lanterns. Some of the dancers represent the dead by wearing black cloths over their faces, others wear white, while fires are lit to illuminate the path of the returning souls, and rekindled to send them on their way. In common with all maritime nations—Greeks, Vikings, and the other wanderers of the South Seas—there's a tradition of sending away the dead in burning boats, either real or made of paper.

yom kippur

Yom Kippur, the Jewish Day of Atonement, is celebrated ten days after new year as a day of fasting and prayer. Although a time to resolve quarrels, pay debts—both spiritual and secular—and give money to charitable causes, it is also a time to remember the dead and light candles in their memory. White clothes, and shoes not made of leather are worn, by both men and women, to the synagogue, observing the principle of not depriving a living thing of life without cause. The evening meal taken on the eve of Yom Kippur is satisfying but bland, says cookery writer Claudia Roden, lacking salt or spice. The Ashkenazim eat chicken soup with matzo balls, or stuffed dumplings. It is said that the dough hides the filling, as kindness covers and softens the memory of misdeeds. The meal is followed by cake, a compote, and fresh fruit.

Although the Sephardim also eat chicken soup, Claudia recalls from her childhood in Egypt that the broth was thickened with egg and soured with lemon, and there was no dessert of any kind.

taboo foods

Religious taboos, as expressed by prohibitions on eating certain foods, rather than the rituals by which foods are prepared, appear in many ways to be a formalization of spontaneous prejudices adopted by one section of a population to distinguish it from another. Some foodstuffs simply tell the neighbors you don't belong to their group, a division that may or may not be useful. For instance, in the Middle Eastern cultures where the differences between one group and another are sometimes hard to distinguish, types of oil used for frying—a pervasive scent difficult to control—indicate a Muslim, Jewish, or Christian household in the same street. In India, garlic and onion are an indication of Muslim cooking, since neither of these great pot-herbs were in use in India until the first Islamic incursions from A.D. 711. In seventh-century India, a Chinese student of Buddhism, Huen Tsang, describes onion and garlic as taboo at a time when ordinary meals consisted of rice, wheat, milk, and little else. Hindus and related faiths for whom onions are also to be avoided use asafetida (*heeng*)—a powder made with dried gum extracted from the rhizomes of a member of the fennel family—which, when heated, has an aroma and flavor similar to that of onions. A household that uses heeng instead of onion as a flavoring can, therefore, be expected to be Hindu, or possibly Jain, and devout.

None of these rules are universal. It must be accepted, says Bengali-born food writer Chitrita Banerji, that India has such a diversity of religion and geography that it is difficult to come up with a single list of dishes that could collectively constitute a national cuisine—still less what can and can't be eaten, and when and where. It would not be possible, for instance, to make generalizations about meat cookery for the whole country. Nor is it strictly true to say all Indians abstain from beef. On the southwest coast of Malabar, there is a substantial Christian minority who ascribe their conversion to the Apostle Thomas—he of the Doubting—who ate beef both before and after their conversion.

Nevertheless, the killing of cattle in India remains the subject of intense debate, both in Parliament and in the press. Meanwhile, cows range freely through every street, treated with the respect due to mothers by sons, a relationship that, to the devout Hindu, is the most sacred of all. The eating of pork is contentious for the usual religious reasons, although, in India, in the heat, where human burial practices can sometimes offer opportunities for scavenging, there is more reason than usual to consider the meat unclean. As always, exceptions can be found. Despite the restrictions imposed by heat, among the Christian communities of Goa state on the western coast of India, roast

right: Young girl in Pongor, southern India, proudly presents an impeccably groomed sacred cow.

suckling pig is the main dish within the traditional Christmas feast, and pork in general is also much enjoyed at other times of the year.

Buddhists, whose religion forbids the taking of life, are by definition vegetarian, although here, too, the rules are open to interpretation. Hindus are subject to similar prohibitions, although these can be equally loosely applied. Until very recent times, the Brahmins of North and South India didn't eat meat, while the Bengali Brahmins were considered somewhat heathen because they ate carp and other large-scaled fish, even though scaleless fish were prohibited.

This taboo is shared by the Jews of India, of whom there is also a considerable community that divides into three groups. The largest of them, the Bene Israel, live on the west coast to the south of Bombay, and were effectively lost to the rest of Jewry until less than three centuries ago. The most Indianized of the groups, since they are the longest established, their legend is that they were the ten lost Tribes of Israel shipwrecked on the coast of India in the days of King Solomon. The other two groups are the Baghdadis—who arrived from Baghdad in Bombay in 1832 during the time of the British ascendancy in India and never felt the need to adopt Indian ways; and the Cochinis of the Malabar coast in southwest India, whose lifestyle and language are indistinguishable from the Malay-speaking peoples among whom they live. Both the Bene Israelites and the Cochinis rightly earned a reputation for excellence in the kitchen, choosing to cook within their regional traditions. Both groups, anxious not to offend the sensibilities of their hosts, adopted Hindu prohibitions on eating beef, which, after many centuries, is not considered *kosher*.

Travel writer David Burton agrees that, in modern times, although Hindus have practiced vegetarianism for more than two thousand years, not all are equally strict. In Bengal, the Brahmins, considered the most devout and therefore the yardstick by which others are judged, eat seafood. Among less devout Hindus, many will eat meat, even beef, while the Kashmiri Brahmins will eat lamb and game, but refuse chicken, seen as an infidel bird brought in by the followers of the Prophet no earlier than the thirteenth century. The Mogul rulers, who established the Delhi Sultanate in what is now Pakistan, encouraged conversion. Nomadic by tradition, they followed their own food ways, and expected their converts to join them. They did not set much store by seafood, were lavish with spices, ate chicken, but made their daily dinner, as befits the pastoralist, on mutton and lamb. To this day, lamb remains the meat of choice among the Muslims of India, eaten either as kebabs—minced or cubed—and threaded on skewers and grilled; or cooked as a *pilaf* or a *biryani*, of which the first is more rice than lamb, while in the other the lamb predominates. All those who converted to Islam were, therefore, expected to change their food customs to match— a daily reminder that, among a population of rice-eating Hindus, the Muslims were very definitely a race apart.

ramadan

Among those of the Christian and Muslim faiths, holy fasting—a sanctified period of voluntary deprivation—serves a double purpose: not only does it do good to both body and soul, it also offers an opportunity for a declaration of identity. This can clearly be seen in Muslim countries during Ramadan—a month of day-long fasts that can only be broken at sunset—when anyone seen to take nourishment in the daylight hours is clearly not of the faith.

The observation of the fasting month of Ramadan is one of the five obligations laid by the Prophet on his followers. All Muslims are expected to abstain from food and drink from sunrise to sunset. "One of the haunting sounds of the East," says Furugh Hourani, writing in the magazine *Petits Propos Culinaires* in 1986, "is the sound of the tabbal, the drummer, passing through the empty streets, waking all people asleep for the *sehour*, the final meal before sunrise…"

No matter how important all other influences may be, Islam, with its dietary laws and restrictions, remains the dominant and most important factor in the eating habits of the Muslim. A true Muslim must adhere to Islamic food laws. He must not eat the meat of animals that have died a natural death: the animal's throat must be cut with a sharp utensil and whoever is doing it must mention the name of God. The eating of blood is prohibited; meat is washed or soaked in water before cooking. Pig meat in any form or shape is prohibited. Insects are prohibited, except for locusts, which were eaten by the Prophet in public so as not to deprive his desert people of a source of food. All alcoholic beverages are absolutely forbidden.

Fasting foods are not necessarily unpalatable. While working in Taroudannt in southwest Morocco in 1972, anthropologists Alan and Anne Meyers observed the importance of good food in the lives of the people whose habits they had come to study: "Food is seen as a sensual pleasure: people speak fondly of favorite recipes and loudly praise their own and other peoples' culinary skills." Meanwhile, they noted, meals were never begun without consecrating the food to God, nor ended without praise for the food that has just been enjoyed.

The dishes they single out as particularly enjoyable—one Muslim, one Jewish, reflecting the makeup of the population of Taroudannt—are *harira*, a soup eaten at nightfall, as soon as food is permitted, to break the fast of Ramadam (*see page 213*), and *dafina*—a word best translated as "buried food"—a one-pot dish that obeys the prohibitions against any orthodox Jew, male or female, performing work of any kind on the Sabbath.

below: Special pancakes prepared with great dexterity during the month of Ramadan for *eid al iftar*—the meal that breaks the fast after sunset: eating and drinking (even water) is not permitted during the hours of daylight.

Harira ramadan chickpea and lentil soup

A hearty lentil and chickpea soup, this is the substantial dish with which the Muslim population of Morocco like to break the month-long fast of Ramadan, stopping off at one of the special harira stalls set up in the marketplace each evening as the sun goes down.

Serves 6–8

1 cup / 250 g chickpeas, soaked overnight, rinsed and drained

8 cups / 2 liters unsalted chicken or lamb broth

½ cup / 125 g red lentils

1 onion, finely chopped

2 lbs / 1 kg tomatoes, skinned and chopped

1teaspoon each of cinnamon, ginger, cumin, turmeric, and dried chilies

Salt and freshly ground black pepper

To finish:

Olive oil

Parsley, cilantro/coriander, finely chopped

Lemon quarters

❶ Cook the chickpeas in the broth for at least 2 hours, till tender. Don't add salt or allow the liquid to come off the boil. Add more boiling water to maintain the volume.

❷ When the chickpeas are perfectly soft, stir in the lentils, onion, tomatoes, and spices, season with salt and pepper, bring back to a boil and simmer for another half hour, till the lentils are mushy and the soup is satisfyingly thick.

❸ Finish with a swirl of olive oil and a generous handful of chopped parsley and cilantro/coriander.

Serve the soup in deep bowls, with lemon quarters for squeezing and a dish of red dates to make the heart glad.

Recipes for *harira* vary throughout the Muslim world. In Morocco, the main ingredients are lentils, chickpeas, and barley, along with a generous addition of beef or mutton—both meat and the bones to strengthen the broth; for flavor, tomatoes, cilantro/coriander, celery, onion, pasta or rice, oil, and turmeric are added. The broth is then thickened at the end of the cooking time with a little flour and sharpened with lemon juice.

During Ramadan, citizens curtail their daytime activities, customarily shutting up shop and returning home for a midday snooze, particularly when the fast falls in the extremely hot summer months. The daily intake of food is reserved for the hours of darkness. In the morning, as soon as they wake and as long as the sun has not yet risen, people eat a light meal of bread with mint tea. This is the only food they will take until the sun goes down at nightfall. Approaching the end of the afternoon, our observers report, the town begins to busy itself in preparation for the activity of the night. As soon as the evening cannon booms, people hurry to break their fast with a light snack of dates, or milky coffee flavored with mint, and then go to the cookshop or make their way home for a bowl of fortifying *harira*.

At midnight, another meal is usually taken—a *couscous* or a *tagine*, perhaps, with a variety of pastries and sweet things eaten in between. Although *harira* is eaten throughout the year, it is at Ramadan that it is most appreciated, despite the fact that the price of the ingredients invariably rise sharply to meet the demand.

left: Arab woman frying donuts—*lokimat*—to be eaten dipped in syrup after sunset during Ramadan; a touch of sweetness breaks the day-long fast.

a one-pot meal

The Jewish *dafina*, while not, strictly speaking, fasting food, nonetheless obeys the rules that forbid the preparation of food on the Sabbath. While *dafina* is the Sabbath meal of Middle Eastern Jewry, the Jews of eastern Europe would not dream of celebrating the Lord's Day without *cholent*—a one-pot meal of similar composition and intent. Both are a layering of different ingredients that together make a complete meal and which, when cooked very gently together for a long period of time, ensures that all the elements remain separate, but each one gives of its best to the others. Although recipes vary—the ingredients are seasonal, and each family will have its own preferences—the basic idea remains the same. Into a roomy pottery cooking pot are placed in layers: meat, onions, chickpeas, rice wrapped in a cloth, and sliced potatoes, both sweet and ordinary. During assembly, each layer is trickled with oil and seasoned with garlic, turmeric, cinnamon, and salt, while buried within are whole, unshelled eggs—an optional extra, familiar to those who appreciate Egyptian *hamine* eggs.

This mighty layering of meat and vegetables must be prepared and set on the charcoal brazier, *mijmar*, before sundown on Friday—the start of the Jewish day of rest. By "rest" is meant that no fires must be lit, no elaborate preparations made for eating, no reading of anything but improving texts, no television, and, of course, no cooking or cleaning. This enforced inactivity makes the midday feast—the *dafina* piled high in a new dish, the rice unwrapped, the rest carefully divided into its different elements—all the more appreciated. After the ceremonies have been observed—the Sabbath prayers, the lighting of candles, the blessing pronounced by the head of the household—the food can be enjoyed to the full, and even more so when accompanied by the Sabbath wine, *giffan*, the Sabbath bread, fresh salads, and something in the way of honey-soaked pastries.

carnival

Carnival—that period of sanctified bad behavior that reaches its climax on Mardi Gras (Shrove Tuesday) with the beginning of Lent—is one of those happy hybrids that is neither strictly Christian nor loosely pagan, but something in between.

In the Christian calendar, the week-long festival precedes the forty days of the Lenten fast, during which neither meat nor fowl may be tasted, which concludes on Easter Sunday, the most important day in the Christian year. Timing is the key. In the northern hemisphere, February is far too early to plant seeds, or even to prepare the frozen earth for planting. Such activities are hardly practical before May. Late February, however, is the first time the fishermen of the Mediterranean might safely leave harbor after the storms of winter. And, in more northerly climes—including those north of the Arctic Circle—this is the time when the harbors and inland waterways might be expected to be free of ice. Carnival, "goodbye meat," say Latin scholars, is therefore the festival that marks the first day of the fisherman's year. For all those who hope to fill their

below: *A Winter's Day in Saint Petersburg* in Tzarist Russia, c. 1890. **Engraving after a painting by Jan Schelminski.**

Russian Buckwheat Blinis buckwheat pancakes

The Russian offering-food taken to the churchyard on the day of the dead is also the daily bread of the rural housewife. Although, these days, the raising agent is more usually baking soda, live yeast has far greater resonance, being the raw material for that magical process by which millions of near-invisible organisms, upon finding warmth and food, surge into life. All the ingredients should be at blood temperature before you begin.

Makes a dozen little pancakes

2 cups / 300 g white bread flour

⅔ cup / 100 g buckwheat flour

1 level teaspoon salt

½ teaspoon dried yeast

Generous 1 cup / 300 ml milk

2 small eggs, whisked

Oil or butter for greasing the pan

To serve:

Sour cream

Chopped scallions

Danish caviar or pickled or smoked herring or smoked salmon (chopped)

❶ Sift the two flours with the salt into a warm bowl.

❷ Crumble the yeast into a little warm water and stir into the milk (it should be in a jug). Whisk in the eggs and blend with the flours, whisking till all the lumps have vanished and you have a smooth, thick cream. Cover with a cloth and leave it to rise for an hour or so in a warm place. You'll see the bubbles; they will tell you the yeast has worked.

❸ To cook, heat a griddle or heavy skillet, grease lightly, and test the heat with a drop of the mixture—it should sizzle and set immediately.

❹ Pour on enough of the mixture to cover the base of the pan. Or you can make smaller pancakes, blinchiki, by dropping on little dollops. Cook over a medium heat until the top looks dry. Flip over and cook the other side. Continue until all the mixture is used up.

Keep the pancakes warm in a clean cloth while you work. Serve with bowls of sour cream, chopped onion, and whatever fishy thing takes your fancy.

larders from both water and land, the opening of the fishing season was a matter for celebration while for those who depended on moving their goods by water, the spring thaw was eagerly awaited—none more eager than the merchants of central Europe who moved their goods along the interlocking waterways of Rhine, the Rhone, and the Danube.

In Tzarist Russia, the pre-colonial-Lent festival, Maslenitsa, "Butter week" was celebrated by the rich with a seven-day holiday. There were trips by troika through the still snowy countryside, picnicking in the frozen woods, or donning skates and taking to the ice. Courting couples bundled themselves up in furs and promenaded up and down the river banks, sipping vodka and nibbling blinis. In imperial Saint Petersburg, on each of the seven days, the Tzar offered a different spectacle, riding out from the palace with his Imperial Guard in full ceremonial dress, all gleaming leather and polished steel, plumed and beribboned in scarlet and gold. On one day, there would be a public performance of Petrushka, on another, the Tzarina herself, resplendent in sables and jewels, would rattle through gates in the imperial carriage to join the common people on the public swings. Butter week would be unthinkable without blini, pancakes made from buckwheat, Russia's only native grain, eaten with butter (of course), caviar for those who could pay the price, salt-cured herrings or salmon for those whose purses were less fat.

It is interesting to note that the same circular breads that are offered to the sun god—rice cakes, tortillas, flatbreads, blinis—are universally considered appropriate for visits to the dead. The reasons given for this preference are many, although the most common is that the sun itself is round and that an offering of round bread is a form of sun worship; others will tell you that round breads are easier to break into pieces and share. It is also true that dough-cakes—made by patting out or pouring a mixture of milled grains softened with water, leavened or not, onto a hot surface—is the simplest form of bread making, the easiest way to transform unpalatable grain-food into something that tastes good and won't easily go bad. Flame applied to the underside of a flat surface produces a circle of heat, never a rectangle or a square. Anyone who appreciates this peculiarity knows that only round breads will cook evenly on top-heat. In other words, if a pancake is the most primitive of grain-foods, a pancake is what the ancestral spirits can be expected to find most acceptable.

When the holy men of Byzantium brought the word of God to the sons and daughters of Mother Russia, *blinis*, the sacrificial food of the pagan dead, became the offering taken by the faithful to the churchyard on Shrove Tuesday. Christianity, a practical religion, overlooked the ancestry and embraced the symbolism—although

Shrove Tuesday Crêpes

Pancakes, *crêpes*, the universal resurrection food, being round, sunny, and made with lavish amounts of eggs. Eat and be thankful on the last day before the beginning of Lent. This version is from the sunny Caribbean, hence the rum and lime.

Serves 4–6

⅔ cup / 100 g all-purpose flour

½ cup / 125 g light brown sugar

1 stick / 100 g unsalted butter

2 large eggs

½ cup / 125 ml tepid milk

Pinch salt

1 tablespoon dark rum

Grated zest of 1 lime

To serve:

Whipping cream, lime juice, sugar, rum

❶ Mix the flour with the sugar in a bowl.

❷ Gently melt the butter and work it into the mixture along with the eggs, lightly beaten. Work in the tepid milk and salt to make a batter the consistency of heavy cream. It's hard to be precise about the quantities, but bear in mind that the crêpe mixture should only run if you tilt it sidewise in the pan. There is no need to let it stand.

❸ Just before cooking the crêpes, add the rum and lime zest, and stir it well in.

❹ To cook, take a small, very heavy-based skillet or frying pan and grease it lightly with butter. Heat till just smoking, and drop in a tablespoon of the batter. Roll it around the pan to make a thin, lacy crêpe.

❺ Turn once, each side should be golden-brown, and pile in a clean cloth while you make the rest. You'll find you have greater success if you make little ones. Always remember that the first crêpe seasons the pan and won't look good, so eat it yourself.

Serve sprinkled with lime juice, with whipped sweetened cream into which you have stirred a little rum.

left: The Shrove Tuesday housewives' pancake race at Olney in Buckinghamshire, England—a modern revival of the old egg-rolling rituals, a period of bad behavior preceding the solemnities of Lent.

the cult of unsanctified spirits was not encouraged. The peasantry, those who depended for their livelihood on the land, continued to do what they had always done, and made sacrifice as sacrifice was due. No one in their right minds, they reasoned, would risk losing the goodwill of those who might intercede with the deity, by whatever name He called himself.

In western Europe, the most enthusiastic celebrants of the carnival are to be found at either end of the religious and ethical spectrum, in easygoing Catholic Portugal and hard-working Protestant Germany. Carnival food must be fast food; eating cannot be allowed to interrupt the courting and mischief-making that is the main order of the day. In Germany, the food of choice is donuts, in France, *beignets*, and in Portugal, salt-cod fritters. The Greeks traditionally eat pork during the first and second week of their three-week carnival, kebabs perhaps, or a cinnamon-flavored *stifado*—though this, a slow-simmered stew, must include neither onion nor garlic, since both are anathema to the cloven-footed gods who rule the feast. But it is in the Americas, where the spirit of Bacchus meets the soul of Africa, that the outrageousness of carnival is truly appreciated. True connoisseurs of carnival head for the spectacle of Rio, Haiti, or New Orleans where the rum is powerful and the food is, well, whatever can be grabbed on the run—street food, dip-in-the-pot, fancies, oysters, fritters, anything that can be eaten on sticks, spicy fingerfood twisted in paper cones, or delicacies dusted with sugar and soaked in rum.

While the Church of Rome could do little about the obdurately pagan nature of Carnival, preferring to let Harlequin have his day and sober up the citizenry in time for Easter, the Reformed Churches held the line at Shrove Tuesday—a day that, though a bit of egg rolling or pancake racing creeps in around the edges, is devoted to using up all the larder stores that might otherwise tempt the godly during Lent. Although pancakes are the most usual use for the eggs and are expressly forbidden during the fast, in rural France (as reported by my own children who attended school in the Languedoc) it is customary for children to steal—or at least remove from the larder without adult consent—the raw materials for the making of a huge omelet. The preparation is done in secret without supervision in a secret place (a hut in the fields, location unknown). The omelet was not the familiar flicked-over bolster every French housewife serves her husband at midday, but a fat, thick egg-cake, yellow and round as the sun. Nor was it tipped out on a plate or cut with a knife, but torn to pieces with the fingers and eaten straight from the pan. What happened afterward was not a matter any of the participants—all of whom had been required to bring stolen goods as a condition of entry—were prepared to discuss.

above: *Venetian Donut Seller* at carnival time. Pen and ink drawing by Jan van Grevenbroeck.

next page: *The Battle between Carnival and Lent* painted by Pieter Brueghel the Elder in 1559 depicts the age-old battle between the forces of asceticism and the human appetite for excess.

Bratwurst **german carnival sausages**

This is the basic German sausage, all-meat, made without bread or rusk, and designed to be eaten fresh. At carnival time, in Freiburg, southwest Germany, as well as during the Saturday market, grilled *bratwurst* is the most popular street snack. If you can't lay your hands on sausage casings, form the mixture into hamburger-size patties. It's easiest if you dip your hands in warm water as you work.

Makes 4 lbs / 1.8 kg

3 lbs / 1.5 kg lean pork (leg or shoulder)

1 lb / 450 g fatback (belly) pork

2 tablespoons salt

3 tablespoons freshly ground black pepper

4 tablespoons chopped herbs: rosemary,

thyme, sage

Sausage casings

Accompaniments:

Sausage-shaped buns

Mild yellow mustard

Freshly grated horseradish

❶ Mince the meat very finely. Put it through the mincer twice (or have your butcher do this for you). Mix with the seasonings and herbs.

❷ Using a funnel, stuff the mixture into well-washed intestines (sausage casings). A butcher who makes his own sausages will be able to sell you a hank of these. Usually, they have been preserved in a great deal of salt, so they will need soaking. When working with sausage mixtures, have a basin of water beside you so that you can rinse your hands frequently. This prevents the fat from sticking to your fingers and making you clumsy. The trick is to roll the casing up the stem of the funnel, like a kid glove up a dowager's arm. If you can't get the casing, no matter—with wet hands, form the sausage mixture into fat fingers or patties and dust with a little flour.

❸ Fry or grill the sausages until perfectly firm. Prick with a knife to check the juices no longer run pink. Serve in sausage-shaped buns and accompany with mild German mustard and horseradish grated into long, thin strings.

Berliners **german carnival donuts**

Deliciously light donuts sold hot from the fryer on market days, but most particularly to revelers at carnival time. They are cooked in such a way that, though golden brown on the outside, they retain a pale center.

Makes about 20

The dough:

Generous 3 cups / 500 g white bread flour

1 teaspoon salt

1 oz / 25 g fresh yeast

(½ the quantity of dried yeast)

3 tablespoons sugar

About ½ cup / 125 ml warm milk

3 eggs

Grated zest of 1 lemon

3 tablespoons melted butter

Fat for deep frying

To finish:

Jelly/jam for stuffing

Confectioners' sugar for dusting

❶ All the ingredients should be as warm as your hand. Sift the flour with the salt into a warm bowl. Work the yeast with a little of the sugar till it liquidizes, then blend with the milk (if using dried, follow the instructions on the packet), and pour into a well in the flour. Sprinkle with loose flour, and leave until it bubbles—15–20 minutes in a warm kitchen.

❷ Work in the eggs, lemon zest, and melted butter to make a soft dough (you may need more warm milk). Knead well, working with the heel of your hand. As soon as it begins to bubble, set aside under a cloth, and leave till it doubles in bulk—about an hour. Rich doughs take longer to rise.

❸ Form into a rope, cut into 20 pieces, and work each piece into a ball. Arrange the balls on a floured tray, cover them with a clean, damp cloth, and set them in a warm place to rise for an hour or so, until doubled in bulk.

❹ Heat the frying fat. As soon as the surface is faintly hazed with blue, slip in the risen doughballs. Fry till golden brown around the edges, but still pale in the center. When well risen, take them out, and drain them on paper towels. Using a small-nozzled forcing bag, squirt in a little jelly/jam and dust with sugar, or dip in a sugar glaze (sugar melted with very little water).

lent

As soon as Ash Wednesday dawns, it's fasting food for the faithful all the way to Easter Sunday. Ever practical, the Christian timetable was tuned to the natural cycle of the seasons—and the principal fast of the year sensibly coincided with a time of reduced agricultural activity and the emptying of winter's larder.

Forty days of enforced deprivation can provide us, in these times of well-stocked shelves, not only with a religious reason to go easy on the rich food and drink, but with a prescription for shedding the winter poundage before spring. A diet of simply cooked fish and vegetables works wonders with the waistline. The medieval housewife who observed Lent as part of the normal cycle of the year baked no cakes or cookies during the period (with the exception of the Mothering Sunday cake that was, in any event, saved for Easter); avoided meat and sweet things; served no alcohol; and used butter, oil, and other enrichments only sparingly. The Lenten timetable was a godsend to the fishermen—providing a ready market at just the right time of year, when the winter storms of the Atlantic abated, allowing those with access to the sea to enjoy the first catches of the year with the church's blessing.

The notion of fast came late to Eastern Orthodox Christians. Rome was not prone to going without dinner until Pope Gregory I, heir to the asceticism of eastern religions and architect of the eventual split between the Patriarchs of Constantinople and the Bishop of Rome, decreed total fast until sundown, with no meat or dairy products to be taken during the forty days. This interdict included eggs from creatures either feathered or scaled. Naturally, the barnyard hens had no such obligations, and continued to lay. Their product had to be stored—hard-boiling was the easiest method—ready to celebrate the Resurrection. Observance was more or less strict according to the historical period and the demands of the established church. Lenten abstinence can range from a single voluntary privation such as a favorite food or drink to a complete day-long fast, with bread and water taken only after sundown. This enforced lean period, strictly observed according to regional habit throughout the Middle Ages, provided our forefathers with a natural balance. It offered the whole population the sanction of church and establishment for an annual physical and spiritual spring cleaning—effectively a chance to recover from the dubious excesses of the winter festivals. The western Church, both Roman Catholic and nonconformist, cut her Lenten clothes to suit her cloth. In the main, she

right: A fourteenth-century Italian manuscript, painted on vellum, provides a visual recipe for fish marinating in vinegar, fasting food for Lent.

contented herself with simply abstaining from meat—both fur and feather—during Lent and on the Friday fasts. Fish, cheese, and milk were usually permitted on these days. Northerners, Scandinavians in particular, were permitted fish, eggs, and cod-liver oil, since there was no other cooking oil available. The mainstay of the diet, particularly among inland populations, was grain dishes, dairy products, and storable winter vegetables, with salted fish the main source of protein.

Nevertheless, observance was by no means uniform throughout Europe. The French were particularly adept at slipping around the demands of the fast, resorting to such underhand tricks as dipping a leg of lamb in the well so that it might qualify, by virtue of its swim, as a fish.

Fish, cheese, and milk were permitted everywhere except to members of the Eastern Orthodox Church where olive oil and all products that come from a living creature—eggs, milk, cheese, and all fish were judged to be red-blooded—were proscribed. Orthodox Russians ate only bread, vegetables, fruit, and honey. In nonconformist northern Europe, through-out the Middle Ages, the first catch of the prodigiously prolific herring—later to be smoked, salted, or vinegar-pickled as a bastion against famine—provided the basic daily dinner of Lent. Meanwhile, the devout Catholics of the Mediterranean got through prodigious amounts of salt-cod. The process by which salt-cured cod, an Atlantic fish never found in the Mediterranean, became the fasting food of all Mediterranean Catholics—both Orthodox and Roman—had something to do with God, but rather more with Mammon. Throughout the Middle Ages, when half the year was fasting, the salt-cod trade was controlled by the Hanseatic League, a consortium of German merchants—Lutheran Protestants, who shared their profits with their Catholic brethren—filling the holds of their returning ships with good Mediterranean red wine. How it all began is harder to unravel. Myself, I incline to the view that salt-cod, the food that from the earliest times provided sustenance for sailors on the high seas, became associated with the passage of the spirit from the world of light to the world of darkness that, in Roman mythology, was reached by crossing the River Styx. The association of death with a voyage across water is common among all creeds and beliefs. It is also, I have found in my own experience, the metaphor that comes most vividly to mind when describing the death of a loved one.

In Ireland, Lent belongs to Saint Patrick. The medieval monks who chronicled the life of the patron of the Emerald Isle recorded that in Lent of A.D. 449, the saint resolved to pass the forty-day fast communing with God in the wilderness of Connaught County. In order to be as close as possible to the divine ear, Patrick climbed the highest hill he could find. Once ensconced on the windy summit overlooking the beautiful Bay of Clew, with the mountains of Mayo stretching to the north, the Twelve Pins to the south, and nothing but the gray-green Atlantic to the west, the saint quickly established contact with heaven. Night after night, throughout the forty-day fast, the messenger angel was kept busy running back and forth with requests—all of which, though greeted with increasing exasperation, were granted. Finally, the exhausted angel called a halt. He would do no more than carry one more request, but that was all.

"What is it to be?" asked the weary angel.

"Nothing much," replied the Irishman. "Just that on the Day of Judgement I myself should be appointed judge over the men of Ireland. I wouldn't like to lose old friends."

Some time later the angel returned, "Out of the question," he said.

"In which case," replied the determined Irishman, "Tell your Master, I shall stay right up here and fast till Armageddon."

The angel sighed and floated heavenward. The following night he reappeared. "The Lord saith," gasped the messenger, "You are the most impossible man he has ever had to argue with—and that includes the Apostles. Your request is granted. Now will you please go home. We're all worn out."

"Excellent." said the saint, clambering up from his knees. "Just one last thing. Let's get rid of all the snakes—and then I'll go home for my cabbage and bacon."

Frijol Blanco con Camaron Seco **mexican shrimp and white beans**

Dried and semidried shrimp, moist and orangey in color, form an important part of Lenten food throughout Mexico. This is a dish from the mountain state of Oaxaca, where fresh fish is hard to come by.

Serves 4–6

1 cup / 250 g dried white beans

Small head of garlic, charred in a flame

½ small onion, chopped

A little sea salt

6 oz / 175 g dried shrimp or 1 lb / 450 g fresh shrimp, peeled

2 large tomatoes, skinned

4–5 garlic cloves, chopped

½ onion, roughly chopped

3 tablespoons sunflower oil

2 leaves epasote or 2–3 fronds of dill

1 small fennel root, roughly chopped

❶ Bring the beans to the boil in 8 cups / 2 liters water in a roomy pot, skim off any gray foam that rises, add the garlic, onion, and a little salt, and simmer gently for about 3 hours, till perfectly soft. Don't let it come off a boil. If you need to add water, make sure it is boiling.

❷ Meanwhile, put the dried shrimp to soak in a little warm water for 10 minutes, then drain. Liquidize the tomatoes with the garlic, onion and a little water till smooth. Heat the oil in a skillet, add the liquidized tomato, and simmer till thick, about 15 minutes.

❸ Stir the tomato mixture into the soft beans along with the *epasote*, or dill and fennel. Stir in the shrimp, add a cupful of boiling water and simmer till the shrimp are tender, 10 minutes, no more.

Eat the soupy beans with soft maize flour *tortillas*. A ripe avocado mashed with a little salt and lime would be an appropriate relish.

Prasopita **greek lenten leek pie**

These delicious pies are sold all through Lent in Greece. Use ready-made phyllo pastry, or make your own by rolling out a flour-and-water dough softened with a little oil so fine you can see the pastry board through it. A worthy task for Lent. The Greeks gather dozens of wild greens from the countryside at this time of year—all fully identifiable by a botanist but not necessarily by the rest of us.

Serves 6–8

20 sheets phyllo pastry

8 tablespoons olive oil

Filling:

8–10 medium sized leeks, finely sliced with their green

1 stick / 100 g unsalted butter

1 large handful finely chopped dill

1 garlic clove, finely chopped

Salt and pepper

3–4 handfuls mixed leaves: turnip greens and spinach

4 eggs

Scant 2 cups / 450 g fresh curd cheese

❶ Preheat the oven to 375 F / 190 C / Gas 5.

❷ Rinse the leeks and put them to cook gently in a heavy pan in the butter with the dill, garlic and salt and pepper. Add the greens, and stir over the heat till all moisture has evaporated.

❸ Beat the eggs with the curd cheese. Mix in the leek mixture when it has cooled a little. Season well.

❹ Line a large, round baking pan—the kind you'd use to bake a birthday cake for a dozen—with 8 sheets of phyllo, brushing between the layers with oil. Spread in the filling.

❺ Finish with the remaining 12 sheets of oiled phyllo. Score the top into bite-sized diamonds. Bake for 30–40 minutes, until the pastry is well crisped and browned. Serve at room temperature.

easter week

It would be impossible to consider the rituals of the Christian Easter, particularly those that commemorate the events of the Last Supper, without a glance at their roots. Since Christians must believe that the authors of the first four books of the New Testament bear witness to real events that happened to real people at a real place in real time, the events of the Last Supper are of paramount importance. When the Gospel givers revealed the details of a meal shared by a man whose claims were in doubt with twelve followers of dubious loyalty in celebration of the Jewish festival of Passover—a force was unleashed that even they, bearing witness to what they heard and saw, cannot have fully understood. All that they needed to say was that Jesus, son of Mary—a man soon to be crucified by the occupying power at the request of his own people—had instructed his followers to remember his presence among them every time they broke bread or drank wine, and that all who participated in this simple feast would, by the act of invoking his name, be consuming his body and blood:

While they were eating, Jesus took bread, gave thanks and broke it, and gave it to his disciples, saying, "Take it; this is my body."
Then he took the cup, gave thanks and offered it to them, and they all drank from it.
"This is my blood of the new covenant, which is poured out for many," he said to them.

This was a statement of such power and complexity that no further words were needed, then or now. By invoking the specter of blood-sacrifice, the appeasing of higher powers with human blood shed in their name—Christ set himself apart from all others of his race and time, possibly of all times and all races. Those who heard the message might confirm or condemn, but they could not ignore, and for the darkest of reasons. If there is one taboo the world holds in common, it is that eating people is wrong. Yet there is ample evidence that our ancestors, both in what became known as the new world and the old, practiced human sacrifice. Once a community was secure enough of its food source to disapprove of cannibalism—since sacrificial meals must be shared, mortal and immortal dipping in the same pot—the main ingredient was replaced with less emotive foodstuffs, an evolution which also supposed that the individual was valuable enough for his own interests to transcend those of the group. It is interesting to note that this particular taboo, once established, became a yardstick by which the humanity of all others is judged. This, the ultimate taboo, was the ghost summoned to the Passover feast. Round the table, twelve men—eleven to witness, one to betray—and the thirteenth, the Lamb of God himself.

God dies that man may live; that is the message of Easter. Powerful stuff, and subversive, as with the sayings of all true prophets. The story is simple enough: in the sharing of bread and wine is to be found salvation. A fundamental idea so simple, a child could understand it. Unfortunately, or fortunately, depending on your view, those who interpret the Holy texts are never children. Two thousand years after that simple supper, the tale has been stitched and patched onto so many other tales in so many other cultures. So intricate is the weave, so tangled the threads, it would be impossible to unravel where one begins and the other ends. The true miracle is that the central idea survives.

left: *The Miracle of Transubstantiation* reverently depicted in a sixteenth-century German engraving.

right: A French nun prepares wafers for Holy Communion—Christianity's central sacrament, commemorating the last meal shared by Christ with his disciples.

pesach

Passover celebrates the exodus of the Hebrew people under the leadership of Moses the Law Giver from captivity in Egypt. As the festival that marks the birth of the Jewish nation, it ranks as the most important festival of the year. The date usually falls in April, and rituals, mirroring the spring-cleanings common in other cultures, center around the need to rid the home of all fermented foods, a reminder of the speed with which the captive Jews were obliged to flee their homes, leaving their bread unleavened. In orthodox homes, everything that might have to do with leavening has to be removed and the house scrubbed and polished until no trace of impurity remains. Proscribed foods include all yeast-raised breads, cakes, and the five grains: barley, rye, oats, wheat, spelt—anything judged capable of fermentation. The prohibition does not extend to the Passover wine, an essential part of the feast.

Matzos, made using wheat that has not had a chance to ferment, and dumplings made with matzo-meal are the unleavened breads of Passover. A children's game, told to Claudia Roden by her father, tells of scouring the house with a feather, candle, wooden spoon, and paper bag, searching with his older sisters for little bits of bread hidden by the grandfathers, and ceremonially burning the findings.

The celebration meal, Seder, the most important event of the holiday, is lamb. The meal can be served twice, on both days of the festival, and while the family is at table, the entire story of the deliverance—3000 years is not long in the history of so ancient a people—is retold in detail, discussed, and related to events of the present day. The Seder tray, on which are placed small bowls (replaced in the sophisticated households of European Jews with a large ceramic dish with compartments) is set out as soon as the household gathers. Meanwhile, a place is laid at the table for the unexpected visitor—the prophet Elijah, it is hoped. Each dish on the tray contains one of the ritual foods that separately and together remind participants of certain historical truths. In one, *karpas*, a green vegetable, parsley, or lettuce serves as a symbol of new growth, but is eaten dipped in salty water as a reminder of the tears of a captive people. In another, *maror*, bitter herbs such as horseradish and chicory serve as a reminder of the bitterness of slavery. There is, *betza*, an egg roasted to represent the sacrifice offered to God in the Temple (one for each person present); *zeroa*, a knuckle or joint of lamb—symbolic or cooked to be eaten—represents the paschal sacrifice offered to God on the Eve of the Exodus. Finally, *haroset*, a paste of dried fruit and nuts, that, to the educated eye and devout heart, is the color of the Nile mud used by the Jews to build the Pharaoh's pyramids. All these things are distributed and examined for their deeper meaning, serving to educate the young and offer comfort to the elderly, who may give thanks to God and be glad.

above: Fish-shaped loaves holding eggs in their mouths baked on the Greek holy island of Patmos at Easter. The fish served as a secret sign exchanged by early Christian converts.

It is certain that the first Christians observed Passover or Pesach—"He passed over"—in accordance with the faith they shared with their founder, by eating lamb with bitter herbs. It is possible to draw a line of distinction between those who call the festival for some variation of Easter—a word derived from the observance of the feast day of Eostre, Norse goddess of spring and rebirth—and those who took their religious lead from the Indo-Aryan system of religious belief and named the festival after the Jewish Pesach—Pasqua, Pascua, Paques. The association with Eostre and the April festival of Eostromonath is also made by the Venerable Bede (chronicler, high in his ivory tower on the edge of the East Anglian marshes, of the vanishing world of Anglo-Saxon England), who made a clear link between Easter egg hunting, egg rolling, and pace egging with the rituals enacted by the hare, Eostre's sacred animal, that served the same purpose as the rites of spring. Meanwhile, the church converted what it

could not eradicate—popping a snow-white apron on top of the scarlet petticoat. However lofty religious intention, the hiding of eggs for young people to find provides a not-so-delicate hint that it's time to get on with the business of choosing a mate. And, if there should still be any doubt of the association, in Germany, bakers bake a special Easter bread in the form of a hare with a whole egg tucked under its tail.

Supplies of eggs for the pace-egging—always a problem at Easter in northern climes—were assured by the rules of the Lent that precluded their consumption throughout the fast. Meanwhile, the hens continued to lay, obliging people to find ways to conserve supplies—mostly by boiling—until the ban was lifted at Easter. Where there's treasure, there's taxes. In medieval times, eggs were offered as Easter tithes to landlords, both secular and spiritual. The custom continues to this day in rural France, where some parishes still make gifts of eggs to their priest on Easter Day.

Some cultures—mostly those of the Mediterranean—bake whole eggs into their Easter breads, while others, particularly Germans and Austrians, bake theirs in the form of figures or animals, with the egg forming the head. Sometimes the bread is braided, with the unshelled eggs nestled neatly in the links. Elsewhere—as with the *kuchlichs* and *babkas* of the Slav tradition—the eggs are included in the dough, which is often braided and formed into a crown or ring. Braided breads have a special spiritual significance since they serve as a reminder of the braid cut off by a young bride on her wedding day—a symbol of virginity lost once but not forever, since it is restored to the faithful wife on the day of her death. The bakeries of Europe are full of regional oddities at this time of year, of which the English hot-cross bun is a somewhat thin-blooded variant. German households still feast on a menagerie of bread beasts—hares, bears, cockerels, wolves, storks, foxes. In Belgium, the shops fill with brilliantly colored marzipan fruit, and in Holland, people used wooden molds to form butter made from the first spring milkings into the shape of the Pascal lamb, dusting the buttery curls with sugar.

palm sunday

Easter week begins on Palm Sunday—the day of Christ's entry into Jerusalem when the cheering populace, so soon to turn against him, strewed a carpet of palm fronds in his path.

On the islands of the Aegean, among the Greek shepherding communities who paid their rent to the landlord in dairy products, Palm Sunday is also known as Cheese Sunday. Anthropologist Margaret Kenna, observing folkways in the 1970s on an island she describes as a day's journey from the Athenian port of Piraeus, recorded the hardships of life on a rocky outcrop too steep and bleak for cultivation, on whose slopes only goats and sheep could be raised: "The shepherds pay the rent for grazing land not in cash but in cheese, the amount being agreed with the owner of the land. The renting year begins on May 18, and cheese-rent for the past year must be paid by this date. As this is usually later than Easter time, most people want the rent to be paid not only in hard cheese which will store well in brine or oil, but also in unsalted soft cheese used in preparing special Easter treats. The soft cheese, called *vrasti* or *mizithra* is made from the afternoon's milk, boiled up with whey from the morning's milk (used to make hard cheese), and sea-water. The most delicious Easter treats are little cheesecakes made like jam tarts in individual pastry cases. The islanders call them *melitera*." The filling is curd cheese set with eggs and sweetened with sugar, flavored with cinnamon. The pastry is an ordinary shortcrust variety, shaped by pinching the pastry together at intervals to form a cup shape: "The pastry-pinching gave rise to a lot of teasing and giggling about who liked to be pinched where and by whom."

In Elizabethan England, Palm Sunday, known as Figgy Sunday, was celebrated with dumplings and puddings made with dried figs. The symbolism of the seed-packed fruit with its scarlet lips and golden juice was not lost on the lewd knaves of Tudor times. In Queen Victoria's day, city grocers sold huge quantities of the dried figs of Smyrna and raisins of Corinth for the servants of the increasingly affluent merchants to bake the cakes without which Easter could not be properly celebrated. Mothering Sunday was the day when serving girls were permitted to bake fruit cakes, as rich and dark as possible, to take home to reassure their mothers of their employers' generosity—no mean thing at a time when eighty-five percent of the working population were employed as domestic servants, inside or out. Of the multitude of traditional puddings and dumplings boiled or baked at this time of year, only the simnel cake survives (*see page 237*). This, a rich fruit cake of the wedding-cake variety, has a layer of marzipan baked through the middle with another over the top, and is usually decorated on the top with thirteen little marzipan balls. Whether these are meant to represent Easter eggs or symbolize the members of the group present at the Last Supper is—in the eye of the beholder—all in the mind.

Simnel Cake

Northern housewives baked the Easter simnel cake—a rich fruit cake with a layer of marzipan through the middle and a topping of marzipan—with the last of the dried fruit and nuts that stocked the winter storecupboard, cleaned out in the course of the yearly spring cleaning undertaken by all responsible housewives as soon as the weather warmed up. There are several theories to explain its curious name, the most likely being that the recipe dates back to Roman times and derives from *simila*, Latin for fine white flour. Those of a Royalist persuasion maintain that the fruity treat is a reference to Lambert Simnel, the unfortunate Roundhead Pretender who came to a sticky end at the hands of Henry VII. And there is a somewhat more fanciful tale of a baker and his wife, one called Simon and the other Nell, who couldn't agree on whose invention it was and were obliged to call it after both. By the way, readymade marzipan won't do—you need the egg yolk to hold the layer together as it bakes.

Serves 6–8

Almond paste:

Scant 2 cups / 250 g ground almonds

2 tablespoons confectioners' sugar

1 egg yolk plus enough water to bind

The cake:

2 tablespoons whole blanched almonds

6 oz / 175g prunes

1²⁄₃ cups / 250 g golden raisins

1²⁄₃ cups / 250 g raisins

²⁄₃ cup / 100 g candied peel

²⁄₃ cup / 100g candied cherries

generous cup / 175 g self-rising flour

²⁄₃ cup / 175 g dark brown sugar

1½ sticks / 175 g butter

1 tablespoon molasses or dark honey

4 eggs

½ teaspoon salt

⅓ cup / 50 g ground almonds

1 teaspoon ground cinnamon

½ teaspoon grated nutmeg

1 small glass brandy or whisky

❶ Make the almond paste by working the ground almonds and sugar with the egg yolk (you'll need water as well).

❷ Chop the almonds roughly. Pit and chop the prunes. Pick over the fruit, checking for little bits of stalk and pips. Sprinkle in a tablespoonful of flour, and toss the fruit in it (this helps prevent the fruit sinking to the bottom of the cake).

❸ Beat the sugar and butter together until light and fluffy—the more you beat, the easier it is to incorporate the eggs without the mixture separating. Beat in the molasses, then the eggs one by one. If the mixture curdles, stir in a spoonful of flour.

❹ Sift the flour with the salt and fold it in. Fold in the ground almonds, fruit, nuts, and spices. Stir in enough brandy or whisky to give a soft mixture that drops easily from the spoon.

❺ Line a deep 8 inch / 20 cm diameter cake pan with buttered paper and spoon in half the cake mixture. Level the surface, and top gently with a circle of almond paste. Spread with the remaining cake mixture. Set aside for half an hour to let the fruit swell. Preheat the oven to 325 F / 170 C / Gas 3.

❻ Bake for 2½–3 hours until the cake is well browned and firm to the touch. If it looks as if it is browning too early, cover with waxed paper. Allow the cake a few minutes to settle. Turn it out and peel off the paper. Store in an airtight tin when it is quite cool. Rich fruit cake improves famously with the keeping.

To finish the Easter Simnel, brush the top with apricot jam and decorate with another circle of almond paste, made to the same recipe as the filling. Decorate with 12 little balls of marzipan in commemoration of the Apostles at the Last Supper, with one for Jesus in the middle. A few fluffy little chicks would add a pagan note that might (or might not) be welcome.

re-enactment of the last supper

Playacting—the re-enactment of the events of Easter and Christmas in the passion plays popular in the Middle Ages, as well as modern Nativity plays—served to bring the stories of the New Testament alive for a congregation that could not read or write. The events of the Last Supper became a favorite subject for the playlets that served not only for instruction, but also, through endless repetition, to provide reassurance that the stories they told were true. The habit was adopted with particular fervor by those communities who found themselves on the far outposts of Christianity. Most vulnerable were the colonizers of the New World. In Central Mexico in the 1930s, reported observer Elsie Clews Parsons, the re-enactment of the Last Supper took place on Holy Thursday, at noon: "The Apostles take their seats on either side of the white-covered table; the priest standing at the farther end, opposite the Nazarene, says a blessing. Thirteen courses are now to be served to the Apostles. Tortillas and all the prescribed viands in small porcelain bowls are heaped high in front of each Apostle. Whatever each man does not eat he bundles up in a tortilla and passes behind his back to wife or daughter to put into her basket and carry home."

Ms. Clews describes the thirteen courses—all meatless, Lent not yet being over—served by the priests, whose business it was to cut up the greens ready for eating. First, a dish of chickpeas with cabbage; second, *nopalitos*, paddles of prickly pear; third, *nopalitos* with pumpkin seeds; fourth, white beans with chili. Then came a succession of vegetable dishes: green peas, green lentils, black beans, lettuce, *chilacayota* (spaghetti squash), green beans. In eleventh place, chickpeas rolled in a *tortilla*; then an *escabeche*—frittered fish bathed in a sharp marinade; finally, the thirteenth, *chillaca de frijoles refritos*, refried beans wrapped in *tortilla*.

"The ritual meal," continues Ms. Parsons, "is served so well and so quickly and so much more is passed into the family basket than into the mouth that in spite of its prescribed length it does not take much time to get through with. There is no conversation, but the cantor chants and the band plays throughout."

easter lamb in greece

At Easter, lamb is the preferred meat in the Christian lands of the Mediterranean. There is a practical reason for the choice: the festival—celebrated according to the lunar calendar on the first Sunday after the full moon that follows the vernal equinox, falls at a time when, on the southern shores of the Mediterranean, the first spring lambs are ready for the spit. Conversely, in the cold lands of northern Europe (with the exception of Britain), pork is the traditional Easter meat. The Hungarians call the Easter celebrations *Husvet*, festival of meat, and dish up the last ham of the winter, or maybe a rich jelly made with a pig's head, the last joint left in the brine-pot. The Romanians and Slavs follow a similar line. The Czechs like a loin of pork roasted with caraway seeds, accompanying the dish with sauerkraut and dumplings.

Easter is to Eastern Orthodoxy as Christmas is to the western Church. This is the time when Orthodox Christians—Slav, Russian, and Greek—go back to their homes to be with their families at a time that conveniently coincides with the spring plantings.

Among the Orthodox Catholics of Greece, the traditional Easter Sunday fast breaker is—as I was privileged to learn when, a few years ago, I spent Easter week in the mountain village of Hora on the holy island of Patmos—spit-roasted lamb. The monks of Hora's monastery founded by Saint John Christodoulos in 1088, hold open house from Palm Sunday to Easter Monday. Eastern Orthodoxy seems more integrated with its supporting communities than western Catholicism, perhaps because many of the monks were married men with families before they took holy orders. At this time of year, the monastery walls reverberate with the happy cries of reunited families. Grandfathers settle down in one corner of the courtyard, while grandchildren tumble up and down the whitewashed steps of the frescoed chambers. Bread for the Host is baked each day in the village bakery below the monastery. Here are no anaemic wafers, but great crusty wheels of *prosforon*—"offering bread"—a full yard in diameter. These are double tiered to indicate the dual nature of God, and made with the finest wheat flour. Only the cross-stamped central piece is distributed from the altar—the rest is laid out in wide, shallow baskets to alleviate the hunger of the worshipers during the long hours of the vigils, or to be taken home to feed the family. The scent which curls down the steep white-washed streets calls the inhabitants to mass more persuasively even than the tolling bells.

right: Presenting the Easter bread on the island of Karpathos in the Dodecanese: fresh marigolds, the color of sunshine, are used to decorate the bread.

In devout Hora, where the monks keep the Easter vigil hour by hour, the people do not like to make too much of the feasting. Not for them the whole lamb carcasses turning on the spit in the open air. On Green Thursday, the day before the silence and solemnity of Good Friday, the young goats (Patmos cannot support a population of sheep) are led up the village street to the slaughter. Friday is a day of bread and water. On Saturday, the innards are made into a special soup, *mageritsa*, in which are included bitter herbs. On Sunday, the meat—packed with oregano, lemon, plenty of potatoes, and garlic, on a large metal tray—is taken up the street, proudly displayed to passersby, en route to the bakery where it is slipped into the oven after the last bread-baking. On Easter Sunday, after the midnight vigil that ends in the acclamation of the risen Christ, the meat is shared quietly with family and friends. Sunday is also a day for visiting, and the accepting

above: Playing the Easter egg cracking game—a family shares the Easter feast on the Greek island of Patmos immediately after the morning celebration of the Resurrection.

and giving of red-dyed eggs. All the trappings of May Day—general jollity, outdoor picnics, visits to the shrine of the local miracle-working image of the Virgin—are kept for Easter Monday. In the morning, the monks from the monastery walk around the houses of the village bearing holy icons, carrying bunches of spring flowers dipped in holy water with which to sprinkle their congregation. To complete the Easter feast, the nuns in the monastery's sister-convent are kept busy all day baking delicious buttery little cookies dusted with sugar and crunchy flakes of almonds, and a delicate honey cake flavored with cinnamon and soaked in a syrup made with orange-flower water.

easter in eastern europe

In the village of Ludomirova in the High Tatras—a mountain range that runs from central Slovakia up to the Polish border—I had the good fortune, several years ago, to celebrate a Russian Orthodox Easter with a family of Ruthenes. Ludomirova—not so much a village in the western sense; more a scattered collection of dwellings loosely linked by a network of muddy tracks, each with its farmyard, cabbage patch, potato field, and surrounding meadows—housed a hospitable, independent-minded population of Russian-speaking Ukrainians marooned in Slovakia by the politician's pencil in the aftermath of the Second World War.

Since Easter is reckoned the most important festival of the Orthodox year, it is the time when everyone goes home to spend the holiday with their family. Throughout eastern Europe, where few urban dwellers are more than a generation from the land, home means back to the farm, providing extra hands at just the right moment for the spring sowing, and at a time when storecupboards are due to be emptied in anticipation of summer's bounty.

A storecupboard still well-stocked by the end of winter is the sign of prudent housewifery—an achievement worthy of celebration on Easter Saturday. Because of this, but also because Easter is the time when ancestor-visiting is in order, custom among the Ruthenes dictated that the Easter food must be brought to church to be blessed, to which end, every household filled a decorated Easter basket with the remaining larder stores as well as the eggs that accumulated during Lent, boiled and painted with pretty patterns in wax. The local ethnologist—a university professor— pointed out with some excitement that these patterns, formed by dipping a pinhead in colored wax and dragging it across the surface in concentric circles, were actually the form of sunbursts.

left: Painting the Easter eggs with delicate traditional designs in paint or wax—the intricate flower and leaf shapes reinforce the Easter message of renewal in Slovakia.

Wax-patterned Easter Eggs

You need plain white eggs, either hard-boiled or emptied by blowing out the contents through a pinhole at either end. For the wax, you need some candle ends, plain and/or colored, and a pin (a lace-pin with a big head is best). Stick the pin into a soft stick or a cork to make a handle. Or tie a pen nib to a stick.

❶ Melt the wax gently, keeping each color separate.

❷ Hold the egg firmly in one hand. Dip the pin-pen in the melted wax, and, starting ½ inch / 1 cm below the apex of the egg, dab on a blob of wax and drag it up toward the apex of the egg to give a tadpole-shaped dash. Do this all around the egg to produce a sunburst pattern. If you alternate the length of stroke and use different colored waxes you get an even prettier pattern.

❸ Repeat on the other end of the egg. Don't hold the egg by the patterned bit or the wax will melt. Make more sunburst patterns around the sides. If you dip the eggs in diluted food coloring, the wax will be thrown into relief, creating a batik effect.

left: Taking the Easter baskets to church to be blessed by the priest—a tradition among Russian Orthodox Catholics that survived throughout the years of communism, practiced within the exiled ethnic minorities.

At that time, Ludomirova supported two churches, one belonging to the Roman rite and the other to the Orthodox Russian. The Romans, in theory at least, served the population of Slav-speaking Slovaks, while the other, a monastery with its full complement of monks, served the Ukrainians. Both establishments, somewhat surprisingly, had survived the years of communism, although the official turning of a blind eye was largely due—explained my hostess—to the money they brought in from the outside. The neighborhood's Easter baskets were delivered to the Ukrainian church on Easter Saturday, just before the Resurrection Mass, and placed in two parallel lines along the wall that separated the churchyard from the cemetery. No explanation was offered for the timing, which elsewhere is always at midnight on the eve of Easter. Mass concluded, the families lined up behind their baskets and drew back the embroidered linen covers. The patriarch then passed down the ranks, sprinkling holy water to the left and right, blessing the food within, thus giving everyone a chance to take a good look in other people's baskets and draw their own conclusions on the neighbors' housekeeping. Many a marriage might be contracted or abandoned on the strength of what the unveiled baskets revealed. Our basket was a sight to be proud of: a large joint of ham, a slab of bacon, hard-boiled eggs dyed scarlet, fresh butter, salt, newly baked bread, and an egg-enriched Easter *babka*.

The contents of the basket joined a remarkable spread on the kitchen table, the preparations for which had been occupying the ladies of the household for several days. The two most important items—essential to the proper celebration of the feast—were the *babkas* and the egg-cheese (*see page 251*), the Ukrainian version of the Russian *paskha*, although they are somewhat less refined than that snowy confection of cream cheese and egg yolks that was once the glory of the Tzar's Easter table. The *babkas*, sweet breads filled with eggs and butter, were the business of the grandmother, who delegated the hard labor of kneading and pounding to her juniors, myself included as an honorary member of the group. The dough had to be beaten for an hour. Leaning with rolled-up sleeves into the huge wooden

trough, the ingredients were mixed—a frothing mixture of snow-white flour, creamy milk, great globs of golden egg yolk, the whites whisked to a froth so that no possibility of lightness might be lost, melted butter, and—finally, crumbled straight into the mix—the levitating yeast. The work was done in relays, twenty minutes at a time—though, not being born to the task, I could only manage ten—until the old lady expressed herself satisfied that the dough was kneaded to a golden smoothness. The dough was then divided and braided into triple braids, folded into tall tins, and set to rise for an hour, until the oven was hot.

Meanwhile, others were making the egg-cheese. For this, a panful of eggs, three or four dozen at least, was mixed with an equal volume of cream and gently scrambled over the heat until thick curds had formed. The curds were then dumped in a clean cloth, tied at the top, and hung on a corner of the stove to drip into a basin till dry. The result—a compact ball, as firm as cheese, that was then glazed with a little more egg and slipped in the oven to form a skin.

Once prepared, all the food was placed on the table, freeing the women, the daughters, mother, and grandmother to enjoy the company of their visitors. With the bowl of decorated Easter eggs set out in the center of the table, and the ceremonial candle lit, everyone tucked into the last of the winter stores with enthusiasm. Little relishes of grated pickled beetroot, pickled dill cucumbers with freshly grated horseradish in sweet vinegar accompanied the cold meats that supported the traditional egg-cheese, the fragrant bread, and the many dishes that had been wonderfully contrived from the contents of the larder. To add to the celebration and to help wash down this splendid feast, homemade liquor, a delicious sticky plum liqueur, flowed freely.

Before the feast could begin, there was a ritual to be observed—a small gesture, barely noticeable, quickly completed, and performed without preliminaries by the grandmother, the senior matron. She drew the youngest child to her and whispered in her ear. The child vanished briefly, to return with a beautiful freckled brown egg. The old woman nestled the egg in her palm and, taking a small sharp knife from her apron pocket, neatly sliced off the top, using the blade to mix the yolk a little into the white. Bright eyes twinkling, she lifted the little cup briefly to her lips, smiled, and sipped. Nodding encouragement, she passed it to the youngest child who, after a moment's hesitation, took a small sip, made a face, and passed it on. And so it continued around the table, until all had shared the golden liquid, bringing with it the sunshine of new life.

Ruthenian Easter Egg-cheese

This is a very unusual dish, a solid sphere of scrambled egg. It looks decorative, slices up neatly, and goes very well with ham.

Serves 6

5 cups / 1.25 liters creamy milk

10 free-range eggs

1 teaspoon salt

❶ Bring the milk to the boil. Meanwhile, whisk the eggs up with the salt. When the milk boils, whisk in the egg. Keep whisking until the resulting custard is thoroughly scrambled.

❷ Tip the mixture into a clean pudding cloth. Hang it in a warm place to drain with a bowl underneath to catch the whey, exactly as you would fresh cheese. Preheat the oven to 350 F / 180 C / Gas 4.

❸ When it is quite drained, tip it out onto a clean dish, paint it with a beaten egg, and slip it into the oven for 10 minutes to glaze. The result should look like a large, shiny yellow Easter egg. Slice it up to serve.

Paskha russian easter cheesecake

Russia's traditional Easter dessert, very rich and delicious, is made with the first spring milkings. The Russians use a special wooden mold to drain the curd. Since the shape should be high and light, a clean flowerpot lined with muslin is a good alternative. No cooking is required, but it's best to start the day before so that the curd has a chance to drain thoroughly.

Serves 8–10

2¼ cups / 600 g well-drained curd cheese

1inch / 2.5 cm vanilla bean, split and scraped

2 large eggs, yolks of both, white of one

1 stick / 100 g softened unsalted butter

Scant ½ cup / 100 g sugar

½ cup / 125 ml heavy cream, well whisked

1 tablespoon chopped candied peel

1 tablespoon chopped blanched almonds

To finish:

Extra blanched almonds

Candied cherries

Candied peel

Raisins

❶ Beat the vanilla into the curd cheese. Whisk the egg yolks with half the sugar until the mixture is white and fluffy. Beat the butter with the rest of the sugar until fluffy.

❷ Combine the egg with the butter, and beat in the curd cheese. Fold in the whipped cream and the whisked egg white. Fold in the candied peel and the almonds.

❸ Tip the mixture into a square of clean muslin and pop it into a well-scrubbed earthenware flower-pot, place it on a plate to catch the drippings, and set it in the fridge overnight to drain. Let the *paskha* drip overnight in the fridge.

❹ The next day, unmold it onto a plate, removing the muslin. Decorate with almonds, cherries and peel, using the raisins to mark out the initials XB, for *Kristos voskryesye*—Christ is risen.

Serve with a slice of *babka* or *panettone*.

Further reading

Adam, Hans Karl, *German Cookery*, The International Wine & Food Society, 1967.

Allatius, Leo, *Recollections of Leo Allatius* ms. 1630, trans. John Lawson in *Modern Greek Folklore*, CUP, 1910.

Andrews, Colman, *Flavours of the Riviera*, Grub Street, 2000.

Banchek, Linda, *Cooking for Life*, Bantam, 1994.

Banerji, Chitrita, *Bengali Cooking: Seasons and Festivals*, Serif,1997.

Basan, Ghillie, *Classic Turkish Cookery*, Taurus Parke, 1997.

Bell, Richard, *The Qur'an*, translated with a critical rearrangement of the Surahs Clarke, Edinburgh, 1939.

Bettany, G.T., *The World's Religions*, Ward Lock, 1980.

Booth, Shirley, *Food of Japan*, Grub Street, 1999.

Brown, Elizabeth Fisher, *Hehe Grandmothers*, Journal of the Anthropological Institute, 1935.

Burton, David, *Savouring the East*, Faber, 1996.

Chamberlain, Lesley, *The Festive Food of Russia*, Kyle Cathie, 1996.

Champion, Selwyn Gurney, ed. *The Eleven Religions and their Proverbial Law*, Routledge, London, 1944.

Cherikoff, Vic and Isaacs, Jennifer, *The Bush Food Handbook,*

Ti Tree, Australia, 1988.

Conte, Anna del, *The Gastronomy of Italy*, Bantam, 1992.

Cooper, John, Eat and be satisfied: *A Social History of Jewish Food, London*, Aronson, 1993.

Dalal, Nergis, *The Sisters*, Hind Pocket Book, Delhi, 1973.

Deh-Ta, Hsiung, *The Chinese Kitchen*, Kyle Cathie, 1999.

Elliott-Binns, Rev. L.E., *Essay on Christianity*, Ulsean Lecturer, Cambridge University, 1930s.

Field, Dorothy Dudley, *The Religion of the Sikhs*, John Murray, London, 1914.

Frazer, James, *The Golden Bough*, Macmillan, 1929.

Galizia, Anne & Helen Caurana, *The Food and Cookery of Malta*, Prospect,1997.

Gallop, Rodney, *A Book of the Basques*, CUP, 1930.

Giles, Lionel, *Taoist Teachings from the Book of Lieh Tzu*, Murray, 1912.

Giles, Lionel, *The Sayings of Confucius*, Murray, 1907.

Gomme, George, *Ethnology in Folklore*, London, 1892.

Graham, Peter, *Mourjou, the Life and Food of an Auvergne Village*, Viking 1998.

Grigson, Jane, *English Food*, Penguin, 1974.

Illyes, Gulya, *People of the Puszta*, Budapest, 1967.

Haroutunian, Arto der, *Middle Eastern Cookery*, Pan, 1982.

Heimann, Betty, *Indian and Western Philosophy, a Study in Contrasts*, Allen & Unwin, London 1937

Henning, *Essay on Zoroastrianism*, Parsee Community's Lecturer in Iranian Studies, School of Oriental and African Studies, London. 1930s

Howe, Robin, *Russian Cooking*, Deutsch, 1964.

Hsiang Ju, Lin and Tsuifeng, Lin, *Chinese Gastronomy*, Norman & Hobhouse, London, 1969.

Jaffrey, Madhur, *Eastern Vegetarian Cooking*, Cape, 1983.

Japan Travel Bureau, *Festivals of Japan*, 1998.

Kato, Genchi, *The Study of Shinto, The Religion of the Japanese Nation*, London, 1931.

Kennedy, Diana, *The Art of Mexican Cooking*, Bantam, 1989.

Kuper, Jessica, ed., *The Anthropologists' Cookbook*, Routledge, 1977.

Lang, George, *The Cuisine of Hungary*, Penguin, 1971.

Leeming, Margaret and Kohsaka, Mutsuko, *Japanese Cookery*, Century, 1988.

Lladonosa i Giro', Josep, *Cocina Catalana*, Antartida, 1992.

Louis, Diana Farr and June Marinos, *Propero's Kitchen*, Athens, 2000.

MacKie, Christine, *Trade Winds - Caribbean Cooking*, Absolute Press, 1987.

Majupuria, Indra, *Joys of Nepalese Cooking*, Bangkok, 1988.

McNeill,F. Marian, *The- Scots Kitchen*, reprint Mercat, 1993.

Parsons, Elsie Clews, *Mitla, Town of the Souls*, University of Chicago Press, 1936.

Petits Propos Culinaires, vols 1-50, Prospect Books.

Roden, Claudia, *The Book of Jewish Food*, Viking, 1997.

Rysia, *Old Warsaw Cookbook*, Spearman, 1958.

Sabieri, Helen, *Afghan Food and Cookery*, Prospect, 1986.

Sahni, Julie, *Classic Indian Vegetarian and Grain Cooking*, William Morrow, 1985.

Shaida, Margaret, *The Legendary Cuisine of Persia*, Grub Street, 2000.

Shoberl, Frederick, *Persia*, London, 1828.

Sing, Phia, *Traditional Recipes of Laos*, Prospect Books, 1995.

Spoerri, Daniel, *Mythology & Meatballs, A Greek Island Diary Cookbook*, Aris Books, 1982.

Steingarten, Jeffrey, *The Man who Ate Everything*, Knopf,1997.

Sullivan, Caroline, *Classic Jamaican Cooking Traditional Recipes and Herbal Remedies*,1893, new ed. Serif, 1992.

Tanttu, Anna-Maija, *Food from Finland*, Otava, Helsinki, 1988.

Thomas, Edward J., *Early Buddhist Scriptures*, AMS, 1935.

Viera, Edite, *The Taste of Portugal*, Hale, 1988.

Viski, Karoly, *Hungarian Peasant Customs*, Budapest 1932.

Warren, Herbert, *Jainism*, Rajputana, India, 1930.

Yen Hung Feng, Doreen, *The Joy of Chinese Cooking*, Faber, 1952.

Yen Mah, Adeline, *Watching the Tree*, Harper Collins, 2000,

Recipe index

picture credits

Chapter 1
Page 2 Hutchison Library/Liba Taylor;
5 Panos Pictures/J Holmes;
8 Corbis; 10/11 Hulton Getty; 13 Bridgeman Art Library; 14 AKG London/Herbert Kraft;
16/17 Robert Estall Photo Library /Carol Beckwith & Angela Fisher; 19 Agence France Presse; 20 Andes Press Agency/Carlos Reyes-Manzo; 21 Panos Pictures/Trygve Bolstad; 24/27 Christine Osborne Pictures;
28 Network/Kazemi/Safir/Rapho; 30 The Art Archive; 32/33 Hutchison Library/Felix Greene; 34 Panos Pictures/Chris Spowers; 36 Corbis/Richard Nowitz; 38 Christine Osborne Pictures; 40/41 Corbis/Penny Tweedie; 42 Werner Forman Archive;
46 Panos Pictures/Caroline Penn; 47 Panos Pictures/Caroline Penn;
50/51 Network/Barry Lewis; 52 Christine Osborne Pictures; 54 Hulton Getty;
56 Panos Pictures/Paul Cevayle; 57 Corbis/Reuters New Media Inc.;
60 Impact/Caroline Penn; 61 AKG London

Chapter 2
Page: 64/65 Bridgeman Art Library/Christies, London; 67 Corbis; 70/73 AKG London;
75 Bridgeman Art Library; 76 Corbis;
80 Corbis; 84 Knudsen; 87 AKG London;
88/89 Corbis; 92 Hulton Getty; 94 Corbis;

96 Werner Forman Archive/Schatzkammer of the Residenz, Munich; 97/98 Corbis;
104 AKG London; 108/109 Hutchison Library; 110/111 Robert Estall Photo Library/Carol Beckwith.

Chapter 3
Page: 116/117 Network/Gerard Stoen/Rapho; 117/118 Corbis;
120 Bridgeman Art Library/The Makins Collection; 122/123 The Art Archive;
124 AKG London; 126 Christies Images, London; 129 Knudsen; 130 Jeremy Hunter;
130/131 Corbis/Hubert Stadler; 134 Corbis;
137 Cephas/Mike Herring Shaw; 138/139 Instituto Português de Museus;
146 Cephas/Mick Rock; 147 Christine Osborne Pictures;
148/148 Network/Christopher Pillitz;
150 Bridgeman Art Library;153 Hutchison Library/Audrey Zvoznikov; 155 Corbis/Paul Almasy; 156 Hulton Getty; 158 Christine Osborne Pictures; 159 Peter Sanders;
160/161 Robert Estall/Carol Beckwith/Angela Fisher; 162 Christine Osborne Pictures; 164 Hutchison Library/JG Full; 168/169 The Art Archive;
171; Corbis/Michael Yamashta;
172/173 Network/Rapho;
174 Hutchison/Hatt; 176 The Art Archive;
177 Corbis/David H Wells; 180 Corbis

Chapter 4
Page: 182/183 South American Pictures;
185 Network/K D Francke/Bilderberg;
186 Hutchison Library/Liba Taylor;
188 Christine Osborne Pictures;
192 Corbis/Underwood and Underwood;
194/195 Hutchison Library/ Isabella Tree;
196 Hutchison Library/ Liba Taylor;
198 Andes Press Agency/Carlos Reyes-Manzo; 200 Impact Photos/Alain Evrard;
202/203 Hutchison Library/C Dodwell;
205 Ann & Bury Peerless; 206 Christine Osborne Pictures; 208/209 Panos Pictures/Neil Cooper; 210 Christine Osborne Pictures; 213 Christine Osborne Pictures;
214 AKG London; 216 Robert Estall Photo Library; 218 Bridgeman Art Library, Museo Correr, Venice Italy; 222/223 Corbis/Francis G Mayer; 224 Bridgeman Art Library/Osterreichische Nationalbibliothek, Vienna; 228 Bridgeman Art Library;
229 Network/Rapho/Michel Baret;
230/231 Network/Nikolai Ignatiev;
232 Impact/Caroline Penn; 233 Hulton Getty;
234 Corbis; 236 South American Pictures;
238 Impact/Christophe Bhuntzer;
240 Impact/Christophe Bhuntzer;
241 Impact/Caroline Penn;
243 Panos/Bob Kauders;
244/245 Impact/Nikoli Ignatiev.;
246/247 Network